Teaching Online

Tech.edu

A Hopkins Series on Education and Technology

Teaching Online

**A Guide to Theory, Research,
and Practice**

Claire Howell Major

Johns Hopkins University Press
Baltimore

© 2015 Johns Hopkins University Press
All rights reserved. Published 2015
Printed in the United States of America on acid-free paper
9 8 7 6 5 4 3 2 1

Johns Hopkins University Press
2715 North Charles Street
Baltimore, Maryland 21218-4363
www.press.jhu.edu

Library of Congress Cataloging-in-Publication Data

Major, Claire Howell.
   Teaching online : a guide to theory, research, and practice / Claire Howell
Major.
        pages cm. — (Tech.edu: a Hopkins series on education and technology)
   Includes bibliographical references and index.
     ISBN 978-1-4214-1623-6 (hardcover : alk. paper) — ISBN 978-1-4214-1633-5
(pbk. : alk. paper) — ISBN 978-1-4214-1624-3 (electronic) — ISBN 1-4214-1623-9
(hardcover : alk. paper)   1. Web-based instruction.   2. Teaching —
Methodology.   I. Title.
   LB1044.87.M245 2015
   371.33'44678—dc23   2014020802

A catalog record for this book is available from the British Library.

Special discounts are available for bulk purchases of this book.
For more information, please contact Special Sales at 410-516-6936 or
specialsales@press.jhu.edu.

Johns Hopkins University Press uses environmentally friendly book
materials, including recycled text paper that is composed of at least
30 percent post-consumer waste, whenever possible.

Contents

Acknowledgments   *vii*

Introduction   1

1   Teaching Online as Instructional Change   7

2   Faculty Knowledge   24

3   Views of Learning   45

4   Course Structure   76

5   Course Planning   109

6   Intellectual Property   131

7   Instructional Time   149

8   Teacher Persona   163

9   Communication   178

10 Student Rights   193

11 Student Engagement   208

12 Community   227

    Conclusion   254

Notes   *259*
References   *287*
List of Contributors   *309*
Index   *313*

Acknowledgments

I get by with a little help from my friends.
—JOHN LENNON AND PAUL MCCARTNEY

The research and writing of this book took place over the span of several years, and I have many people to thank for their support along the way. I appreciate the sponsorship that I had while completing the research and writing of this book. In particular, I am grateful to the Spencer Foundation, which provided funding during the early stages of this work as I searched for information about best pedagogical practices in online courses. I also appreciate assistance from The University of Alabama, which came in the form of a sabbatical leave, during the initial portions of my research. I am grateful to the individuals who helped me with the research that went into conceptualizing this book, in particular Stephanie Blackmon and Austin Ryland.

Once I had the manuscript in draft form, several individuals offered useful suggestions; because of this, I offer them my thanks. In particular, my editor, Greg Britton, was supportive of this manuscript throughout its development. He encouraged me to write the book and to be creative with it, and he offered exceedingly useful suggestions for its development and improvement. I also am grateful to those who reacted to early drafts of the manuscript: Elizabeth Jones, Lisa Lane, Susan Lucas, Marilyn Staffo, Geri Stone. Likewise, I appreciate the efforts of those who read later drafts of this work, including Amanda Brunson, Jennifer Humber, Susan Lucas, and Maggi Savin-Baden. Moreover, the book went through a rigorous review process, and I offer my gratitude to the two external reviewers who gave their time and energy to reading the manuscript and offering suggestions for improving it.

I did not write this book alone; rather, forty-seven individuals also contributed their own writings to the text. I deeply appreciate the following colleagues who contributed their ideas and opinions about online learning in the sidebars to this book, listed in order of their appearance in the volume: Margaret Soltan,

Eloise Tan, Chuck Eesley, Matthew Koehler, Lisa Lane, Kenley Obas, Katrina Meyer, Valerie Irvine, Norbert Pachler, Curtis Bonk, Dave Cormier, Robert Bernard, Gardner Campbell, Alec Couros, Howard Rheingold, Lisa Lane, Patrick Biddix, Cris Crissman, Alan Levine, David Evans, Laura Paciorek, Rose Marra, Wendy Drexler, Giulia Forsythe, Charles Miller, Aaron Doering, William Cross, Neal Hutchens, Chad Tindol, Alex Tabarrok, Marilyn Staffo, Maggi Savin-Baden, Bonnie Stewart, Norm Friesen, Stephanie Blackmon, Susan Lucas, André Denham, Tisha Bender, Amanda Brunson, Ted Major, Jesse Stommel, Wanda Sullivan, Fil Arenas, Bryan Alexander, Terry Anderson, Jim Groom, Eric Rabkin, and Todd Conaway.

Finally, I'd like to thank my family for their support, encouragement, and patience throughout the process of writing this book: Ted Major and Christopher Major.

Teaching Online

Introduction

Change is such hard work.
—BILLY CRYSTAL

This book is about change. In particular, it is about the myriad changes that faculty face when we teach online. Teaching online means altering the ways in which we conceive of our work as teachers. It means rethinking our views and our abilities. It means developing new knowledge about teaching and media, new forms of pedagogy, and new communication patterns. It means reconsidering what we hope that students will gain and how we might know that they have gained it. It means rethinking how we develop materials as well as how we spend our time. Given its growing importance as a form of instruction in higher education, it is time to take stock of such changes. The purpose of this book, then, is to provide sound *information about changes* that faculty face when we teach online and to outline *strategies for managing these changes*; the purpose is not to convince faculty to take up online teaching, nor is it to provide a how-to manual for teaching online.

To be most useful, information about the shifts and alterations that teaching online entails should be more than anecdotal. Instead, educators need reliable information that is grounded in evidence as well as documented in pedagogical practice. Fortunately, thousands of faculty have now taught online, and many of them have shared their experiences in different types of publications, both formal and informal. Likewise, many researchers have given their scholarly attention to the practices of online teaching. Together these works compose a robust and ever-growing body of practical information about teaching online. Thus sound information from which we can learn does exist. The challenge with existing research related to teaching online is that currently it is unwieldy and spread across multiple sources. As such, the information is difficult to discover, manage, consume, and apply. Educators need a solid synthesis and explication of information grounded in the best available practice-based evidence to date.

The book responds to this need by presenting a synthesis of theory, research, and practice related to the instructional changes faculty experience when we teach online as well as a review of strategies for managing them. I first examined and synthesized the body of research on faculty experiences of online teaching. This search produced an extensive list of studies (more than a thousand) related to this primary focus.[1] I also drew on hundreds of other sources, culling and collating information from theoretical position papers, books, and chapters as well as blogs and other social media to identify the primary changes that faculty encounter when they teach online and key change-management strategies. The intent was to condense this information into practicable form and share it with educators who can use it for better decision-making, planning, or teaching. These works also provide extensive documentation for the arguments and conclusions presented in the chapters.

I come to the task of writing this book from a combination of vantage points. I am a professor of education at the University of Alabama, a large, on-ground, research university located in the southeastern United States. As part of my responsibilities, I conduct studies that have prepared me to write this book. These efforts center on teaching and learning at the college level, and I specifically investigate instructional change;[2] I also focus on providing faculty with advice about how to go about instructional change based on the findings from my research.[3] I have written about several different teaching approaches, including online learning.[4] The subject areas in my teaching also have prepared me to write this book. I offer courses on college and university teaching, distance learning, and technology in higher education, providing students with a sound, theoretically grounded knowledge base combined with hands-on exposure to technological tools and other resources that can help them learn to teach online. I consider myself intellectually interested in online learning, but not necessarily a booster for it. I taught my first online course in 2004, and I have continued to teach online and have blended courses for almost a decade now, although I do not do so every semester. To hone my knowledge and skills about this form of teaching, I recently completed an open course on online teaching, Pedagogy First.[5] Thus I have gained theoretical and research-based knowledge as well as practical experience. Moreover, I have expertise in research synthesis, which is the process I used to develop and write this text.[6] These myriad areas of my work have converged and compelled me to undertake the task at hand: developing a roadmap for faculty on the changes they will experience when they teach online and about specific strategies for dealing with them. I come to this book, then, as a scholar who has sufficient knowledge and experience to understand the changes that accompany teaching online and provide suggestions for managing instructional change.

In addition to bringing my own perspective to bear on this work, I also have drawn on the direct experiences of others. Colleagues with practice and expertise in online teaching—teachers, technologists, and researchers—have shared their ideas related to these changes with readers of this book. Their words appear alongside mine, featured in sidebars contained within each of the chapters. In sum, this text presents multiple perspectives on the changes faculty probably will experience when they teach online and on how they might best manage these changes.

Many different audiences should find this book useful, including faculty members, researchers, instructional designers, faculty development professionals, students, administrators, and policy makers. In short, it should be helpful to any change makers who engage with online learning in higher education. Faculty members who have thought critically about teaching online and who seek sound information about the changes they will face could use this book to weigh the potential benefits and challenges of doing so. Information contained in this volume can allow them to make more-informed decisions about whether to teach online. Many of us who have already made the choice to teach online are finding the adventure to be an intellectually stimulating and exciting change, and many of us likewise are discovering that we are not fully prepared to take on the challenges of teaching in a completely new and different way. Thus faculty who are planning to teach online can find ideas and information that should help prepare them for adjustments they most likely will need to make when they teach online. This book also will provide faculty who have experience teaching online with a frame of reference for the challenges and issues they have encountered; an assurance that they are not alone; and evidenced-based, practice-improving suggestions that they may not yet have considered. For faculty who do not plan to teach online but who are interested in it for other reasons, such as intellectual curiosity, this book can still serve as a valuable source of information.

Instructional designers and faculty developers who work directly with faculty members to help them prepare for and support their teaching online should find this text to be useful for understanding the changes these teachers will confront. It highlights areas of faculty concern, including those that are barriers to faculty buy-in as well as to faculty success. It provides suggestions for how to best manage these potentially problematic areas, which instructional designers and developers may use when working with faculty members. In short, this book can help instructional designers and developers better assist the faculty with whom they work. In turn, the benefits that faculty and instructional developers gain from this text can result in improved online teaching and learning, which is a boon to students.

This book can be a useful resource for individuals who have scholarly interests in the topic of online learning, such as students who are enrolled in programs like instructional technology, learning systems, learning design, or higher education. Indeed, a goal of this volume is to highlight the most critical issues to date related to teaching online. These issues have the potential to spark ideas and conversations in academic settings, which in turn can contribute to the quality of future dialog by these individuals. Researchers who study online learning or higher education should also find this book to be of use. The theories and extensive bibliography presented in it should aid those who are conceptualizing, planning, and carrying out new studies related to online teaching and learning. Here researchers can find a concise synthesis of the existing body of knowledge, which hopefully they can use as a springboard for advancing teaching online as a field of inquiry.

Individuals and groups who have decision-making responsibilities that influence the future and direction of online learning in higher education also might find this book to be a valuable resource. In addition, it can help administrators who make decisions about technology understand the various changes that teaching online requires of faculty. This knowledge, in turn, should allow administrators to make more-informed decisions, which can shape institutions. The book could also be of use to policy makers, foundation officers, and agency leaders, all of whom influence higher education in a number of ways, to augment their understanding of the issues related to online teaching and learning. Such information can help them make better decisions about the kinds of research and practices to encourage and support.

This book contains twelve chapters. Chapter 1 provides a theoretical grounding for understanding the nature of the changes that can happen when teaching online. Each of the remaining chapters focuses on a specific educational issue, and each chapter has a similar structure: an introduction of the educational issue, an explication of the issue, a description of the changes that attend the issue when teaching online, and strategies for managing these changes.

Following the first chapter, the next two chapters present changes to faculty members' personal perspectives and views as they relate to online learning. In chapter 2, "Faculty Knowledge," the focus is on the concept of teacher knowledge, the ways in which teaching online changes what faculty need to know, and what adaptations are necessary. I present strategies faculty might use to develop critical knowledge necessary for teaching online. Chapter 3, "Views of Learning," looks at the ways in which our perceptions of teaching may change when we teach online, expanding and broadening the means by which we can conceive of student learning. I describe strategies for discovering and articulating our views of learning.

The next three chapters highlight issues of change related to designing and developing courses. In chapter 4, "Course Structure," I explore the emergence and development of different approaches to teaching online. From traditional online courses to massively open online courses (MOOCS), online learning comes in myriad shapes and forms. Chapter 5, "Course Planning," presents information about how planning processes differ when teaching online as well as strategies for managing these changes. In chapter 6, "Intellectual Property," I describe questions of ownership, particularly those related to course materials and products, and how we experience these ownership issues differently when teaching online. I also outline strategies for navigating the various factors associated with intellectual property in online courses.

The following three chapters cover changes related to the direct instructional experience. In chapter 7, "Instructional Time," I address issues related to whether teaching online requires more time than teaching in fully onsite environments and consider the ways in which teaching with technology alters patterns of instructional time, extending and fragmenting it as it changes the pacing and rhythm of classes. I suggest strategies faculty members may use to manage time when teaching online courses. The focus of chapter 8, "Teacher Persona," is on how faculty who teach online compartmentalize their personas, make choices about whether they project a real or an imagined persona, and communicate their personas. I also describe strategies faculty members can use to create authentic online personas. Chapter 9, "Communication," centers on the ways in which teaching online alters patterns of communication with and among students, thus changing our experience with instructional communication. I suggest strategies for improving communication when teaching online courses.

Chapters 10–12 focus on changes in how we manage the student experience. In chapter 10, "Student Rights," I consider issues of access, privacy, and ownership of student products. Chapter 11 focuses on the concept of student engagement and how faculty experience this educational issue differently when they teach online. I provide suggestions for recognizing and enhancing student engagement in the online classroom. Chapter 12, "Community," discusses how a sense of community happens in a different way in online courses. I suggest strategies for gauging and enhancing community in online courses.

The format of the chapters is unconventional, in part due to the contributions from other authors. Moreover, this volume has comprehensive endnotes that contain citations from the text, brief reports of research studies, and discursive analyses of ideas. Readers may wish to engage with this text differently than they do with others. In order to use this book effectively, consider the following suggestions:

- Appraise the themes in the various chapters. Consider whether the highlighted changes "ring true." Consider which aspects of the changes are most central to teaching and learning in higher education.
- Analyze the contributions from colleagues for additional insights about the topic detailed in the chapter. These sidebars feature informative and inspirational information about teaching online. Consider them for their pedagogical merit (i.e., what readers can learn from them) as well as for the practical suggestions they offer.
- Compare the main text with the endnotes, which provide extensive documentation from existing literature along with discursive analyses of ideas. Consider bookmarking the endnotes to make it easier to flip back and forth between the main text and the notes, or alternately consider reading the chapter text first and then reading the endnotes that support that chapter.

Upon completion of this volume, readers should have a solid understanding of the issues involved in teaching online, an idea about the changes faculty experience when teaching online, and a set of strategies for dealing with these changes effectively.

This book, then, is a research-based resource for faculty who are interested in teaching online. It treats teaching online as instructional change and, as such, is a necessary addition to the scholarly and practical literature in this field. I invite readers to view this work as a theoretical introduction to instructional changes that attend teaching online as well as a practical guide to managing those changes. I also invite readers to review the ideas and information contained herein and question whether and how it relates to their own experiences as well as whether and how the issues will evolve in the future. I recognize that through these invitations, this book probably will raise as many questions as it answers, but that, too, is part of its intent. I hope that this volume will spark many conversations and many debates about online learning, faculty work, and change.

Chapter One

Teaching Online as Instructional Change

When people are ready to, they change. They never do it before then,
and sometimes they die before they get around to it.
—ANDY WARHOL

O ver the many centuries of higher education's existence, faculty have taught
in myriad ways, and over the past hundred years, technology has become an
integral part of the educational enterprise. This period of history also includes several examples in which technology is what *enables* instruction in higher education.
That is, the intervening agency of communication technologies has allowed instruction in higher education to happen across time and space without the physical co-presence of the instructor and students. Formal approaches to this type of
instruction, known as "distance education" or "distance learning," began with correspondence study and developed rapidly alongside advancing technologies. Radio in the 1920s, television in the 1950s, and computers in the 1980s are communication technologies that have allowed educators to offer higher education to
students who participate in the instructional process at a distance.[1]

Online learning, currently the most in-vogue form of distance learning in
institutions of higher education, has experienced a period of remarkable growth
as students have flocked to online courses. In 1998, too few fully online courses
existed for researchers to take student enrollment in these classes into account.
Yet the most recent Sloan Foundation report, which presents results from a survey of more than 2,800 participating institutions of higher education, indicates
that by fall 2013, the number of students taking online courses was 7.1 million.
This figure represents 33.5% of total enrollment.[2] Moreover, 77% of the institutions involved in the survey were offering online courses.[3]

Students are taking online courses in increasing numbers, and high-ranking of-
ficials likewise have signaled the growing importance of online learning in higher
education in several ways. In the Sloan Foundation surveys, fewer than 50% of
all institutions of higher education reported in 2002 that online learning was

critical to their long-term strategy, while by 2011 that number was 66%.[4] In the 2013 survey, 90% of administrators indicated a belief that it is "very likely" or "likely" that all students will be taking at least one online course in the next five years.[5] It seems clear that administrators believe online learning is occupying an increasingly important role in institutions of higher education.

With the growing significance of online learning as an instructional form, ever-increasing numbers of faculty are teaching online courses. Findings from a 2013 survey of more than 2,200 faculty members indicated that 30% of them have taught online. Faculty at all career ranks, part- and full-time faculty, and faculty teaching at a range of institutional types have developed and taught online courses.[6] With evidence to suggest that almost one-third of faculty members are teaching online and more are planning to do so in the future, this instructional form appears to have reached what Everett Rogers calls the "tipping point" in the diffusion of an innovation, and in this case, the innovation is an instructional one.[7] That is, online learning appears to have become a common instructional practice among higher education faculty.

Despite the increase in faculty uptake of this instructional form, there is surprisingly little information available about what teaching online really means for them. And while what it means for them necessarily is bound to educational contexts, it is safe to say that when teaching and learning happen in the absence of the simultaneous physical co-presence of the instructor and the students, the instructional experience changes in myriad ways. Indeed, teaching online is a constitutively different way of offering instruction in higher education. The dearth of accessible information about such changes is problematic, since without sound information, faculty are not best prepared or equipped to navigate change successfully. Thus faculty need solid information about the instructional changes that accompany teaching online, and highlighting these changes is the goal of this book.

Critical context to understanding the specific changes we experience is understanding the nature of the change itself. That is, to truly come to grips with what changes, it is important to understand how and why such change happens. The concept of technological mediation of instruction, and its necessary consequences, provides a foundation for understanding the instructional changes that are part and parcel of teaching online. Thus I turn to a discussion of technological mediation for the remainder of this chapter in order to set the stage for the specific changes I describe in the chapters that appear hereafter.

Table 1.1   Technologically mediated perceptions

Unmediated perception	I—world
Mediated perception	I—technology—world

Mediated Instructional Realities

When teaching online, technologies do not simply serve as functional instruments that can assist with instructional work. Instead, they serve to mediate our realities and, in so doing, become part of them.[8] Existential phenomenologist Martin Heidegger has argued that our technological tools are what make "connections" or "linkages" between humans and our realities.[9] Don Ihde, a philosopher of science and technology, elaborates from Heidegger's work and suggests that technology serves as a mediator of reality.[10] Artist Nam Jun Paik makes a similar point: "Skin has become inadequate in interfacing with reality. Technology has become the body's new membrane of existence."[11] That is, technology intervenes between us and realty, as illustrated in table 1.1, which is drawn from Ihde's work.

When teaching online, our instructional realities are similarly mediated by technology. That is, technology stands as an interface between us and our instructional worlds; our perceptions of our realties are altered by it. Such mediation can happen in several ways, and Ihde discerns four important human/technology relations that inform how technology serves as a mediator when we teach online.[12]

TECHNOLOGY AS CONTEXT

Technological tools often provide a background for human experience. An electric light, for example, is a background of experience for an individual in a room that is lit by it. In serving as background, technology is simply part of the world, part of our surroundings, and we are as aware of it as we are aware of anything else. It is an aspect of the environment that individuals can see, hear, and experience directly, but we may not think much about it. When we teach onsite, technology serves as such a background. We typically teach in lit and heated or cooled rooms so we can meet at any time of the year or day. Like it or not, even when we teach onsite, we are never truly "teaching naked," or teaching sans machines.[13] Rather, technology is background to our experiences.

When teaching online, technology not only serves as background, but also as a context for instruction, since it functions as the place where teaching and learning happen. That is, the *place* of the course is cyberspace, as that is where instructors and students interact, exchange information and ideas, make course products, and otherwise carry out the work of the course. It is not a place in the physical sense of the word, but nonetheless it is the place where the course happens. Not all courses have a central hub, but even in decentralized and distributed courses,[14] technology still shapes the interactions, providing the contextual framework for them—an instructional infrastructure—as instructors and students meet "out there" in cyberspace to accomplish the work of the course. Thus technology creates the digital microcosm that is the course itself. It is both background and foreground; technology not only illuminates instruction but also gives it a place, and in so doing becomes part of the instructional experience itself.

TECHNOLOGY AS AN EXTENSION OF SELVES

Technological tools can serve to increase an individual's capacity within a given environment or context. As technology is incorporated with humanity, it becomes an extension of the human body, for example by looking through a pair of glasses. In such embodiment relations, the technology is effectively a part of us, a part of our bodies, as is wearing glasses. In the ideal, we are not aware of it; the technology is transparent. When we teach onsite, we experience this type of relationship with instructional technology. We may use microphones so more students can hear us, or laser pointers to better illustrate important concepts in our audiovisual materials. When we teach online, however, the relationship becomes even more closely knit, since technology is the interface with instruction. We are even more bonded to it because it is necessary for the instructional offering. Our computers or tablets or smartphones are nearly always with us. We are tethered to them, as we must be in order to do our jobs.

TECHNOLOGY AS AN INTERPRETIVE LENS

When technology serves as an interpretive lens, we experience the quality or value of a concept or object without experiencing that quality directly, but rather by perceiving a technological representation of reality, such as seeing a thermometer and understanding that it is cold outside without necessarily experiencing the cold physically. We are removed from the world; thus the world requires some sort of interpretation, which we make with and through technology. We are aware of this technology. It mediates our experiences with phenomena; thus these experiences are changed. When teaching onsite, faculty typically experience the instructional processes directly, and we rarely need technology to help us interpret them. We talk with students. We see what they look like and construe their expressions accordingly. We observe them as they interact with each other. When we teach online, we interpret the instructional experience *with* the technology. We decode text, for example, to see how students communicate. If we have images of them, we do not experience their expressions the moment they occur; rather, we see them as they were at the time of the picture, which is a curated experience, since students select pictures based on the images they want to share with others. We see interactions in discussion boards or on blogs or other social media, but often after they have happened. In short, we are removed from the experience of the moment, and we interpret things like feelings, thoughts, and relationships with and through technology.

TECHNOLOGY AS A HUMANLIKE INTERFACE

In some cases technology can replace interactions between humans with a humanlike interface. For example, when an individual uses an ATM to withdraw cash, that person interacts with technology as if it were a person distributing cash. When we teach onsite, we do not often interact with technology as if it were human. But when we teach online, it is a possibility. When a student receives an immediate response and grade after taking a quiz, the technology serves as a humanlike interface, resembling a teacher distributing a grade. A pedagogical agent, or a software agent that typically takes the form of an animated person in order to help learners, is an example of technology serving as a humanlike interface.[15]

Mediated Instructional Forms

Not only does the mediation of instruction alter the way in which we, as instructors, are present in our instructional worlds and how these are present to us, but it also alters instructional forms. Several of these forms change, including instructional interpretations, instructional actions, and instructional products.

INTERPRETATIONS

When faculty teach online, technology mediates our interpretations of what we are experiencing. In some instances this mediation leads to foregrounding, and in others backgrounding, of what it is we are trying to perceive and understand; in still others it means rendering visible what would have been invisible, and likewise invisible what otherwise would have been visible.[16] As Ihde indicates, this is a process of amplification and reduction. Thus when we perceive with technology, our interpretation changes. In this way, rather than simply transmitting or mirroring experiences, technology actively shapes interpretations.

There are many examples of how this shift happens in practice in an online course. We cannot see a student's happiness at answering a question well or puzzlement over another student's response (reduction), but we may be better able to view their logic in their written responses and thus have a better sense of whether they understand important concepts (amplification). A student's negative comment may seem much worse in print than the intent behind it would warrant (amplification), and we might later overlook a more neutral or positive response (reduction) because it feels diminished or minimized in an online or text-based environment. Technologies, then, are not neutral but instead play an active role in the relationship between us and our worlds, which affects how we interpret events.[17]

ACTIONS

Technological mediation can move beyond influence on interpretations to influence on actions. Our tools can introduce a cognitive bias that can lead us to wield them based on how they are *intended* to be used rather than how they *could* be used, which has direct implications for our instruction. Indeed, when inventors develop a new technology, they tend to have a specific goal in mind. There is an implied functionality inherent in a technological tool, which can influence our view of what it does or what it should do. This functional fixedness can cause us to focus on the way we believe that the object should be used rather than focusing on how to apply it in a new way in order to solve a problem.[18] A PowerPoint presentation might allow us to create audiovisuals for a lecture that might not have been possible without this technology. The same technology, however, may have prompted the redefinition of the lecture as a teaching tool.[19] PowerPoint asserts a certain cognitive style and nudges our thoughts into outlines and bullet points. If we are not careful, we can omit important details or treat all issues as if they are of equal weight, regardless of whether they actually are. Formatting slides and finding or creating images may take away time that could have been spent on fine-tuning arguments and conceptualizing issues. Arguably, we could apply PowerPoint more effectively than we generally do, such as by using its multimedia capacities to evoke a different kind of response from the audience, but the process of employing this tool is one of give and take, a fine balance between maximizing the possibilities of technology without letting the implied use of the tool overwhelm instructional decision making.

Beyond functional fixedness, however, technologies have "intentions," often built in by their designers; these intentions may also drive our actions.[20] They may have "scripts" which guide what it is we do with them. In keeping with what philosopher of technology Peter-Paul Verbeek argues, our actions are changed. Verbeek's notion of praxis, following that of philosophers Bruno Latour and Madeleine Akrich, suggests that technologies can "invite" certain actions and "inhibit" others. Verbeek explains: "Like the script of a movie or theater play, artifacts prescribe to their users how to act when they use them. A speed bump, for instance, has the script 'slow down when you approach me'; a plastic cup, 'throw me away after use.'"[21] That is, technologies are so imbued with purpose that they suggest actions to us, and these actions seem so natural that we follow them.

When we teach online, then, the tools we take up suggest actions to us. In her article "Insidious pedagogy," history instructor Lisa Lane makes this argument by suggesting that learning management systems, rather than simply making technology easier for faculty to use, instead encourage certain choices. Lane argues that while such systems are improving and adding capabilities that support teaching from a range of perspectives, she also notes that these features may be hidden from faculty, and thus default settings within the system may drive pedagogical choices:[22]

> The built-in pedagogy of the big systems is based on traditional approaches to instruction dating from the nineteenth century: presentation and assessment. This can be seen in the selection of features which are most accessible in the interface, and easiest to use. In Blackboard/WebCT, the simplest tasks are uploading documents and creating text in boxes. Although the Discussion Forum is at the top level of access, most other non-traditional features are buried deep in the system.

Thus the technological tools we take up for teaching, with their intentions and their defaults, invite and inhibit our instructional actions.

PRODUCTS

When technology intervenes in instruction, instruction is changed. The medium becomes part of the message.[23] An artist who uses a brush goes about the process of creation in a particular fashion and necessarily produces a different product than she would have done had she used a pencil. A musician who plays a musical score on a piano creates very different music than he would have produced had he played the same score on an oboe. An instructor who teaches online, even if using the same objectives and the same content, has a decidedly different product than an instructor who teaches onsite. Similarly, an instructor who uses Blackboard as a platform has a significantly different product than an instructor who uses social media.

Mediated Attitudes about Instruction

Using the technologies that we need to teach online necessarily changes our experiences, or at least our attitudes toward them, and this alteration may be positive or negative, depending on the contexts and specific changes. Two texts offer analogies that help clarify how faculty members' attitudes toward instruction may change when they teach online. In his text *Transforming technology: A critical theory revisited*, Andrew Feenberg argues that that there are two alternative conceptual technological models of postindustrial education: the factory model and the city model.[24] In her now classic work, *In the age of the smart machine*, Shoshana Zuboff asserts that computer-based technologies are not neutral. Rather, technology imposes as well as produces new patterns of information and social relations, which, in turn, have implications for our work.[25]

Feenberg's factory model suggests that learning-technology initiatives are focused on efficiency, mechanization, standardization, and reproduction. This model theorizes that technology is a medium of automation. In education, this means that technologies may be deployed to make education a technocratic commodity, automated and delivered in bite-sized modules. Feenberg asserts that the driver for this automated perspective is financial, and technology serves as a centralizing managerial delivery tool. Traditional, skilled, teacher-led educational tasks, methods, and artifacts may be replaced by technological means. Likewise, Zuboff says that technology may "automate" work, which involves replacing human labor and physical motions and leads to dull jobs that lack meaning. Drawing these two perspectives together, when we teach online, some of our work becomes more automated. While automation can be empowering—perhaps we have time to focus on more interesting aspects of our job—if we do not find a balance, it has the potential to make aspects of the job feel less exciting.

On the other hand, Feenberg's city model represents a society reflected in an "urban logic" of societal interaction and communication. It emphasizes freedom and variety over efficiency and encourages new ideas. According to this model, technology may be used to open up the educational process and is aimed at liberating individuals by distributing informational resources more equitably. It permits student-centered qualities, such as flexibility and individualization. This mode theorizes that technology is a medium of communication. Human and computer capabilities are complementary. While technology may be best suited to accomplish some operational tasks, faculty are best suited to manage complex activities and communications in the college classroom. Zuboff suggests that technology may "informate" jobs, replacing human contact with collecting information and data but potentially leading to more stimulating, challenging jobs and greater satisfaction. In its ability to "informate," Zuboff suggests that information technology substitutes a technological interface for sensory or expressive relationships with objects or persons. Thus the sensory- or expressive-based skills diminish, while new skills that allow effective management of the new interface should be developed to harness the full power of the technological tool. Zuboff's work holds relevance for faculty teaching online. In particular, the notion of "informating" skills provides a theoretical frame for understanding faculty perceptions of the changes that may occur when adopting web-based instructional technologies. Specifically, faculty in classrooms rely on interpersonal skills that, when changing to a web-based environment, are replaced by what Zuboff calls "intellective skills," such as abstraction, inference, and procedural reasoning. Finding the balance between the factory and the city models, between automating and "informating," is key to a positive attitude toward teaching online.

Strategies for Deciding Whether to Change

Teaching online is a form of change that involves our instructional realities, forms, and attitudes. When faced with a specific change, such as the kind that teaching online inevitably brings, it can be useful to reflect on what is at hand before making a decision about whether to proceed with that change. Several strategies for considering change follow.

STRATEGY #1: CONSIDER CORE VALUES

Faculty deciding whether to teach online should consider what we hold dear about teaching and what we truly would deem too great a sacrifice to do without, and then we should think about whether we can accomplish what is essential to us when teaching online. Our overarching consideration should be whether we believe we can retain and even enhance what is important to us in onsite teaching when teaching online or, alternately, replace these with things that are equally or more meaningful, even if different. We should be able to retain who we are and what we deem valuable as real human teachers when we are in an online environment, or even develop a better set of values. Margaret Soltan

A Poetry MOOC

MARGARET SOLTAN
Associate Professor
English
George Washington University, US

I'm often called a "traditionalist," and it is true that I do things like ban laptops in my classrooms.

And I did come to online teaching warily. I refuse suggestions from my expensive private university that I teach this or that class online, because I think students paying tens of thousands of dollars every year in tuition deserve teachers right there in front of them, immediately present physically and mentally. Students of this sort also deserve the energy, the presence, and the inspiration of other students around them in real time.

But when Udemy, a MOOC provider, approached me for its Faculty Project, I said yes.

I like the way MOOCs democratize things: Students pay nothing, and these courses are available to anyone in the world. I wanted to be part of that sort of outreach. My poetry course has no grading or accrediting component (yet), but I respond to student comments and questions.

Now that I've conducted my course for a year, I have learned that "quality" also means an elusive, precious sense a teacher can get that she is not just conveying ideas and techniques, but forging an intense connection with far-flung, very diverse people.

This sense of connection does not have to be on a grand scale. While some MOOCs do not consider themselves a success until hundreds of thousands of students have enrolled and passed tests and initiated online discussions, for me the success of my course (it currently enrolls close to two thousand students) is already there. To take one instance, a woman in China commented: "Your reading of [Edward Thomas's] 'Adelstrop' is beautifully illuminating, and you make modern poetry matter to me. A million thanks!"

Poetry is intense, intimate, enigmatic. Yet it is also something that pro-vokes intensities we can share. For me, there's joy and gratification in re-alizing that I am making a connection with the globe via poetry—a diffi-cult but universal form of human expression. This joy and gratification inspire me to do better with each lecture; thus they are part of the quality built in, if you will, to the MOOC.

---

describes her decision to teach online and how her values influenced her deliberation.

STRATEGY #2: CONSIDER THE CATALYST FOR CHANGE

When considering change, we should contemplate what is spurring us to teach online. It may be that we simply *want* to do it, that we think it will be exciting and invigorating, which is a good reason to consider teaching online.[26] If we are excited by teaching and find it a creative endeavor, then we probably will invest the time and energy to do it well. Another catalyst, however, may be that we *need* to do it. We may need the experience of teaching online, as doing so can enhance our ré-sumés. We may need it for the salary that teaching online can provide.[27] We may need to do it because we cannot relocate to take an onsite position. Finally, we may *have* to do it, because our administrators require us to do so or because we work at online institutions. There are a host of good prompts for teaching online, just as there are reasons *not* to do it. We may believe that the time spent will be too great.[28] We may not believe we can offer the best-quality course online.[29] We may have professional concerns, such as questions about intellectual-property rights.[30] Another issue is a lack of perceived value for online courses in promotion and ten-ure decisions.[31] Our ultimate and personal answers to the question of whether we should teach online depends on whether we are taking it up for the right reasons. Eloise Tan describes her rationale for developing an online course (see p. 18).

STRATEGY #3: CONSIDER THE SPECIFIC GOALS FOR CHANGE

We may find that we want to teach online in order to help us accomplish a spe-cific goal. We may want change for the benefit of students, in order to provide edu-cational access to students who might not otherwise have it.[32] We may wish to teach

Why Teach Online?

ELOISE TAN
Lecturer and Teaching and Learning
    Developer
Learning Innovation Unit
Dublin City University, IE

In 2010 the president of Dublin City University (DCU) launched DCU Online, a strategic initiative to substantially increase the amount of courses we offer through blended and fully online environments. For someone who works in a department that carries out research and provides continuing professional development in the area of higher education pedagogy, that meant one thing: I was going to need to learn how to teach online and, what's more, to teach others about online pedagogy.

So the honest answer to why I started to teach online is that I was asked to. I was nervous and unsure of the challenge. While comfortable with technology, I had my fair share of PowerPoint presentations not working or dodgy wireless in the lecture hall to know that a course constructed and delivered online would present a challenge to anyone. What if I can't manage the technology? What if the students can navigate the space better than I can? Or what if they can't even figure out how to log in? The "what ifs" are endless when you embark on designing and teaching online. Yet there are rewards. The reasons I will continue to teach online are that I enjoy the online interaction and environment, I believe I can provide an equally or more enriched pedagogical experience for students online, and I know that online education can reach people that the traditional "students in seats" model of higher education simply cannot.

I wrote about my journey in a short piece for the *Chronicle of Higher Education* titled "Bitten by the online bug."[1] The readers' responses say much about our colleagues' fears and concerns. While we have all experienced education at a brick-and-mortar university, we can be hesitant and unsure of how to lead students in an online journey we may have yet to go on.

When teaching continuing professional development (CPD) modules on pedagogy in higher education, I often hear from participants who state that they unconsciously model their teaching after their learning experience. Those that had a mostly rote education often share that form of learning in their approach to pedagogical concepts. Encountering reflective practice, learning-centered models, or even being exposed to a variety of educational theories "opens their eyes" to new ways of teaching and being in the classroom. As a CPD lecturer, I see firsthand that many higher education instructors come to the task of lecturing with an impressive depth in their research expertise but little formal education in pedagogy. In that reality it is understandable why some struggle with or oppose online teaching.

For me the journey as an online educator is ongoing. I am constantly learning and questioning ways of being in the online environment. Now, instead of "what ifs," I ask myself "hows." How do I know they are learning online? How can I balance content with space for students' reflections? How can I bring inspiration and passion to online pedagogy? I now see online teaching not as a requirement, but as a new frontier in higher education that I am ready to explore.

Note

1. Tan (2012) also describes her reasons for teaching online in her *Chronicle of Higher Education* article.

---

online because we think it can lead to better interactions with students and allow us to use new technologies to improve our teaching.[33] We may choose to teach online because we think doing so can help us achieve something pedagogically that we could not accomplish by teaching onsite. Chuck Eesley, who teaches a large online class on technology entrepreneurship, describes how he thought this form of teaching could help him reach his educational goals.

STRATEGY #4: CONSIDER READINESS FOR CHANGE

When deciding to make an instructional change in the form of teaching online, it is important to consider readiness. At a fundamental level, readiness means being prepared: knowing and understanding what changes are required and what practices will be necessary in order to change. Table 1.2 (see p. 21) provides a readiness assessment for teaching online.

Venture Lab Online Education

CHUCK EESLEY

Assistant Professor and Morgenthaler Faculty
  Fellow
Department of Management Science and
  Engineering (MS&E)
Stanford University, US

My experiments with online education have been motivated by the desire to expand the impact of my teaching. The nature of my course, Technology Entrepreneurship (E145), which I've adapted from the same course pioneered by my colleague, Tom Byers, demanded innovations in online education. Early on, Byers began putting his course information online, and I see myself as continuing in that tradition of openness and experimentation. I normally teach E145 to undergraduate engineers at Stanford University. When I first began talking about putting my class online, it was my colleague Amin Saberi, an expert in network algorithms, who first got excited and offered to help. He crystallized the idea that what is distinct about the type of class I teach is the team-based, experiential-project nature of the course. This was also the aspect of the online education problem that had not yet been solved, and we set about to tackle it.

In my class, students form teams and work together on a real-world start-up project during the course of the ten-week class. Saberi and one of his doctoral students, Farnaz Ronaghi, built the Venture Lab (https:// novoed.com) platform to offer team-based, experiential education, which provides more of the social and peer-learning aspect of university education, but at web scale. In our initial class we had eighty thousand students sign up, and thirty thousand formed teams and worked on the team projects. We have students do an initial assignment in algorithmically assigned teams before enabling them to search among their classmates and build their own teams.

There are always some challenges in working with teams, particularly globally distributed ones where some students do not finish the course.

Yet these challenges mimic the real-world challenges of working in teams. The team and peer-review functionality enable students to better learn from their experience working together, more closely approximating real-world problem solving. It also fosters a greater sense of obligation to one's peers, which enhances the learning experience. My belief is that with the data gathered through online education, we can improve the curriculum to the point where we can begin to close the 2 sigma gap, which is the improvement in learning outcomes that results from one-on-one tutoring.[1] Not only does online education hold out a possibility to reduce educational costs, but it also offers a chance to improve the quality of education by mixing online and offline learning.

Note

1. Bloom's (1984) study notes that there is a 2 sigma gap between large group and individual instruction. He suggests that we seek instructional methods that can help bridge this gap.

Table 1.2   Readiness assessment for teaching online

Assess your technology. Teaching online requires adequate technology. In order to be successful at change, your institution has to provide or you have to be willing to purchase equipment suitable to do the job. The following questions can help us to assess our readiness for teaching online:

- Do you have a reliable computer?
- Do you have high-speed Internet access?
- Do you have access to a learning management system (LMS) or other tools you could use to support online instruction?
- Do you have access to technologies that will support many different pedagogical approaches?

Assess your support structure. One of the most important aspects in making a successful change is having an adequate support structure. For this reason, when preparing for change, faculty may wish to consider whether their institutions, departments, and programs will be supportive of such changes, and, if so, how. Faculty preparing to teach online may consider the following questions when gauging their readiness for change:

- Do you have the support of policies that determine promotion and tenure or merit increases?
- Do you have training opportunities available?

(continued)

Table 1.2   (continued)

- Will your institutions support course development through release time or financial compensation?
- Do you have support from colleagues who could answer questions about the technology or pedagogy required for teaching online?

Assess your dispositions. While there is no one particular type of online instructor who is successful at change, faculty may wish to engage in self-interrogation to determine whether they are, in fact, good candidates for taking up online teaching. This form of teaching requires time on task as well as an innovative spirit. Faculty thinking about such a change may consider the following questions when assessing their readiness for change:

- Do you like learning new technologies?
- Do you have the self-discipline to spend hours on the computer?
- Are you happy spending time communicating online?
- Do you believe the quality of online learning can be comparable to or better than onsite instruction?
- Are you comfortable with change?

Assess your skills. Faculty who teach online need a set of skills in order to be successful. For this reason, faculty who are assessing their readiness for a shift to online teaching may consider the following questions:

- Do you have good organizational skills?
- Are you good at time management?
- Are you good at giving quick and frequent responses to student questions?
- Can you convey your thoughts in writing?
- Do you understand basic computer terminology?
- Do you have the technical skills you would need to teach online?
  - Basic computing (e.g., keyboarding)
  - File management (create and name files; organize and manage files)
  - Word processing (e.g., insert tables, graphs, and graphics into documents)
  - Presentation software (add multimedia to a presentation)
  - Social networking (e.g., use Facebook or Twitter)

Assess your preparation. There are some general questions faculty who are thinking about teaching online might consider when assessing their readiness for making this change:

- Have you taught online previously?
- Have you participated in any faculty-development activities for online teaching?
- Can you create a course site that is accessible both in layout and to students with disabilities?
- Do you know about different instructional strategies you can use to teach online?
- Do you know how to moderate online interactions?

Assess student readiness. A given group of students may be either more or less ready to participate in online learning. For this reason, faculty would do well to consider the learners' level of preparation.

- Do they have the necessary tools?
- Do they possess the skills they will need to be successful?

STRATEGY #5: CONSIDER THE SPECIFIC KINDS OF CHANGES
THAT ATTEND TEACHING ONLINE

In this chapter, I have described why and how faculty experience change when teaching, drawing on the philosophy of technology to support my argument. In the remaining chapters, I discuss the educational issues that faculty experience differently. Each of the chapters after this one focuses on a specific educational issue. When considering whether and how to teach online, faculty will want to examine and weigh these specific changes (i.e., consider *what* it is that changes) in order to determine whether they are willing and able to do so.

Conclusion

Teaching online is a fundamentally different way of engaging with instruction, and it requires an interpretation of our experiences, which is an act that, by its nature, changes them. I hope this book will encourage faculty to think about what we face if and when we move from teaching in an onsite learning environment to an online one. Unlike other texts on the topic of online learning, the implicit question I address in this book is not *how* faculty should teach online, but rather *whether* we should teach online, particularly given the changes that we will face. The question at hand is asking whether these changes are worth it, which is something for each individual to ponder. It is worthy of considered attention, and knowing and understanding the kinds of shifts that will be required is important in weighing whether we truly want to teach online.

Chapter Two

Faculty Knowledge

> Before you become too entranced with gorgeous gadgets and
> mesmerizing video displays, let me remind you that information is
> not knowledge, knowledge is not wisdom, and wisdom is not foresight.
> Each grows out of the other, and we need them all.
> —ARTHUR C. CLARKE

Those of us in traditional teaching roles typically have some notion of what we are to do as teachers prior to teaching for the first time. We have gained such knowledge over decades and in a number of subtle ways. We probably have seen good and bad teaching on television shows and in movies, and thus have learned from the examples of Michael Douglas in *The Wonder Boys*, Fred MacMurray in *The Absent-Minded Professor*, Russell Crowe in *A Beautiful Mind*, Michael Caine in *Educating Rita*, and John Houseman in *The Paper Chase*, to name just a few.[1] Most of us also have had decades of practice in face-to-face classes as students. In college and in graduate school, we learned about our disciplines from professors who ultimately served as our role models for our teaching. In particular, we often remember and emulate those professors who taught in ways that best advanced our learning, and we avoid strategies that did not work as well for us. We thus have front-row (sometimes back-row) experiences of watching good and bad onsite teaching, as well as role models who have shown us what teaching in a face-to-face setting requires. Through these models and experiences, we have developed at least some knowledge of onsite teaching.

Unlike the case with onsite courses, however, few of us have the knowledge we need in order to teach online, particularly when we first start. Rarely have we had many deep or sustained opportunities to learn about how to teach online through the observation of successful practices. Good online courses are not often the subject of television programs or movies. We typically have not experienced online courses firsthand, as only a few of us have taken an online course prior to setting out to teach one ourselves for the first time, although this will soon change, along with shifting demographics in the professoriate. We may have read "how to" books about it or even attended workshops to learn to use a specific technology, but doing so does not supplant seeing a model course or actually experiencing online teaching. As a result, we often do not have a good, practical sense of the look, pacing, and feel of online courses. We simply do not have mental examples of what teaching online should be. When we teach online, the knowledge that we need changes, and we experience faculty knowledge in new ways.

About Faculty Knowledge

The term "professor" dates back to the fourteenth century and typically refers to a person who possesses expert knowledge in a specific discipline or field and has the ability to profess it. Over the years, becoming a member of the professoriate has required increasingly specialized knowledge as well as certification of that knowledge through graduate degrees. When we hold master's degrees, we are thought to have undergone intensive study and demonstrated mastery of a body of content knowledge befitting the degree. Possessing a master's degree also signals that we have developed advanced knowledge of theoretical and applied topics in these areas, as well as higher-order skills as they relate to that knowledge, including critical thinking and problem solving. When we hold doctoral degrees, we are thought not only to have developed further knowledge but also to have deepened our understanding of our disciplines or fields. We are also thought to know how to interpret this knowledge base and, as authorities, to share it with others. Thus when we enter the teaching profession in an institution of higher education, we are thought to have expert-level knowledge in a particular area and analytical skills that we can share with students.

In addition to a mastery of content knowledge, faculty members are assumed to have acquired some knowledge of pedagogy. We generally know about the purpose of teaching, and we know that we will be sharing academic knowledge and skills with students. We know about the students we teach and the cultural contexts in which we work, whether geographic, institutional, or departmental. We know about a variety of teaching methods and techniques, having both experienced and practiced several of them ourselves. We have a sense of the kinds of things we might do in a class, ranging from lectures, to discussions, to group work. We have some ideas about how to manage classrooms and ensure students are attending and participating. The level of knowledge may differ from faculty member to faculty member, but on the whole, faculty are expected to be equipped with some knowledge of pedagogy.

As scholars have begun to consider the concept of faculty knowledge, they also have started to see the various kinds of knowledge not as discrete areas, but rather as coherently integrated ones. Lee Shulman, an educational psychologist and former president of the Carnegie Foundation for the Advancement of Teaching, made this conception clear in his work during the mid-1980s. According to Shulman, faculty possess content knowledge (CK), which comprises the theories, principles, and concepts of a particular discipline. On the other hand, faculty also have a general pedagogical knowledge (PK), or knowledge about teaching itself. Of these two areas of knowledge, Shulman asks the question, "Why this sharp distinction between content and pedagogical process?"[2] For Shulman, then, having knowledge of two distinct areas—faculty members' knowledge of the content of their specific disciplines and their knowledge of general pedagogical techniques—is insufficient. He instead argues that there is an overlap between those areas, which is where effective teaching happens.

Shulman's concept of pedagogical content knowledge (PCK) is the blend where subject-matter knowledge and general pedagogical knowledge resides. He states that PCK is "that special amalgam of content and pedagogy that is uniquely the province of teachers, their own special form of professional understanding."[3] He then describes his conception of pedagogical content knowledge:[4]

> For the most regularly taught topics in one's subject area, [PCK includes] the most useful forms of representation of those ideas, the most powerful analogies, illustrations, examples, explanations, and demonstrations—in a word, the ways of representing and formulating the subject that make it comprehensible to others. . . . Pedagogical content knowledge also includes an understanding of what makes the learning of specific topics easy or difficult: the conceptions and preconceptions that students of different ages and backgrounds bring with them to the learning of those most frequently taught topics and lessons.

Pedagogical content knowledge, then, is a way of knowing that is unique to teachers, who take an aspect of subject matter; organize and present the material; and, through pedagogical choices, transform it into something that the learners can comprehend. The concept of PCK is a useful idea that indicates a space in which good teaching happens. It is the singular combination of knowledge both of content and pedagogy combined with a deep understanding of how to convey these elements to students. This notion gives rise to the question of what happens when one area is not as well developed as another; given that few faculty have had formal training in pedagogy, the implications seem clear. If our knowledge of pedagogy is diminished, then the space in which the potential for truly good teaching happens could be reduced as well. Moreover, PCK demonstrates the fundamental nature of faculty knowledge, which is not solely content or pedagogy; rather, is a unique blend of knowledge areas that not only are inseparable but also are necessary to each other. Shulman's notion of pedagogical content knowledge provides a framework for understanding the areas of knowledge that teachers need.

Changes to Our Experience of Faculty Knowledge When Teaching Online

When we teach online, our knowledge necessarily differs in several key ways. We express content knowledge differently. We apply pedagogical knowledge differently. We necessarily add a dimension to our knowledge bases: technological knowledge. Given these shifts, we also integrate these three areas of knowledge differently.

EXPRESSION OF CONTENT KNOWLEDGE

When we teach online, the way in which we express content knowledge differs from the way we express it when we teach onsite. This seemingly simple alteration, however, makes it a different form of knowledge altogether. When we decide to teach online, we shift away from tacit knowledge, which we cannot easily explain or communicate, to a formal and explicit expression of knowledge. Our knowledge of course content is no longer something that resides somewhere in our heads, invisible, with students trusting that it is there and that we will convey it to them. Rather, we have to make it visible and tangible. We have to think through the manner in which we will store, review, update, and communicate knowledge in a formal way. Expressing knowledge in an online course also requires us to have a different set of skills for sharing that knowledge with students. We may not need as much of our sensory or expressive skills online as we do onsite to communicate an idea. On the other hand, we do need high levels of sensory skills such as abstraction, inference, and procedural reasoning in order to determine how to communicate knowledge online.[5] Thus our knowledge of content and the ways in which we will share it necessarily change.

APPLICATION OF PEDAGOGICAL KNOWLEDGE

When we think about pedagogy onsite, what we tend to think about is embodied pedagogy, which includes both embodied teaching and embodied learning. It is not just our minds that are engaged when we lecture, discuss, have students work in groups, and so forth; rather, our bodies are an integral part of the process. We picture ourselves and our positioning in relation to the students. We are physically present as we are acting, interacting, and relating. The physical act of participating in the pedagogical moment affects the mind; it is part of the learning process, whether we are aware of it or not. Max Van Manen, a noted expert on both qualitative research and pedagogy, argues, however, that pedagogy cannot be found "in observational categories"; rather, pedagogy is felt by its presence in a given encounter. Pedagogy may be "cemented deep in the nature of the relationship between" the self and others.[6] When teaching onsite, this presence includes our bodies in the pedagogical act. Embodied pedagogy is relational, since it occurs between teaching and learning and between teacher and learner.

When we teach online, our physical bodies are not part of the pedagogical process in the same way that they are when we teach onsite. When we teach online, students are more directly connected to the knowledge, or the substance, and less to the substrate, or the knowledge bearer. It is an intellective form of engagement rather than an interpersonal one. In addition, as Norm Friesen, an expert on e-learning practices, argues, individuals experience pedagogy differently online and onsite.[7] They will, for example, encounter virtual artifacts and objects, such as texts and other information, that, when compared with those onsite, "manifest a pliability, brilliance, discontinuity, and disposability that can have an educational value. At the same time, . . . [they] present certain limitations that prevents some styles of experiences . . . from being adequately simulated or represented."[8] Similarly, while we may employ the same pedagogical approaches online as we do onsite, when we strive to infuse technology with pedagogy, we do not simply simulate these approaches. Rather, they are constitutively different. Instead of physical areas, our pedagogy happens in liminal spaces, at the threshold where the boundaries between the human and the technological begin to dissolve.

As cyberprofessors, we are becoming more adept at technology; the boundaries between us, our tools, and our pedagogical practices are increasingly blurred. Thus our knowledge of pedagogy necessarily changes as the technology becomes an extension of ourselves. If planning an online discussion, we might think about how we will structure conversations (e.g., whether through chat or threaded discussions), how we will acknowledge student contributions (whether naming individual students or commenting on the group response), and how we will respond to comments (e.g., whether we will respond to each post, weave several of them together, or ask students to take turns summarizing them). We may even think about the space between interactions and how we might deal with the virtual silences. Thus, in a pedagogical act, how we would engage onsite—almost without thinking as we position ourselves among students and acknowledge and encourage them with both verbal and nonverbal signals—becomes mediated by technology, and the knowledge of pedagogy that we have requires changes.

ADDITION OF TECHNICAL KNOWLEDGE

When we teach online, we typically need to know about technology, but we may feel that we do not have this kind of knowledge.[9] Technological knowledge both arises from and simultaneously is embedded in human activity.[10] It has its own abstract concepts, theories, and rules, and these are essentially applications in real situations. Knowledge is at the heart of the technological process, and the process itself is "the acquisition and application of a corpus of knowledge concerning technique, that is, ways of doing things."[11] Technology, then, is an embodiment of human knowledge; at its most fundamental level it is organized knowledge for practical purposes.[12] It is through activity that technological knowledge is defined; it is activity that establishes and orders the framework within which technological knowledge is generated and used.[13] Our conception of knowledge, then, changes and is changed by our relationship with and understanding of technology once we begin to comprehend that technology both embodies and requires knowledge. The process is an iterative one, and it alters the nature of work.

The iterative process—in which technological knowledge is linked to a specific activity and that activity, in turn, conditions the use of knowledge—is evident in the use of technology for teaching. What we know changes what we do, which then changes what we know. In this fashion, the ways in which we use technology in teaching, particularly when teaching online, are an extension not only of what we know but also of the activity involved in our teaching. In turn, the technological activities that we take up convey our knowledge to the learner through the very fact of their use.[14] Teaching online ultimately changes our work as teachers; it is a specific kind of activity, different from teaching onsite. Because of these changes, teaching online requires an alternative kind of knowledge as well as new ways of relating to and employing that knowledge.

Instructors teaching online need differing levels of technical knowledge. The degree of technical knowledge we need depends on other course characteristics, such as how much of the course we will offer online, what platform or learning environment we will use, how much assistance our institutions will provide, and so forth. A faculty member who is working with a group of instructional technologists to put a course online will probably not need the same level of knowledge as a faculty member who is taking a do-it-yourself approach to using social media as a learning environment in a course. The level of technical knowledge and the skills faculty will require depend on the level of support they will have, the tools they are using, and so forth.

INTEGRATION OF FACULTY KNOWLEDGE: CONTENT, PEDAGOGY, AND TECHNOLOGY

Extending Shulman's ideas about pedagogical content knowledge,[15] educational technologists Punya Mishra and Matthew Koehler suggest that when teaching online, instructors need not only content knowledge and pedagogical knowledge but also technological knowledge, and that the interaction among these three bodies is important.[16] The authors argue that these interactions represent new forms of knowledge. They illustrate their concept of technological pedagogical content knowledge (TPACK) in figure 2.1.[17] TPACK advances the notion that faculty who teach online need new and different knowledge and expertise than those who teach

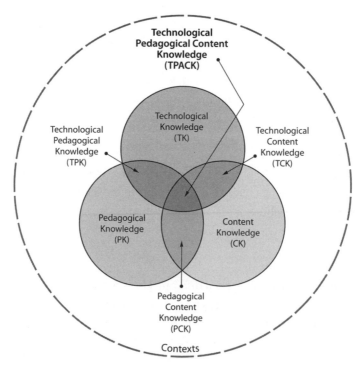

Figure 2.1. Technological pedagogical content knowledge (TPACK)

onsite. Such knowledge transcends the three individual knowledge areas and represents a different form of integrated and synthesized knowledge.

The TPAK model adds two new dimensions to Shulman's notion of PCK. In particular, technological content knowledge (TCK) results from the interplay of knowledge of technological tools (TK) and the content of a discipline (CK). Koehler and Mishra suggest that new technologies can afford new and varied representations of content as well as improved navigability. They also note that the technology may change the knowledge itself.

For example, an English professor who uses YouTube to teach Shakespeare, asking students to create their own mashups (a blend using content from more than one source) of Shakespearean plays to demonstrate key themes, may make these themes more accessible to students. But the new technology does more than teach the concepts; rather, it allows changes in the nature of learning about drama by having students create their own technological adaptations, which is a form of learning that did not exist prior to this technology. Thus the technology alters the learning, and vice versa.

In addition to TCK, technological pedagogical knowledge (TPK) concerns the interplay between knowledge of technological tools (TK) and knowledge of teaching practices (PK). It also requires knowledge about various technologies and what they do, an ability to select the technology that will best accomplish the goal, and awareness of how these elements might best be employed in teaching and learning. It also requires knowing how these technologies might include teaching. For example, an online teacher wishing to engage students in a discussion would need to know about various messaging, chat, and discussion-board options; to think about whether the goal of the discussion is to develop an initial understanding and facility with terms or instead to promote deeper thought and reflection; and to formulate how the discussion might be catalyzed, facilitated, and assessed.

Thus instructors who teach online need content knowledge, pedagogical knowledge, and technological knowledge. They also need knowledge that represents the intersections of pedagogy and content, of technology and content, and of technology and pedagogy. If any of these areas are not as well developed as they should be, then interactions among them are, at best, not as powerful as they could be (at worst, the interactions could fail to occur), and teaching and learning could both suffer. This latter point is essential. Discrete knowledge of any of the three main areas is insufficient for effective online teaching. It is the overlaps that are critical. Instead of simply adding new knowledge regarding technology to content knowledge and pedagogical knowledge, faculty instead should develop knowledge about the ways in which technology and content interact, as well as the interplays between technology and pedagogy.

It is easy to see the usefulness of this model for explaining what kinds of knowledge faculty need when teaching online. We can know what a discussion board is, have a general idea of how one works, and technically learn how to post questions and responses. If, however, we do not understand the ways in which using a discussion board interacts with the content of the discussion itself, either extending or limiting it, then we cannot be as effective in our roles as discussion facilitators as we would be if we do comprehend it. Moreover, if we do not know how technology and pedagogy interact (e.g., if we have not considered how to frame discussion prompts differently, know how many to frame, understand how to ask students to respond, and so forth), then we will not be as successful as we would be if we did have this knowledge. We need, then, not only to have knowledge of content, pedagogy, and technology, but also to have knowledge representing the interrelated and interdependent blending of these knowledge bases. Thus teaching online requires new forms of knowledge, which influence and are influenced by the technology.

Strategies for Developing Faculty Knowledge for Online Teaching

Developing knowledge for teaching online is not an easy task, and faculty who are aware of this fact often would appreciate opportunities for developing that knowledge for their online teaching.[18] Educational researchers have concluded that thinking about the connections between these areas, and thus having integrated knowledge of teaching with that of technology, is something that occurs over time and with some effort.[19] For those of us who choose to teach online, we need sound ways to develop knowledge, which typically requires moving beyond one-shot approaches. Instructors learn by studying, by doing and reflecting, by collaborating with others, by looking closely at students and their work, and by disseminating their ideas and findings. Thus, when trying to learn about teaching online, there are several key ways to go about it.

STRATEGY #1: KNOW WHAT YOU KNOW (AND WHAT YOU DO NOT)

Faculty members would be well served by assessing their levels of knowledge about teaching online. Knowing where we stand gives us the necessary information to begin the process of knowledge development. Table 2.1 outlines four dif-

Table 2.1 Levels of knowledge and skills

Level	Skills		
	Developing knowledge and skills	Choosing appropriate tools	Communicating knowledge and skills
Basic	Maintains and demonstrates [content, pedagogical, technical] knowledge and skills necessary to teach online	Chooses appropriate [content-related, pedagogical, technical] tools for teaching online	Has the capability to share [content, pedagogical, technical] knowledge and skills with others
Intermediate	Maintains and demonstrates [content, pedagogical, technical] knowledge and skills necessary to teach online at a high level of accomplishment	Chooses appropriate [content-related, pedagogical, technical] tools for teaching online; experiments with new processes, tools, or technologies to determine their applicability	Provides opportunities for others to learn [content, pedagogical, technical] skills and concepts
Advanced	Demonstrates an active interest in enhancing current [content, pedagogical, technical] knowledge skills and learning new ones; applies advanced knowledge for teaching online at a high level of accomplishment	Chooses appropriate [content-related, pedagogical, technical] tools for teaching online; improves or redesigns processes, tools, or technologies to determine their applicability	Consistently shares [content, pedagogical, technical] expertise with others, both in teaching skills and explaining concepts
Expert	Demonstrates a strong interest in continuously improving current skills and developing new ones; applies advanced [content, pedagogical, technical] knowledge to innovation and problem solving; demonstrates exemplary accomplishments when teaching online	Insightfully selects, combines, or invents appropriate [content-related, pedagogical, technical] tools or technology for teaching online; improves or redesigns processes, tools, or technologies	Is sought out by others for one's [content, pedagogical, technical] knowledge and skills and demonstrates expertise in troubleshooting complex issues related to teaching online

Source: I adapted this table from Microsoft's functional/technical skill competencies, at www.microsoft.com /education/en-us/Training/Competencies/Pages/technical_skills.aspx.

ferent levels of knowledge, from basic to expert. Instructors may wish to self-assess which of the four levels they belong in for each of the three skills areas (content, pedagogy, and technology) separately.

STRATEGY #2: PARTICIPATE IN ANY FORMAL OPPORTUNITIES AVAILABLE

Faculty-development opportunities oftentimes are available at one's home institution. Many institutions offer lectures and workshops aimed at helping faculty members master specific technologies, such as learning management systems. Fewer institutions offer sessions about pedagogy and technology. Many colleges and universities have formal coursework in the areas of instructional design and learning technologies. These could provide us with the theoretical expertise that can form the basis of our technological pedagogical content knowledge. Matthew Koehler, one of the developers of the TPACK model, gives an example of such a course.

STRATEGY #3: ENGAGE IN SELF-STUDY

Consider a do-it-yourself (DIY) approach to learning how to teach online. A DIY approach puts us in charge of what to learn, allowing us to assess what we know and what we do not and letting us make key decisions about how to fill in the gaps. Lisa Lane, an expert in online teaching who facilitates a free online course on teaching online,[20] describes some of the approaches to self-study (see p. 37).

STRATEGY #4: PARTICIPATE IN OPPORTUNITIES FOR SOCIALIZATION

Socialization is a process of coming to know and understand norms, customs, and ideologies. It provides individuals with the skills and habits necessary to be effective participants within their cultures. A faculty member interacts among several different cultures, including professional, disciplinary, institutional, and personal ones, and these various areas provide opportunities for faculty socialization to online teaching. Kenley Obas, an instructional technology leader, explains how to take advantage of such opportunities (see p. 39).

STRATEGY #5: DEVELOP A PERSONAL LEARNING NETWORK

Developing a personal learning network (PLN)—a group of people who can help guide learning, identify learning opportunities, answer questions, and be a center of knowledge and experience[21]—is especially useful in providing a source of support when teaching with the Internet, whether someone is an early adopter or

Learning by Design

MATTHEW J. KOEHLER
Professor
College of Education
Michigan State University, US

In 2006 we proposed the technological pedagogical content knowledge (TPACK) framework as a way to think about the kinds of knowledge teachers need to grasp in order to effectively teach about technology.[1] We argued that teachers needed to understand content (what to teach), pedagogy (how to teach), and technology, as well as comprehending how these three bodies of knowledge interact in teaching.

The TPACK framework has been helpful in shedding some light on what teachers, including faculty, need to know, but less attention has been paid to how they are supposed to learn it. In theory, there are multiple ways in which teachers could develop TPACK, and many such approaches have been proposed (see www.tpack.org for a listing).

Our work has focused on an approach we have called "learning technology by design."[2] In this approach, which has been successful over time, teachers work collaboratively in small groups to develop technological solutions to authentic pedagogical problems. In a specific example of this approach, faculty development by design was used in a faculty-development model to help prepare university faculty to teach online.[3]

In our faculty-development-by-design approach, six tenured faculty members became "students" in a regular master's-level educational technology course. Design teams (one faculty member, and three teachers in the master's program), worked together to design an online course to be taught by the faculty member the following year. Class periods had some whole-group time to discuss the theory and practice of online teaching, and smaller-group time to work on the project.

(continued)

Learning through this approach is, in some key ways, qualitatively different from what might be expected. First, we emphasize learning all of the components in the TPACK framework equally and at the same time, instead of initially prioritizing technology. Second, in this approach learning is implicit. For example, participants learned about web design by designing web pages for their online course. Third, learning is self-directed and project driven. For example, one group focused on how technology could be used to provide feedback, while another group concentrated on how to present and organize lessons.

How does this approach lead to learning the components of the TPACK model? Consider for a moment the traditional approach to helping faculty develop their understanding and use of technology: the target audience is directly taught (via a workshop or a similar technique) some specific skills or technology, in the hope that they can somehow later go back and integrate this new technology into their specific content areas and pedagogical expertise. In practice, this approach has failed, as the TPACK frame suggests it would, because the participants' understanding of technology is not linked to pedagogy or content.

In contrast, the learning-technology-by-design approach honors the rich connections between technology, the subject matter (content), and the means of teaching it (the pedagogy). As teachers create solutions to problems (e.g., how to design an online course), they learn the technology (e.g., how to make a web page) in the context of their content knowledge (i.e., the course they are teaching) and pedagogical understanding (i.e., how they are teaching it). Thus the design process helps builds the connections outlined in the TPACK framework, and every act of design is always a process of weaving technology, content, and pedagogy together.[4]

Notes
1. Mishra & Koehler (2006).
2. Koehler & Mishra (2005b).
3. Mishra, Koehler, & Zhao (2007).
4. Koehler et al. (2004).

(Photo credit: CC A-NC-SA
Lisa M. Lane)

DIY Approaches to Faculty Development

LISA LANE
Instructor
History
MiraCosta Community College, US

Many faculty teaching online learn the ropes by taking training sessions in how to use a learning-management system (LMS), like Blackboard or Moodle. But ending their preparation there (or sometimes even starting it there) can limit the creativity of professors in implementing their own ideas and pedagogies. Online course creation should be initiated from the strengths, ideas, and goals of the professor, not from the design and intentions of a course-management system. Yet it is so easy to just start plugging things in and uploading files.

All the best ways to avoid a cookie-cutter course involve a faculty member branching out in his or her professional development. This may mean taking workshops in pedagogy, or being mentored by an experienced online instructor. But there is even more benefit from the do-it-yourself (DIY) approach, which leads to greater confidence. Some elements of this approach include:

- *Becoming an online student.* There is little that is more educational than ceasing to be a teacher and becoming a student in an online class. You quickly realize what is right and what is wrong in terms of approach, schedule, tasks, and individuation. Taking a course in one's discipline or in an area of interest can help, and there are now many online classes in learning how to teach online, which serve double duty.

(continued)

- *Living on the web.* The lack of experience that stymies most new on-line instructors is not an inability to use an LMS. Rather, it is a lack of time spent in the open environment of the web. Professors who publish openly online, who participate in social networks online, and who engage in professional communities online make better online instructors. Those who habitually create materials and videos to post to websites tend to be equally creative when designing an online class, as well as more comfortable in the online teaching environment.
- *Doing some reading.* There is a great deal of research currently being published on the effectiveness, design, and pedagogy of teaching college students online. Articles about brain science, educational reform, or web usability can all inform online teaching.

At my community college in California, a small group of experienced online faculty formed a group to provide pedagogical workshops for faculty who were new to teaching online. Our current offering, an open online class in teaching online, attempts to fulfill all three of the above elements. In the class (called the Program for Online Teaching), which is designed and facilitated by our group, faculty have the opportunity to be online students, with readings and assignments due weekly. They create and post on their own blogs and try various tools for networking. This experience, currently in a year-long iteration (two twelve-week semesters), is designed to increase confidence when teaching in the online environment.

Such confidence makes it possible for professors to put their own pedagogy first, adopting and adapting online tools (including the LMS, if used) to fulfill their pedagogical objectives, rather than being "led" by the technology. Such an approach results in greater creativity, better teaching, and more engaging online classes.

a novice. PLNs lend themselves particularly well to those who are teaching online, since they often are accomplished through such Web 2.0 tools as social networking to maintain social contact (e.g., Facebook), microblogging to hear about best practices in short bursts (e.g., Twitter), wikis to find information related to the subject area (e.g., Wikispaces), blogs to follow longer discussions on best practices (e.g.,

Faculty Socialization

KENLEY OBAS
Assistant Professor
Associate Vice President of Information
    Technology
Alabama State University, US

Socialization is a key component for faculty success in both traditional and online teaching. While the socialization process is well constructed for traditional faculty, it is not structured as adequately for online instructors. Departmental meetings, office hours, or casual "water cooler" encounters do not occur naturally in an online environment. Therefore, participating in formal socialization opportunities is essential for faculty teaching online.

After carefully researching how traditional faculty socialize at Alabama State University, we developed several means that foster socialization online. First, we examined the obligatory course-orientation meeting for faculty members, since it is a key element in the formal socialization process. We then developed an online course-orientation session for all faculty teaching online courses. While we created this orientation for faculty teaching only online courses, we also invited faculty teaching traditional and hybrid courses to participate. We held the orientation in a synchronous environment, using web-conferencing technology. The session included presentations from college administrators and a review of procedures at the institution. The opportunity for faculty to interact in a formal setting, however, was the most important factor. We requested that all faculty members have a webcam, since it was essential to put a face with a name. We also encouraged faculty to use the chat feature to learn more about each other during the session. Finally, we purposely allowed time for informal conversations prior to the start of the online course-orientation session. We found that these conversations were candid and

(continued)

informative, providing insights for the institution. Several faculty members exchanged contact information and even ventured into virtual breakout sessions. In addition to the orientation, we added other socialization opportunities, such as online forums, online workshops, and mentoring.

In the event that a given institution lacks a formal orientation and socialization process for online educators, several other options are available to assist online faculty in this regard. Professional organizations, such as the United States Distance Learning Association (USDLA), are a viable means to provide opportunities for socialization. Organizations like USDLA offer workshops and seminars that allow online faculty to communicate and discuss their experiences. In addition, faculty attending these events represent a variety of backgrounds, which could help create a rich and diversified experience for participants. Another opportunity to socialize exists in social-media outlets, such as Twitter, Facebook, and Tumblr. Several online faculty have used Twitter as a means of sharing their experiences and strategies in teaching online. Following these faculty members on Twitter offers an informal forum in which to exchange ideas about and even express frustrations with teaching online. Facebook and Tumblr also provide opportunities to communicate with faculty throughout the world who are teaching online. It is important for faculty to identify an arena where they can communicate with other faculty members.

Faculty need positive socialization. Online educators are no exception, as they can become detached and isolated from both their peers and their institution. Developing formal and informal socialization opportunities for online faculty has to be intentional and deliberate for online programs to be successful.

---

using Technorati as a search engine), real simple syndication (RSS) readers to keep up with multiple blogs in one place (e.g., Google Reader), social bookmarking to learn what others are bookmarking (e.g., Delicious, Diggo), and webinars to listen to live, online presentations and participate in real-time chat with subject experts (e.g., TedTechTalkLive). These all help us with learning to use communication tools while becoming informed about online teaching from those who do it regularly. In some ways PLNs provide a model of online learning that many of us need. Face-to-face teaching circles, which are informal and regular discussion groups held on campus with faculty members who have similar interests in teaching online, also can help faculty work with the kinds of changes they are experiencing online. Such groups can generate and share ideas, discuss problems and solutions, and serve as an informal advisory committee.

STRATEGY #6: LEARN FROM THE WISDOM OF PRACTICE

While gaining knowledge from what others have done can be an effective approach, we ultimately learn from our own practices, assessing what works for us and what does not. If we consistently seek to develop better online practices, in a sense we are acting as leaders. Learning from the wisdom of practice is a less codified approach than other methods of developing knowledge,[22] but it consists of the basic process of trial-and-error coupled with reflection. Developing and sharing the means to reduce the "collective amnesia" that is common with teachers would be a contribution to research and practice.[23] Many instructors use blogs for this purpose, both as a way to keep a personal record about the course and as a means of sharing information with others.

STRATEGY #7: LEARN FROM THE PRACTICES OF OTHERS

One important way to develop faculty knowledge for teaching online is to learn through the documented practices of others, which often are captured in research studies. One of the most recognized examples of documenting teaching practices in higher education is Arthur Chickering and Zelda Gamson's widely cited article, "Seven principles of good practice in undergraduate education."[24] These principles, aimed at suggesting instructor actions, are:

1. Encouraging contact between students and faculty.
2. Developing reciprocity and cooperation among students.
3. Encouraging active learning.
4. Giving prompt feedback.
5. Emphasizing the time spent on task.
6. Communicating high expectations.
7. Respecting diverse talents and ways of learning.

Several authors have adapted Chickering and Gamson's principles for the online environment. Chickering himself, working with Steve Ehrmann, wrote one of the first of these, "Implementing the seven principles: Technology as a lever."[25] More than a decade later, Maria Puzziferro and Kaye Shelton have suggested the need for faculty development for online faculty to help them adopt the seven principles.[26] Other researchers have also documented good practices in teaching online. Katrina Meyer, an expert in higher education and an educational researcher, describes her research on the practices of effective online teachers.[27]

STRATEGY #8: USE TEACHER RESEARCH TO DEVELOP KNOWLEDGE

Teacher research has much to offer in the field of online learning. While existing research is replete with direct comparisons of students on exams, grades, standardized tests, and the like, there is surprisingly little in the way of in-depth analyses of particular courses. To ameliorate this dearth, faculty who are interested in a specific question about a given course could gather data in an attempt to answer this question. Different queries about issues such as the ones described in this book could be studied across disciplines, across educational levels, and across institutional types, to name but a few possibilities. Additional attention to context would be a useful supplement to the knowledge base. Providing detailed information about the maturity of the course, such as faculty experience, student demographics and experience, and the pedagogical approach would be a welcome addition to the research. Data collected from students or faculty could include:

- interviews
- focus groups
- activity logs
- time logs
- self-reflections
- journals
- virtual field notes
- communication patterns

Faculty teaching online not only can improve our own knowledge but also contribute to the knowledge base related to online learning by developing presentations, course monographs or articles, or course portfolios.[28]

STRATEGY #9: LEARN FROM STUDENTS

Students can sometimes be a terrific source of information and expertise for learning a new technology. They are usually eager to show you a trick or tip. Treating students as experts has multiple advantages, including boosting student self-esteem ("I taught my professor something she didn't know today!"), and moving the class closer to an instructional model in which everyone is learning together.

Research on Faculty Stories about Teaching Online

KATRINA MEYER
Professor
College of Education, Health,
   and Human Sciences
University of Memphis, US

Experienced online instructors know something beginners often do not. In 2009 and 2010, I interviewed twenty-one experienced online faculty in tenured or tenure-track positions at public master's/doctoral institutions and community colleges. These faculty had each taught more than ten on-line classes and had offered instruction in basic disciplines (humanities, social sciences, and sciences) as well as several professional fields (e.g., nursing, education, computer science). They were asked a deceptively simple question, "How do you attempt to increase student-learning pro-ductivity in your online courses?" Student-learning productivity was de-fined as learning that happened faster or better, or was more in depth. Faculty members' stories of what they did to bring about this type of learning produced four common themes.

First, faculty stressed the importance of the abundance of online re-sources available for their courses. They used material from the Library of Congress, web-based learning games, virtual labs, and faculty-developed content to add richness to their courses. Second, they noted the impor-tance of online tools (e.g., email, texting, and tweeting) to provide one-on-one attention to students, answers to questions, guidance on next steps, and feedback on student work. Third, they stressed the learning re-sulting from student interactions with other students, be they through participating in a discussion board, working collaboratively on group proj-ects, or preparing a wiki. The fourth theme was the faculty's focus on time. This included the need to routinize instruction into time segments—such as into seventeen-day cycles, seven-day cycles, and even

(continued)

forty-eight-hour cycles—plus choosing a deadline for handing in assignments that would be consistent throughout the class. Additional ancillary themes were (1) finding creative ways to engage students in the subject, including the use of experiential learning and problem-based learning, and (2) making the students' learning active rather than passive. Most importantly, these faculty were certain their efforts were affecting student learning—they had seen the evidence in their students' work.

Conclusion

Teaching online requires and instills new ways of knowing, new types of knowledge, and new ways of developing knowledge. These supplemental forms of knowledge add to what teachers typically should know and do in order to fulfill their roles as teachers. In particular, teaching online requires us to learn about technology and the ways in which it intersects with both content and pedagogy. Doing so requires additional effort, but it can also help us to understand both content and pedagogy in new ways. Adding in technological knowledge has the potential to develop our knowledge bases and ultimately has the means to help us improve as teachers.

Chapter Three

Views of Learning

You live and learn. At any rate, you live.
—DOUGLAS ADAMS

S tudent learning is one of the key responsibilities of most college and university faculty members. To be competent in our instructional roles and best enable student learning, we need a general understanding of what learning is, or at least a good idea about what we think it is. Deep in our core belief systems, we carry convictions about the essential features and elements of learning as well as ideas about how students can best accomplish it, whether we explicitly acknowledge these views or not. It is our notions of learning that inform and drive our teaching practices. Thus when we teach, we necessarily are taking a stance, or position, on learning. Teaching online changes not only the circumstances but also the processes and products of learning, which, in turn, requires us to reposition our views about the best ways to create the conditions that foster it. As online teachers, we necessarily (re)consider our views of learning when we make decisions about how to teach in this new instructional format.

About Views of Learning

There are many differences of opinion about what learning is, what the goal of learning is, how learning occurs, and what factors influence learning. There are, however, a few things on which scholars do seem to agree. Most scholars concur that, at its most fundamental level, learning is a form of change. They also agree that learning involves acquiring or developing new (or modifying existing) knowledge, behavior, skills, attitudes, or values. Learning is a process that may occur as a part of educational or personal development. It may take place consciously or subconsciously. The way in which scholars believe that these things happen in practice, however, varies widely.

Many theories of how individuals learn were developed in the field of psychology and have been subjected to clinical tests and efficacy trials. These theories predominated views of learning in the nineteenth and twentieth centuries and are still widely accepted today, with evidence of their importance being visible throughout the educational landscape, represented in the ways in which instructors develop, teach, and assess courses. Among the key theories are behaviorism, which holds that learning is a change in behavior; cognitivism, which holds that learning is a change in mental structures; and constructivism, which holds that learning is a change in an individual's internally constructed realities. Table 3.1 depicts the primary features of these theories.

Expanding on the ideas of the constructivists, a group of learning theorists have recently turned their attention toward the interactions that happen between and among individuals and technologies. That is, their theories hold that knowledge resides not only within individuals but also within technological objects and tools. Learning is or may be mediated by technology, which, in turn, takes on significance as a critical component of learning. Learners interact with each other and with technology; they engage in joint activities and have shared tools, and their interactions with technology are, by nature, social ones. Learners use their objects and tools, and they think and learn with them. They construct a common language and a shared understanding while they simultaneously are engaged in the pursuit of individual and collective objectives. Individuals learn as they construct a network of both human and nonhuman actors, including technological tools. Thus they are active agents in a sociocultural and sociotechnological environment. Tools both enable and constrain their actions and interactions. From these perspectives, then, learning is the set of connections between people, tools, and the environment. Learning is something beyond an individual act; it is groups of individuals tapping into and building a networked intelligence, which may become even more explicit in an online learning situation. As such, these theories, typically branching from constructivism, portray a sociotechnological view of learning. Table 3.2 (see p. 49) provides an overview of three such concepts of learning.

Given the development of our understanding of the role of technology in learning and the growing influence of the sociotechnological constructivists, we have new opportunities and fresh challenges involved in reconsidering learning in a novel and connected environment that values both the creation and sharing of knowledge. The idea that learning is something human, individual, and personal has expanded to include a view of learning that occurs through connections with others and with technologies, one that is not only facilitated but also potentially augmented by technology. No longer do we see technology simply as a tool, or an aid to learning; rather, we learn *with* and *through* technology so learning can and

Table 3.1 Overview of psychological theories of learning

	Behaviorism[1]	Cognitivism[2]	Constructivism[3]
Variations	• Classical conditioning (Skinner; Pavlov)[4] • Operant conditioning (Thorndike)[5] • Social-learning theory (Bandura)[6]	• Gestalt psychology (Wertheimer)[7] • Information-processing theory (Atkinson; Shiffrin)[8] • Schema theory (J. Anderson)[9]	• Cognitive constructivism (Piaget)[10] • Social constructivism (Vygotsky)[11] • Social constructionism (Pappert)[12] • Sociotechnological constructivism (see table 3.2)
What learning is	A change in behavior	A relatively permanent change in a learner's schemata or in the way that the brain processes information	A process during which a learner draws on current and past knowledge to construct new ideas, at times with other human or non-human actors
Goal of learning	Acquiring knowledge (e.g., facts)	Changing mental processes (e.g., problem solving)	Constructing new knowledge (e.g., a new internal reality); the convergence of knowledge between individuals
How learning occurs	Stimulus and response	Duplication of the knowledge constructs of the knower, who organizes information for the learner	Experience of an individual acting and engaging with others; learner-to-learner interactions
Factors that influence learning	Rewards/punishments	Existing schemata and prior experiences	Prior experiences

Sources: I developed this table by distilling information from a wide range of resources on learning theory; an overview of these theories/sources appears in Savin-Baden & Major (2004). See also Siemens (2006b).

1. Online computer-assisted instruction (CAI) is an example of a behaviorist educational approach, with its emphasis on the delivery of content and on frequent testing to determine whether the content has been learned. There are many studies about CAI that have taken place over decades that document the effectiveness of CAI as an instructional approach (e.g., Pear, 2004).

2. Cognitivism often relies on the image of the computer as a model of mental processes and holds that learning is a process of acquiring and storing new information, resulting in a change in an individual's internal mental state as short-term knowledge is transferred to long-term memory. Information-processing theorists, including many early CAI proponents, believe that several factors can affect rote learning, such as the organization of prior learning, practice, and mnemonics. Theorists who focus on information processing specifically include R. Anderson (1984); Gagne & Dick (1983); Rothkopf (1970); Newell, Shaw, & Simon (1958); and Miller (1956).

(continued)

Table 3.1   (continued)

---

3. Many online instructors are turning to constructivism as a learning theory underpinning instructional design.

4. Classical conditioning holds that a neutral stimulus can become associated with a different stimulus that elicits a response, which can be either positive or negative. Ivan Pavlov demonstrated this phenomenon by finding that after conditioning, a dog can associate a neutral stimulus, such as the sound of a beating metronome, with food. The dog can then respond to the neutral stimulus by salivating.

5. Operant conditioning suggests that consequences control behavior. That is, a subject will probably repeat behaviors that are rewarded but will not repeat ones that are punished. When Edward Thorndike placed a cat in a "puzzle box," the cat learned to pull a ring, which allowed it to escape through a side door. The cat would repeat the behavior to free itself from the box.

6. Social-learning theory indicates that people learn within a social context through observational learning, which occurs via live observation, verbal instruction, or symbolic systems (e.g., television, movies, or the Internet). See Bandura (1977).

7. Gestalt psychology suggests that human consciousness cannot be broken down into elements; rather. it should be considered as a whole. The brain is holistic, with self-organizing tendencies.

8. Information-processing theory holds that the human mind is like a computer, in that it is an organized system that processes information. The mind applies logical rules and strategies as it moves information from short-term to long-term memory. The mind, just like a computer, has a limited capacity for storing and processing information.

9. Schema theory holds that an elaborative network of abstract mental structures, or schema, represents the way in which an individual understands the world. According to schema theory, schemata are the core elements of cognitive processing. This theory attempts to explain organized knowledge as a process of encoding information in long-term memory. According to schema theory, existing knowledge provides a framework into which newly formed structures are fitted. See J. Anderson (2004).

10. Piaget (1985) describes his concept of cognitive constructivism.

11. Vygotsky (1978) describes his notion of social constructivism.

12. Social constructionists believe that learning happens when students are engaged and share information with others (Papert & Harel, 1991).

does happen in new and different ways. Table 3.3 illustrates several recent shifts that may be enabled by technology.

Faculty teaching in different environments can occupy various places along each continuum. While one might argue that onsite faculty tend toward the categories on the left-hand side and online faculty tend toward those on the right, in reality faculty teaching onsite may position themselves toward the right end of any of these continua. Likewise, faculty teaching online may position themselves toward the left.

Changes to Faculty Views of Learning When Teaching Online

Teaching online, however, can and does aid (and sometimes requires) movements toward the right along the continua in table 3.3 (see p. 51) in several important ways. First, teaching online can *support* a shift in perspective. An individual who moves toward the right in his or her perspective may take up teaching online

Table 3.2   Socio-technological constructivist views of learning

	Distributed-learning theory (distributed cognition)	Situated-learning theory (situated cognition)[1]	Connectivism
Where knowledge resides	Knowledge resides in and is distributed across systems composed of a human agent and his or her peers, teachers, and socioculturally constructed cognitive objects and tools[2]	Knowledge is both bound to social, cultural, and physical contexts and is situated in activity[3]	Knowledge exists in the world
What learning is	Learning, or knowledge development, is attributed to the system of human agents interacting dynamically with artifacts	Learning is a social process in which knowledge is co-constructed; it is situated in a specific context and embedded within a particular social and physical environment	Learning is making connections between information and being able to regularly access that information
Goal of learning	Coordination of representational cognitive estates	Social construction of knowledge	Creation of a capacity for learning
How learning occurs	Learning, or cognitive achievement, is a process in which cognitive resources are shared socially, so an individual can accomplish something he or she could not do alone	Learning is unintentional and situated within authentic activity, context, and culture. Learning takes place in the same context in which it is applied	Learning requires making connections between human and nonhuman knowledge sources.[4] The learner does this by connecting with and contributing information to a learning community.[5] Learning is thus a process of developing a network and creating connections within it[6]

Note: It is my argument that these theories fall within a constructivist paradigm and form a new sociotechnological constructivism. The scholars who developed these theories have not claimed to be constructivists.

(continued)

Table 3.2   (continued)

George Siemens, one of the developers of the notion of connectivism, has claimed that connectivism is a new and distinct type of learning theory, comparable to behaviorism, cognitivism, and constructivism (see Downes, 2005, 2006, 2007; Siemens, 2005a, 2005b, 2006a, 2006b, 2008). Other scholars, however, suggest that connectivism does not constitute a theory of learning; rather, it is either an analogy, a pedagogy, or a curriculum (see Kop & Hill, 2008; Verhagen, 2006).

1. This type of learning often is associated with communities of practice, which are groups of individuals who share a common interest. A community of practice can exist onsite, such as at work, or online, such as with discussion boards or newsgroups. Members of the community share ideas, information, experiences, and so forth. See Wenger (1998) and Lave & Wenger (1991).

2. Salomon (1997, p. 112) describes distributed learning.

3. Lave & Wenger (1991, p. 50) describe situated learning as a process of "legitimate peripheral participation." Their view of learning is one of "an evolving, continuously renewed set of relations." As a novice moves from the periphery to the center of a community, he or she becomes more active and engaged and, if the process continues, eventually assumes the role of an expert. The authors believe that "increasing participation in communities of practice concerns the whole person acting in the world" (p. 49). Through continued social interaction and collaboration, learners ultimately become involved in a community of practice that embodies the beliefs and behaviors that a learner should acquire. J. Brown, Collins, & Duguid (1989, p. 34) suggest that cognitive apprenticeship is an aspect of situated learning: "Cognitive apprenticeship supports learning in a domain by enabling students to acquire, develop, and use cognitive tools in authentic domain activity. Learning, both outside and inside school, advances through collaborative social interaction and the social construction of knowledge."

4. A learning community serves as a node and is always connected to other nodes (learning communities). Nodes vary in size and strength, and they are dependent on the number of individuals who are navigating through a particular node as well as on the concentration of information in a particular cluster. Ties are what connect nodes. Siemens (2005a), one of the developers of this perspective, outlines the major ideas of connectivism:

- Learning and knowledge rest in a diversity of opinions.
- Learning is the process of connecting specialized nodes or information sources.
- Learning may reside in nonhuman appliances.
- The capacity to know more is more critical than what is currently known.
- The ability to nurture and maintain connections is needed to facilitate learning.
- The ability to identify connections between concepts is important.
- The purpose of connectivist activities is to maintain current and accurate knowledge.

Decision making is a learning process, as information can change and what is viewed as correct one day may be incorrect the next. Siemens (2008, paragraph 10) asserts that "the ability to see connections between fields, ideas, and concepts is a core skill."

5. Siemens (2005a) suggests that "a community is the clustering of similar areas of interest that allows for interaction, sharing, dialoguing, and thinking together."

6. According to Siemens (2008, paragraph 6), "the capacity to know is more critical than what is actually known."

because it can best accommodate that change in perspective. Second, teaching online can provide faculty with new experiences that can *prompt* shifts in their perspectives; it is easier to see the timing of learning as being in a state of flux when instruction can occur asynchronously. Third, teaching online can *compel* shifts in perspectives. An individual who starts at the extreme left-hand end of the continua who, for reasons beyond individual choice, takes up teaching online

Table 3.3   Potential shifts in one's views of student learning

	Starting from ⟶	Extending to
Timing	fixed	flux
Locus	single	multiple
Type	formal	informal
Route	prescribed	emergent
Duration	completable	continual
Activity	consumption	production
Product	invisible	visible
Outcomes	accepted	uncertain

(e.g., if a faculty member needs a job that requires online teaching or if an administrative decision necessitates teaching an online course) will necessarily make some movement to the right across most of these categories, simply in order to accomplish teaching an online course.

The extent of an individual's move along a particular continuum depends on the instructor's unique circumstances; faculty can move incrementally or dramatically along each continuum. An individual who teaches a blended course may be positioned only a little bit toward the right, edging slightly toward seeing the timing of learning as being in flux. On the other hand, an individual who teaches a fully online course may be positioned further to the right, toward seeing the timing of learning as being in a constant state of flux. Table 3.3, then, depicts several continua illustrating the kinds of changes to views of learning that teaching online can support and facilitate and, in some cases, may require. In the following sections, I provide further details about and examples of each of these changes.

TIMING AND LOCUS OF LEARNING

For hundreds of years, members of academe casually functioned under the myth that learning happens within a set time of the day, for a fixed duration during a semester or quarter system, at a stable location. Students walked to brick-and-mortar buildings, entered hallways and then classrooms, and plunked down in their seats at a predesignated time. That perspective is changing as we are beginning to conceive of knowledge as something that resides in the world, across systems, and is bound to social, cultural, and physical contexts.

When we teach online, we necessarily move beyond traditional considerations of the timing and locus of learning. While we might value the interpersonal interchange that can occur within a set space and in real time, a view of learning as something that happens at a fixed time and in a single location can be difficult to maintain when teaching an online course. Students "come" to the course, or access it, in multiple ways and at myriad times. We have begun to view learning, then, as something that extends beyond the limits of time and space. Learning anywhere, anytime, is reality.

Valerie Irvine is a pioneer in anywhere, anytime learning through what she has dubbed "multiaccess courses." In such courses, students have multiple points of entry for a course; they may attend an onsite session, or they may attend with an offsite cohort, or they may login from home. She describes three different multi-access courses:

1. Teacher as Leader (ED-D 410)
2. Social Media and Personalized Learning (EDCI 338)
3. e-Research: Harnessing and Understanding Technology in Research (EDCI 515)

When teaching online, students reside in multiple places and access the course when and where they can. The development of handheld technologies is pushing the boundaries of access to learning even further. Learning does not have be done at a fixed setting, or even an alternative one; rather, it can be mobile.[1] That is, students need not sit at a desktop computer to participate in a course; they may learn wherever they are, whether in their homes, in libraries, on a bus, at a coffee shop, on campus, and whenever they like, even when climbing a mountain, working in a warzone, or taking a vacation in a remote area.[2] Norbert Pachler, an educational expert who studies mobile technologies, indicates how these technologies are allowing learning to happen beyond its previous limits of time and space.

TYPE OF LEARNING

Learning traditionally has been associated with a formalized system of higher education. More recently, alongside the advent of communications technologies and new views of learning using technological artifacts, we have begun to realize that learning can be unintentional, situated, and can take place in the same context in which it is applied. This realization has led us to recognize nonformal and informal approaches to education, or education that occurs outside the bounds of a formally recognized curriculum.[3] Scholars have identified several types of informal learning, including self-directed learning, which is intentional and conscious; incidental learning, which is unintentional but conscious; and socialization, or tacit

Example of Three Multiaccess Courses

VALERIE IRVINE
Assistant Professor
Education
University of Victoria, CA

I started teaching open online courses in 1998 at the University of Alberta, under the leadership of David Mappin and Craig Montgomerie. These courses began with EDPY 487 (Virtual Schooling) and EDAL 547 (Educational Administration with Computers) and continued at the University of Victoria in 2001 with the Computers in Education Certificate Program. While all of these courses ran off open web pages, using modules with a link to a conference board that supported access for credit learners and guest access for open learners, the most exciting part was receiving email submissions of assignments from a diverse group of open learners, ranging from K–12 students in British Columbia to university students at Coventry in England. We did not track the visits to the page, so it is unclear how many learners accessed it. This course occurred long before the MOOC phenomenon, and the mix of for-credit and open-access participants always fascinated me, but I also became drawn to the immediate obstacles to online courses within brick-and-mortar institutions. I had moved from one province to another to enroll in a face-to-face graduate program, only to find my courses were online in the first term of my graduate program. Similarly, when I began my academic appointment, I had interest from strong potential graduate students who could not study with me because they were unable to relocate to my campus and could not take our core courses online. The problem here was the rigidity in the modality used to offer courses. My research program was formed to examine ways to move control of course access to the Internet. In 2009, I created the term "multiaccess learning" to describe this mixing of

(continued)

modalities for course access, timing, group formation, personalization, and social-media integration, as well as for blending synchronicity and flipping (presenting taped lectures in advance of the class session).[1]

In 2012, prior to the practicum for students who were BEd majors, we offered a multiaccess course—with nine face-to-face students on campus and seventeen students coming in by webcam from around western Canada—for a conversation-based seminar on ethics in teaching and learning. Our campus registration system was modified to allow a learner to choose between access modes for a single course section. A more detailed multiaccess framework was also created, outlining the four tiers of access (face-to-face, synchronous online, asynchronous online, and open). It was published, along with a study of this education course that covered perceptions of course quality and learner preferences for modes of course access.[2]

In 2013, this core course was expanded to six out of eight sections, and I then taught EDCI 515, a graduate-level Educational Research Methods course offered in multiaccess mode. We were soon joined by a Computer Science Research Methods course, so we co-located half of the students from each course in two on-campus rooms, while the other half of the learners in each course joined in via webcam. Because we had enough

BEd course on Teacher as Leader, with seventeen remote and nine face-to-face learners

EDCI 515: An Educational Research Methods class, with two co-located courses from education and computer science. One class had twelve learners while the other had twenty-two. Approximately half of each class joined via webcam, and the other half joined face-to-face.

EDCI 515: Separate co-located room, with a Computer Science Research Methods class

(continued)

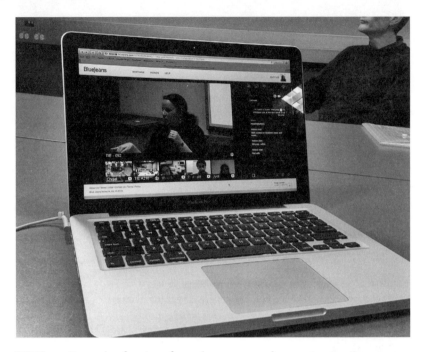

EDCI 515: Example of an interface when a remote learner is accessing as an individual node. Content is maximized or minimized using a slider bar.

endpoints free, learners (or myself as the instructor) could choose from day to day whether to come to campus or join online.

In 2013 I also taught EDCI 338, another education course, with four learners in the face-to-face classroom and twenty-two students joining via webcam. Because we were near the maximum use of endpoints, the students who lived in town had little flexibility in choosing a mode from class to class; they were required to confirm if there was enough room to move between face-to-face and online. We also often brought in guest speakers from around the world, such as Bonnie Stewart.

In the two courses discussed here, we also blended the timing (one hour synchronous and two hours asynchronous via discussion, using the course hashtag on Twitter or blog postings and comments mixed with personalized open-learning pursuits and course projects). We also sometimes flipped the classroom, with guest lecturers sharing videos of their talks for viewing in advance, so we could use our hour to converse with

EDCI 338, with guest speaker Bonnie Stewart

University of British Columbia / University of Victoria Island Medical Program lecture hall, showing webcam access from the interior of the province

(continued)

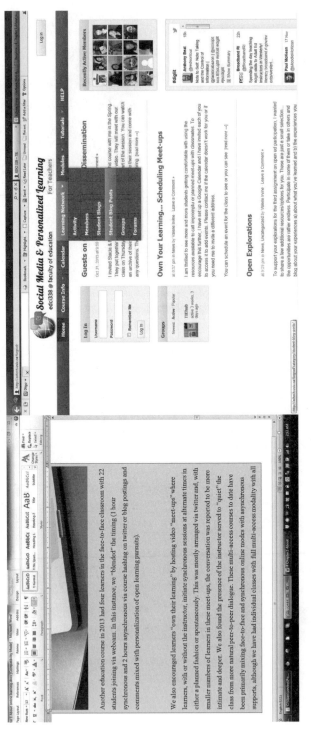

EDCI 338: Open course blog using WordPress Multisite with BuddyPress

them instead of receiving a lecture. Twenty-two learners were remote, while four were in the classroom with the instructor.

The course blog and most student blogs for EDCI 515 and EDCI 338 were hosted via a multiuser site (WordPress Multisite with BuddyPress) created by Dr. Jillianne Code, and a rich site summary (RSS)[3] aggregation that syndicated all student posts (hosted or external) on one page.

I also encouraged learners "own" (become actively involved in) their learning by hosting video meet-ups, where learners (with or without the instructor) initiated synchronous sessions at alternate times in either a planned fashion or spontaneously. I also found that the presence of the instructor served to quiet the class, steering them away from more natural peer-to-peer dialogue. These meet-ups were mostly arranged via Twitter and, because of the smaller numbers of learners in these meet-ups, the conversation was reported to be more intimate and deeper.

Multiaccess learning conveys to the learner that they have control over how they wish to access the course within the designated tiers that are being offered. It is a way to support these diverse access-mode preferences within one course offering, while allowing the brick-and-mortar university to engage in online and open learning while retaining face-to-face offerings.

Notes

1. See Irvine (2009).
2. See Irvine, Code, & Richards (2013).
3. RSS is a format for delivering regularly changing web content. Many news-related sites, weblogs, and other online publishers syndicate their content as an RSS feed so whomever wants it can subscribe.

---

learning, which is neither intentional nor conscious.[4] When engaging in informal learning, the learner sets the learning goals and objectives and may achieve them through self-study, mentoring, and the formation of communities of practice. Informal learning provides students with opportunities for greater reflection and greater control over their learning; such opportunities, in turn, give students a chance to practice self-regulation and individual reflection on that learning, which is important, since informal learning is not necessarily measured by or subjected to tests.

Mobile Learning

NORBERT PACHLER
Professor and Director of International
    Teacher Education
Institute of Education
University of London, UK

The influential New Media Consortium's (NMC) Horizon Project produces an annual report in which it identifies and describes emerging technology it considers likely to have a significant impact on education and educational practice in the near future.[1] These yearly reports have featured mobile technologies with an increasing degree of emphasis over the past few years. This trend is a reflection not only of the rapidly evolving technological prowess of these devices—multifunctionality, computational power, convergence, and resource ecology, to name but a few—but also, equally importantly, of their integration in people's everyday lives. New practices have also emerged, with mobile devices and the artifacts and services created with and accessed through them becoming legitimate cultural and learning resources.

   This new attitude toward and our expectations about learning are characterized, among other things, by our experiences in using a growing range of material, social, and cultural resources to acquire something of personal relevance. This shift is particularly significant for online learning, as it reflects the increasing desire of people not only to work, shop, and be entertained wherever they are and whenever they can and want to do so, but also to harness the potential these mobile devices have for promoting learning in informal contexts. Therefore, it is essential for providers of formal learning opportunities, such as higher education institutions, to also foster a serious engagement with mobile devices, such as smartphones and tablets. Otherwise, they risk a fundamental disconnect with the expectations of learners and the sociocultural realities of their worlds and lifestyles.[2]

Notes

1. Information about the Horizon Project is available at www.nmc.org /horizon-project/.

2. Pachler, Bachmair, & Cook (2010) and Kress & Pachler (2007) provide additional insights into the concept of mobile learning.

Online learning offers us opportunities to recognize informal learning. Massively open online courses (MOOCs) are a good example of this shift in our perspectives on learning.[5] Thousands of individuals have flocked to courses that are offered, at least currently, outside the bounds of a formal credit structure. They have done so for personal or professional reasons and to achieve their own goals, which extend beyond the bounds of what a formal program encompasses. Informal learning takes advantage of the extended views of learning across place and time, but truly recognizing, measuring, and rewarding this kind of learning remains a challenge. Curtis Bonk, a leading researcher in the field of educational technology, describes how various types of informal and extreme learning are growing and thus are increasing our opportunities to conceive of learning in new ways (see p. 62).

ROUTE OF LEARNING

The route of learning in higher education typically has been associated with didactic instruction, in which a professor leads a group of students through the process of acquiring a predetermined body of content knowledge and related skills. That is, the educational institution or the instructor sets the learning goals and objectives, and learning is an intentional process in which the students participate by doing what is expected of them. This type of learning lends itself to assessment and evaluation. With the development of new views of learning, we have begun to see that cognitive resources can be socially shared, so an individual can accomplish something he or she could not do alone. Moreover, we have begun to recognize that learning can require making connections within a network of human and nonhuman actors.

Prescribed learning can be the norm in online courses, as is evident through many such courses developed from a behaviorist perspective. This form of learning has the advantages of being familiar, contained, and measurable. A growing number of individuals, however, have come to the idea that learning in online courses is an emergent activity, one that can scarcely be prescribed or controlled

Informal and Extreme Learning

CURTIS J. BONK
Professor
Instructional Systems Technology,
    School of Education
Indiana University, US

Online learning is changing the face of higher education. Whatever your role, be it instructor, instructional designer, program manager, learner, or some other, you now have access to countless free and open resources, tools, and websites to enhance and potentially transform learning. There is an influx of open courses that learners can browse, enroll in, or download and share with others. Most recently, there is much interest in the possibilities of massive open online courses (MOOCs) with thousands or even hundreds of thousands of learners in a single class. Instead of being enamored with the raw enrollment numbers, however, my research team and I feel that there is a need to collect stories about some of the individual life changes brought about by this type of online learning. Each human learner matters.

For example, open educational resources might be accessed by someone in a hospital bed or in prison who, in turn, gets inspired by the content and decides to complete an unfinished degree or start a new one. Along these same lines, a person who is unemployed or recently retired, as well as a young adult in career transition, might find MOOCs and other free and open resources invaluable in igniting new passions and skills. With online content, such people can learn when in a bookstore, café, nursing home, or train. We are currently collecting stories about such learners.

Think back to the late 1980s, when videoconferencing projects were established between high school students in New York City and Moscow, Russia. These intercultural exchanges were considered pretty extreme, at the far edges of learning possibilities. Today, such instructional activi-

ties commonly occur in online webinars, video chats, and web conferences. For instance, in a project called Soliya, new technologies are
used to encourage college students in the United States and the Middle
East to engage in critical thinking, collaborative projects, and significant
cross-cultural dialogues and debates. Websites such as the Khan Academy, TED Talks, and even YouTube shift such video-based learning opportunities from live events to stockpiles of videos that can be watched at
any place, at a time one chooses, and used for myriad educational purposes. As an example, school children in India who lack qualified
teachers are using Khan Academy videos to learn math, science, and
English.

Shared online videos and MOOCs are just two forms of extreme learning. People who want to learn a new language can use the award-winning
BBC *Learning English* program, or they could join an international community of language learners using Palabea or italki to have individualized
learning interactions. Other online learners might be working on a master's degree in education while fighting in a war zone in the Middle East.
Younger learners might seek an online high school degree while playing
professional tennis or participating in Olympic training. Extreme learning
can also be witnessed on the interactive program *Nautilus Live*, where primary and middle school students use the web to ask questions of scien-
tists and engineers aboard vessels like the E/V *Nautilus*. In 2012, live
video and data feeds were sent from this ship as it traveled the Black,
Aegean, and Mediterranean Seas detailing various research and scientific
discoveries.

The formats for open, informal, and extreme learning are increasing.
We are attempting to document some of these forms and the opportunities they offer, so online instructors and learners can take better advantage of them. We also want to detail the motivational factors involved in
selecting them. If successful, the stories we collect in our research might
serve as inspirations to others hoping to learn from open educational resources, be they the more casual, informal variety like Wikipedia and
YouTube or those that are a bit more unusual or extreme.

other than by the learners themselves, although it certainly may be encouraged, promoted, and nurtured by the instructor.[6] This form of learning is, by definition, messy and uncontrolled. Dave Cormier, an educational theorist who was instrumental in the development of MOOCs, describes this as "rhizomatic learning," an organic view of learning as an emergent activity.[7]

DURATION OF LEARNING

In the past, educators have considered information or skills to be static concepts. Once the learner had acquired a set bit of content or a specific skill, the learning process was deemed complete. The focus of this type of learning is on "learning about," and it is the focus of most higher education institutions. Douglas Thomas and John Brown, experts in technology and learning, suggest that there are two more senses of learning that, instead of being static, are directly related to the perspective where learning is a form of change; that is, knowledge and skills are in a constant state of flux, so learning is and must be continuous.[8] One of these senses of learning is "learning to be," which requires engagement with a community and involves processes such as socialization and enculturation. Students learn new social norms and develop media literacy, and they need guidance about how to belong. They need space to "hang out" with others so they can become socialized as members of the learning community. The other sense of learning as continual change is "learning as becoming," which is the idea that learning is never fixed and formalized and always involves the learner in a process of becoming. Individuals, Thomas and Brown believe, need to move beyond mere knowledge and awareness of others to involvement as part of the group. They also should learn disciplinary, institutional, and course norms in order to situate themselves within a group. They need to acquire knowledge in new ways and have it become their own. To this end, Thomas and Brown argue that what is almost completely missing in education is the concept of play, or the idea of learners as tinkerers. Play allows individuals to delve into systems, figuring out how and why they work and what rules underlie them. By understanding systems at this level, individuals can begin "hacking" them to get results, even if a system is not explicitly designed to produce these results. Play can lead to either surface levels of understanding or deeper ones; the latter facilitate the transformation from learning to know, to learning to be, and then to learning to become.[9]

Teaching online can enhance our opportunities to see the character of learning as a process of continuous change. Students often have to "learn to be" in an online course. They should learn new social norms in a different environment,

Rhizomatic Learning

DAVE CORMIER
Manager
Web Communications and Innovations
University of Prince Edward Island, CA

(Photo credit: Kate Inglis,
www.kateinglis.com
/photography/)

The rhizomatic-learning approach developed in response to my experiences working with online communities. In 2005, some colleagues and I started meeting regularly online for live interactive webcasts at EdTech-Talk. We learned by working together, sharing our experiences and our understanding. The outcomes of those discussions were more about participating and belonging than about specific items of content—the content was already everywhere around us on the web. Our challenge was in learning how to choose and how to deal with the uncertainties of the abundance of information and the choices presented by the Internet. In transferring this experience to the classroom, I try to see the open web and the connections we create between people and ideas as the curriculum for learning. In a sense, participating in the community *is* the curriculum.

A rhizome is the underground stem of a plant (like hops, ginger, or Japanese bamboo) that helps the plant spread and reproduce. A rhizome responds and grows according to its environment, not straight upward like a tree trunk or a corn stalk, but rather in an apparently haphazard yet networked fashion. As a story for learning, this type of rhizome is messy, unstable, and uncertain. It is also, as anyone who has ever had a rhizomatous plant in the garden will tell you, extremely resilient. A rhizomatic learning experience, like a rhizome itself, is multiple; it has no set beginning or end. Instead, a rhizomatic approach fosters learning through the act of experimentation.

(continued)

The web is an ideal place for this kind of learning. By exploring a community or a context, you can get to know how language is used, what the customs are, and how decisions are made. You can get a feel for the knowledge that exists in that field. The idea is to think of a classroom/community/network as an ecosystem in which each person is spreading his or her own understanding among the pieces of information available in that ecosystem. Publically wending one's way through that accumulation of knowledge (by content creation and sharing) provides a contextual curriculum to remix back into the existing research/thoughts/ideas in a given field. An individual's own rhizomatic learning experience creates a curriculum for others.

---

norms that are not necessarily the same as they are onsite. Often students need to acquire new tools to develop and demonstrate literacy in these changed environments. To be successful, students have to grasp how to situate themselves in a group. They should determine whether they are lurkers, contributors, commenters, linkers, or a combination of these varied and continually changing roles. In some online environments, students have opportunities to hack the system and create new combinations of information and technology, thus using content and technology in novel ways. If we empower students for learning and provide them with the appropriate technological tools, then learners have opportunities for play, that is, for using technologies in ways in which they were not intended in order to get new results. Students can have opportunities for tinkering with and hacking systems online that they might not have in onsite environments.

ACTIVITIES AND PRODUCTS OF LEARNING

For hundreds of years, educators labored under the assumption that learning happened by way of an individual's consumption of information and ideas. This "banking model" of education presumed that the learner was an empty account waiting to be funded.[10] The products of learning were deemed invisible, with evidence of learning believed to be embedded in the minds of individuals. Individuals might not even be aware of possessing a certain kind of knowledge and might not know how to demonstrate what it is they know. On the other hand, somehow this learning should be signaled through a person's performance on tests and assessments. Thus, under this view of education, learning is a transient event that leaves very little evidence of having taken place. Over time, however, educators began to question and challenge this perspective, asserting that students are individuals who should necessarily be active agents in the process of learning and who can demonstrate measurable learning outcomes.

Teaching online provides an additional opportunity to allow learners to make flexible use of knowledge and become producers of visible information and knowledge. That is, students can create informational products more easily in an online environment than they do onsite. They can create e-books, videos, animations, and so forth that document their knowledge, making it visible to others. When learning online, individuals have opportunities to demonstrate and explain in a tangible way what it is they have learned and how they have learned it. The online learning environment also allows us to make the processes of learning more durable, through the creation of learning artifacts. When online, these learning moments and artifacts—such as emails, discussions, or chats—are captured. Learners can engage in problem solving and critical thinking as they create new and remix existing knowledge to solve a practical problem. Internet technologies have also allowed more-experienced learners to engage novice learners in areas of expert thinking, such as through video production. These expert approaches traditionally have been invisible to novices, but technology makes them more explicit and more attainable. Learning is contextual; it is both practical and creative, reflexive and socially accountable.[11] A record of the events exists, which we may revisit and reflect on. The products of learning are also explicitly and visibly rendered, providing evidence of the processes of their creation.

OUTCOMES OF LEARNING

When we teach onsite, we have decades of educational research studies that document learning from lectures, collaborative learning, problem-based learning, and a host of other approaches; thus we need not feel we are entering into unchartered territory when we teach an onsite class. On the other hand, we are also developing a well-documented body of evidence that suggests that online learning is an effective method of improving learning outcomes. Between 1998 and 2012, more than two thousand research or evaluation studies on the effectiveness of online learning at the higher education level were published in peer-reviewed journals.[12] Just over two hundred of these studies involved a direct comparison between online and offline program models, suggesting that by and large, online and offline courses often have similar outcomes in the area of cognitive gain. Some results have shown that online courses are slightly better, and others that offline ones have a modest edge.[13] Such findings, sometimes referred to as the "no significant difference" phenomenon, have gained the attention of many educators. In particular, researchers have compiled a bibliography of hundreds of studies that compare online courses (or other form of distance education) with onsite ones.[14] As the name of the phenomenon suggests, in most cases the mode of instruction does not lead to a significant difference in the amount of content students learn.[15] Some researchers have done meta-analyses of such studies, reanalyzing the published data to determine an effect size (a statistical measurement of how robust a particular factor is), and in general have confirmed the "no significant difference" indication. One of the most recent meta-analyses of these studies was conducted by the US Department of Education, where researchers found that *"on average, students in online learning conditions performed better than those receiving face to face instruction"* [emphasis in the original].[16] This difference was slight, but statistically significant.[17] The researchers also found that *"the effectiveness of online learning approaches appears quite broad across different content and learner types"* [emphasis in the original].[18] In other words, online learning was effective for undergraduates, graduates, academics, and professionals. Several scholars claim that research aiming at a comparison between online and offline courses has been largely exhausted.[19] Robert Bernard, well-known for his work using meta-analyses to examine learning outcomes in online courses, discusses this belief, along with ideas about the future of such research.

We have also taken strides toward documenting learning outcomes in online courses. Online learning provides optimal conditions for capturing significant data from a large number of students, and many scholars advocate learning analytics as a way of examining and interpreting them. The 2012 *Horizon report* states that learning analytics is "the interpretation of a wide range of data produced by and gathered on behalf of students in order to assess academic progress, predict future performance, and spot potential issues."[20] The process of learning analytics involves gathering data and subjecting them to statistical analyses, as well as explanatory and predictive modeling, to gain insights into and to act on complex issues. Various analyses can be employed, such as social-network analysis, content analysis, discourse analysis, information visualization, and so forth. Researchers have begun to use learning analytics to study different questions and issues, from identifying at-risk students in online courses to looking at learner experiences during a MOOC, as well as to gauge e-mentoring relationships.[21] These tools have been heralded for their potential in documenting online learning outcomes, but some educators have urged caution.[22] For example, Gardner Campbell, an educational technology leader, suggests that we remember the human side of learning (see p. 71).

Future Research in Online Learning

ROBERT M. BERNARD
Professor
Educational Technology, Centre for the Study
    of Learning and Performance
Concordia University, CA

It is difficult to predict where research in web-based online learning is heading, mainly because it is hard to know where online learning itself is going. But there are some trends that suggest the kinds of research models that we are likely to see in the future.

Some older patterns of research are diminishing, hopefully to be replaced by more productive approaches. For instance, I believe that the old stalwart of research questions, "How does online learning compare with traditional classroom learning?," will finally be laid to rest. There are at least four meta-analyses that answer this question fairly definitively.[1] Each found an average effect size of between 0.12sd and 0.15sd favoring online learning, so it is relatively clear that online learning can be as effective as classroom instruction, if not more so. What is not clear is what makes the difference—the distance, the media, the instructional strategies, or all of these in various combinations? Answers to these questions are not likely to be forthcoming unless we change the direction of our comparative research.

Two other studies have proposed that for quantitative research to advance beyond simplistic comparisons, a new paradigm is required, one that compares one online condition with another around some substantive instructional question.[2] This may lead us to a clearer understanding of which instructional strategies, characteristics of media, patterns of interaction and engagement, and supporting facilities can make online learning the best that it can be, in and of itself, without reference to classroom instruction.

(continued)

In the domain of qualitative research, Janette Hill, Liyan Song, and Richard West provide a perspective that focuses on the role of social-learning theory in the design and execution of web-based learning environments (WBLEs). In particular, they suggest the following implications for future research and practice: "(1) examining learners' individual characteristics in WBLEs, (2) identifying strategies for promoting social interaction in WBLEs, and (3) developing effective design principles for WBLEs."[3]

The world of educational research is no longer divided as much as it once was between quantitative and qualitative paradigms. There are now mixed models that combine the strengths of each approach, allowing researchers to address big questions ("Is it this, or that?") while investigating more nuanced issues relating to learning processes. I expect to see more mixed-methods studies in the online research literature in the future.

Notes

1. See Cook (2009); Means et al. (2009); Sitzmann et al. (2006); Bernard et al. (2004).
2. See Bernard et al. (2009); Cook (2009).
3. See Hill, Song, & West (2009, p. 97).

While we have a strong and growing body of evidence to suggest that students can learn disciplinary content knowledge in well-designed online courses, and we possess some cutting-edge techniques that are showing potential, we have not significantly redefined the concept of what it means to learn in an online environment. Because of this, we still have a long way to go to document how students do and do not develop in online courses. Several researchers have conducted surveys of faculty members to gauge their opinions about the quality of learning in online courses. Their findings are mixed. Some studies document that faculty think online courses lead to higher levels of learning;[23] many other studies suggest that faculty believe there is no difference between online and offline learning;[24] and several studies that included both faculty who were experienced and those who were inexperienced with teaching online have documented the faculty members' opinion that online courses are of a lower quality than those taught in a face-to-face environment.[25] A recent survey by the Sloan Foundation, notable for including more than 10,700 faculty at sixty-nine public colleges and universities, found that

Caution in Learning Analytics

GARDNER CAMPBELL
Vice Provost for Learning Innovation and
    Student Success
Virginia Commonwealth University, US

(Photo credit: D'Arcy
Norman)

With so many markers of our external lives now stimulated by and fed back into the digital realm, we live in a world in which "big data" get bigger and apparently more comprehensive by the second. We seem to be on the verge of quantifying, within cyberspace, a record of our lives so accurate, identifiable, and predictive that the stories of our lives will simply write themselves. The determinist's dream will come true: everything will be fully quantified and therefore fully understood.

Much of what is currently discussed as "analytics" in education represents learning in this way. What we know about brains and cognition, however, suggests instead what anthropologist Gregory Bateson terms an "ecology of mind."[1] The questions Bateson proposes about mind and learning concern not behaviors but epistemologies, the assumptions and strategies through which we make and share meaning. Can these be analyzed? Certainly. But we must be careful not to think that measuring or tracking a single set of actions—clicks on a web page, or even answers on a test—tells us everything we need to know about the complex processes of learning and understanding. Nor should we think that numbers alone can offer us an adequate representation of that complexity. Numbers are powerful symbols. But we have other symbols available to us as well, no less powerful and useful: stories, images, music, and the humanities in general. These endeavors are interpretive and expressive, and, singly and together, investigate meaning within the experience of our lives. Part of

(continued)

the significance of quantitative data is that they help us question and, when appropriate, revise our assumptions. But they are not meaningful in themselves, any more than a list of events is meaningful outside the context of our lived experience.

If we are not very careful, "learning analytics" may lead us into the trap that Bateson articulates: "*Somebody gets paid to make the pathological trend more comfortable. We treat the symptoms—we make more roads for the more cars, and we make more and faster cars for the restless people; and when people (very properly) die of overeating or pollution, we try to strengthen their stomachs or their lungs. . . . That is the paradigm: treat the symptom to make the world safe for the pathology*" [emphasis in the original].[2] Will the vendors whose products track our students' "behavior" make the world safe for the pathologies of standardized curricula and regimented instruction? Will their agents be a cadre of apparatchiks left behind after the colleges and universities replace their unruly intellectuals with compliant proctors of compliant students for whom "student success" means only "success at being a student"? As Charles Dickens wrote in a different context in *A Christmas Carol*, "the shadows of the things that would have been, may be dispelled." There is still time for our spirits to burn more brightly and prevent such a future. The humanities and the sciences, in their largest human contexts, must be partners in these acts of illumination.

Notes

1. See Bateson (1991).

2. See Bateson (1991, p. 295), in his chapter on his chapter on "Symptoms, syndromes, and systems."

---

a full 70% of all the faculty surveyed believed that online courses are inferior to offline ones, and 48% of those who had taught online believed that online courses are inferior. Somewhat surprisingly, the study author also found that the majority of those who feel the learning outcomes of online education are somewhat inferior nonetheless have recommended online courses to students.[26] In short, much research remains to be done to reframe the concept of learning in a new environment and document these outcomes. At a fundamental level we, as faculty, know that, but while we may be hopeful, we are still uncertain.

Strategies for Taking a Stance toward Learning

The changes to the ways in which we view learning in online environments are significant. For this reason, we should come to terms with what we believe about learning as well as with our views about learning with technology. We can use our understanding of learning—from what it is theoretically to how it happens on-line—to serve as a guide for our instructional practices. Our views necessarily drive what instructional approaches we adopt. Thus comprehending our own views toward learning can help us better understand why we do what we do as teachers and allow us to make better instructional choices in the future, which, in an iterative cycle, can influence student learning. There are several strategies that faculty can employ to better prepare for and manage these choices.

STRATEGY #1: TAKE STOCK OF YOUR VIEWS OF LEARNING

In order to begin this process, we should think of ourselves as learners. While the adage states that "teachers teach as they were taught," it seems reasonable to assume that we may instead teach as we best learned. That is, knowing how we learned can provide insight into why we go about things in the ways in which we do as teachers, even—or perhaps especially—in a new environment. Learning styles have received some attention in the educational literature as of late, and while there is no evidence to support the idea that matching teaching approaches to learning styles improves learning, there is some evidence that different learners have preferences for doing certain kinds of activities.[27] For this reason, some instructors can benefit from both taking a learning-style inventory themselves and having their students take one. Doing so can provide instructors with a sense of how they and the students may prefer to learn. Inventories such as the Kolb Learning Style Inventory (LSI); the Grasha-Reichmann Student Learning Style Scales (GRLSS); Barbara Soloman and Richard Felder's Index of Learning Styles; or Neil Fleming's Visual, Auditory, Reading/Writing, Kinesthetic Learning Styles (VARK) can be a good starting point.[28] While it is not possible to accommodate all students' learning styles at any one time, it can be useful to know their different preferences toward learning, even if it simply triggers the idea that such knowledge can be helpful in varying our teaching approaches.

STRATEGY #2: IDENTIFY A PERSONAL THEORY OR THEORIES OF LEARNING

We can seek to identify a theory of learning that meshes with our own. A good exercise for instructors is to review learning theories and identify those that are

Table 3.4   Assessing readiness for changing one's views of learning

		Level of readiness					
	Starting from	1	2	3	4	5	Extending to
Timing	fixed						flux
Locus	stable						mobile
Type	formal						informal
Route	prescribed						emergent
Duration	completable						continual
Activity	consumption						production
Product	invisible						visible

most compatible with their own perspectives and experiences, both as learners and as teachers. Based on what we glean from theory, we can challenge our underlying assumptions and either embrace or reconsider them as we determine how to structure online learning experiences. In short, where our knowledge of how to do something falls short, theory can help us bridge the gap. Once we have an understanding of our views, it can be helpful to put them into writing. Developing a formal statement that reflects a personal view of learning allows us not only to refine our thinking about our views of learning, but also to use them in a new way. It also provides us with an avenue for making our views more transparent to students by sharing this information with them.[29]

STRATEGY #3: ASSESS READINESS FOR ADOPTING NEW VIEWS

Given what we know about the ways in which teaching online requires us to change our views on the processes and products of learning, we would do well to consider our levels of readiness for such changes. Instructors can consider the shifts outlined in table 3.3 for where they fall along the continua. Rating each change for a level of readiness from 1 (happy with the old view) to 5 (highly ready for a new view), as illustrated in table 3.4, can provide teachers with a better understanding of their own perspectives and thus help them assess whether, and how, they might choose to teach online.

Conclusion

Living in a state of constant change has presented us with new opportunities for revisiting long-held notions of learning as well as for considering new directions about the ways in which we conceive of learning. Our views of learning are important, since what we believe about the means people use to learn has a direct influence on what we do in higher education as well as on how we determine whether we are doing it well. Teaching online adds some new questions and new implications for how we understand learning, particularly in online courses. Conceptualizing learning in an online environment demands that we consider the relationship between technology and learning and their influence on each other, and it requires taking a stance toward learning in this new environment.

Chapter Four

Course Structure

The whole is more than the sum of its parts.
—ARISTOTLE

Instructional systems may be understood in part through an examination of the essential features and elements of various instructional phenomena, as well as in the ways in which these interact with each other. Faculty may consider how the courses we teach are situated within an institution, department, and program. We may also strive to understand how they are similar or dissimilar to other courses that we are aware of. In addition, we may consciously or unconsciously compare elements within and across our own courses. And all for good reason. Understanding course structure, which comprises these elements and interrelations that faculty intuitively seek to understand, can help us to grasp the meaning of a complex instructional system. From that understanding, we can make better decisions about our teaching and thus create better courses. When we teach online, there are new structures for us to consider and understand, however, and these differences can lead us to new patterns of making decisions and eliciting meaning.

About Course Structure

A course is a unit of instruction, typically fixed not only by the subject matter but also by the organizational parts, or elements, through which the course is offered. Common organizational elements of courses include course term (e.g., semester, quarter, or a set number of weeks), course credit hour (e.g., fixed or variable), course enrollment (e.g., small or large), course curricular designation (e.g., prefix or section number), and course type (e.g., lecture or seminar). These elements signal the interrelation of courses and other organizational units in institutions, and many of them have been determined prior to the assignment of an instructor to teach the course. Course structure, then, comprises the basic organizational elements of a course and their arrangements and relations to other elements.

Changes to Faculty Experience of Course Structure When Teaching Online

When reading literature related to online learning, the structures of different types of courses are not always readily apparent. Indeed, it would be possible to conclude from this literature that "online learning" is one specific thing: a monolithic approach to any teaching that takes place over the Internet. In the past decade, authors have used many different terms seemingly interchangeably to signal teaching by means of the Internet, thus bolstering this perception. These terms include online learning, e-learning, web-based teaching, Internet-based teaching, computer-based learning, virtual learning, and countless combinations of these terms. In practice, however, the diversity that exists among online courses is impressive, demonstrating the myriad ways in which individuals teach online courses. New elements associated with teaching online include enrollment, timing, amount, platform, and pathway. A host of different combinations of these elements are possible for individual online courses; thus these elements signal course composition at a fundamental level. Table 4.1 outlines the different structural elements along a continuum, in the form of a classification chain.

While the table illustrates extremes, many courses fall somewhere in between, offering a combination, or middle ground, thus increasing the number of possibilities. Knowing more about the different elements and their potential combinations can help faculty better understand the current state of online learning and provide a foundation for understanding the ways in which making choices among these elements is an aspect of instructional change.

Table 4.1   Classification chain of online course structures

Structure	Completely ◄————————————————————►	Completely
Enrollment	closed	open
Amount	online	blended
Timing	asynchronous	synchronous
Platform	provider-offered	do-it-yourself
Pathway	centralized	distributed

ENROLLMENT

One of the most currently discussed structural elements of online courses is enrollment, which may be closed or open. A closed course is available only to those who formally sign up for it through a recognized institution. An alternative term that some use to describe closed-enrollment courses is "traditional online course," which marks a notable shift away from stakeholders viewing only onsite courses as a traditional form of higher education. This term thus demonstrates a growing awareness that online learning has been in existence for a sufficient length of time (in this case, decades) to be considered mainstream.[1] While what counts as traditional online teaching is extensive and loosely defined, the common ground among these courses is that they mirror the enrollment structure of the onsite classroom. In short, only those students who register through an institution of higher education and who pay tuition can enroll in the courses.

On the other hand, an online course may have open enrollment. Open-enrollment courses have had some history as an option within higher education, but they have rapidly gained visibility with the relatively recent development of massively open online courses (MOOCs). The core feature of these courses is that they are available to anyone who has adequate technological tools, who wishes to learn something about the topic, and who has the time to participate. Thus thousands of participants potentially could enroll in them. Some courses are both closed and open: a small group of students can enroll for course credit, but the course is also open to a larger group of participants who will not earn credit, such as the model described by Alec Couros. Couros is credited with being a foundational influence on the MOOC movement, and he enthusiastically describes an open course he taught in 2007.

While open courses have been around for some time, Dave Cormier of University of Prince Edward Island is credited with coining the term "MOOC" in 2008 while teaching a course with fellow Canadians George Siemens of Athabasca University and Stephen Downes of the National Research Council.[2] More than two thousand students enrolled.[3] As their model suggests, MOOCs typically are large-scale open courses (or have the potential to be large-scale ones). Participation in these courses typically is free, unless participants wish to use them for credit, at which point various kinds of fees attach to them. These differ by course provider and user purpose and could involve payment for a transfer credit to a MOOC-accepting institution of higher education or for taking and passing a certifying examination.

Open Courses

ALEC COUROS
Associate Professor
Education
University of Regina, CA

In 2007, I facilitated Social Media & Open Education, an open online graduate-level course now seen as a fundamental influence for the early MOOC movement. The design of the course was heavily influenced by my research on the open-source software movement and, more specifically, on the individuals and the networks they formed to solve difficult and elaborate problems. The development of GNU/Linux, an incredibly successful endeavor, was a testament to how a problem as complex as an operating system could be addressed through the weak ties of networks. I wanted to leverage such networks for teaching and learning.

When the course began, I had twenty registered students, which was above the norm for enrollment. But then, in a discussion with my students, we decided to invite the world to participate. I put out a "call for network mentors" on my blog, sent out a tweet, and soon we had over two hundred mentors for my students—a 10:1 mentor-to-student ratio. And these "outsiders" weren't your average students: they included professors, teachers, instructional designers, educational researchers, and several university administrators (one of whom was a university president).

The role of mentors was multifaceted: participation in course events, feedback on student work, resource sharing, and a number of other activities. But it was their role as informal learners that really made a significant difference. These were professionals, role models to my students, who were participating in the class as learners without the motivation of earning course credit. These were individuals who were genuinely interested in the material and in supporting the learning of my students. Their

(continued)

presence added an enormous motivational aspect that would have been difficult to replicate.

But there was another student who also made a significant impact. He was a sixteen-year-old high school student from Scotland who stayed up late every Tuesday so he could participate in this graduate course emanating from Canada. One night, during an Elluminate session on student digital literacies, this Scottish student pulled out his bass guitar, added a few loops from GarageBand, and gave us a live performance. The chat room lit up with amazement at what we had just experienced.

Open courses provide opportunities and connections that can serve as inspiring supports for students. The serendipity of networks is one of the reasons I'm a huge advocate for openness in course design.

Currently there are at least two distinct forms of MOOCs: cMOOCs and xMOOCs.[4] The differences between the two have the potential to influence the future directions of open courses. The first, cMOOCs, are associated with the notion of connectivism, a theory of learning that uses the metaphor of a network made up of nodes and ties to describe learning.[5] What characterizes this type of MOOC is openness, diversity, autonomy, and connectivity across a network of distributed knowledge. In cMOOCs, the learner is expected to discuss, debate, discover, and produce.[6] The second form, the xMOOC, emerged largely from the work of Stanford University professors Sebastian Thurn and Peter Norvig, who taught a course in artificial intelligence in which over 160,000 participants enrolled.[7] The three leading providers of xMOOCs currently are Coursera (started by Daphne Koller and Andrew Ng), a for-profit company with Stanford roots and many university partners, including many ivy-league institutions; Udacity, a for-profit with Stanford roots but with no university affiliation; and EdX, a nonprofit run out of the Massachusetts Institute of Technology (MIT) and Harvard University, along with the University of California at Berkeley and the University of Texas system. Early forms of xMOOCs differed dramatically from their cMOOC predecessors, particularly pedagogically. Many of the xMOOCs started with somewhat traditional pedagogy, in which learners watch video lectures and participate in objective online assessments (e.g., quizzes and exams). These courses have evolved over time, however, as some xMOOCs rely on team-based learning and participant reviews of each other's work, while others, particularly those taught in the humanities, are thought to be moving closer to the methodology of the cMOOC by using more constructivist pedagogical approaches.[8]

MOOCs have captured the attention of journalists, administrators, faculty, and students, all of whom have striven to understand more about them. These courses have been hailed for their potential to make higher education scalable as well as free and affordable to anyone interested in enrolling.[9] They also have been criticized for possibly being able to create a stratified educational system that provides onsite education to a privileged few and online education to those who cannot afford it otherwise.[10] Some have argued that these courses will disrupt higher education as we now know it.[11] Others claim that they will not matter much in the long run.[12] While these several perspectives offer intellectually interesting and important arguments, those who describe the potential influence of MOOCs on higher education do not typically consider the differences between various kinds of MOOCs, which can influence the future development of online courses. Combinations with other elements create myriad possibilities for their structure, however, and understanding the differences among various types of open courses can allow educators to have some influence on their development and, thus, a hand in shaping how they might affect higher education.

AMOUNT

Another structural element of online courses is the amount of the course that occurs by way of the Internet. In fully online courses, all of the content is delivered and all of the interactions and activities happen through the Internet. There are no required onsite meetings. Orientations and examinations, however, may be either onsite or online, depending on institutional requirements. Teaching a course in this fashion often requires dramatically rethinking that course from the bottom up, providing instructors with the capacity to accomplish something different and unique when teaching fully online. But they also lose some of the benefits of onsite teaching, such as seeing students in real time and having visual cues, such as eye contact and body language.

In blended, or hybrid, courses, part of the content is delivered and some of the course activities and interactions take place at an onsite location, while other parts of the content and some interactions occur online, in a learning environment supported by the Internet. There is no firmly established rule about how much of the course has to happen over the Internet for it to be blended, although some of the sessions that normally would be held onsite would take place online instead. In short, putting a syllabus online and exchanging some emails with students is not blended learning. Rather, substantive and direct instructional activity should take place over the Internet in order for a course to be considered blended learning. Teaching a blended course purports to be the best of both worlds, allowing faculty and students to meet in real time and space and to be supported virtually. When alternating between online and onsite teaching, however, the continuity of the class can feel somewhat broken.

There are some differences in the literature about whether there are two or three classifications related to the amount of an online course that occurs by way of the Internet. In an influential Sloan Foundation report, I. Elaine Allen and Jeff Seaman suggest a percentage allocation to determine the type:[13]

- *Online.* 80% or more of the course happens on the Internet.
- *Blended or hybrid.* 30%–79% of the course happens on the Internet.
- *Web-assisted.* 1%–29% of the course happens on the Internet.

Other researchers seem to favor a simple distinction between the terms "fully online" and either "blended" or "hybrid." While the former approach has the advantage of making finer distinctions, the latter seems to be the most useful and wieldy for faculty who teach online. Fully online is a fairly clear description, while 80% or more online leaves that classification more open for interpretation. In addition, the difference between a course that is 75% online and one that is 80% online is probably small, if even detectable. Finally, 1% online is such a tiny amount that it seems questionable to count such a course within the category of courses taught through the Internet. Certainly many of us who teach online do not make a distinction between 29% and 30%, nor would we be likely to consider a course with 1% offered online as a web-assisted course. As a practical matter, it seems most accurate to label a course that never meets onsite as fully online and designate one that has some meetings onsite and some activities conducted over the Internet as blended.

TIMING

Another structural element of an online course is related to how the course unfolds over time. In synchronous courses or sessions, students and instructors are required to be online at the same time. That is, the course has a regularly scheduled meeting time, and the instructor and students participate in the course then. Lectures, discussions, and presentations thus occur at that predetermined time. Synchronous courses provide students with the opportunity to participate in a real-time class experience, as well as to have fairly instant responses to their questions and comments. In asynchronous courses or course components, instructors supply materials—including lectures, assignments, tasks, and tests—that students can access at any time. Students complete assignments at different times, although they often are given a timeframe for finishing the assignments, such as a one-week window. They may watch a video or respond to a discussion prompt within their own timeframe. Instructors also respond to and interact with students at different times. Asynchronous courses allow students to have a longer period in which to form their thoughts and compose comments and responses before having to contribute them to the class, while synchronous classes can favor quick thinkers and fast typists.

PLATFORM

A learning platform is the foundation on which a course is built. A platform provider offers a prebuilt product that can handle many online learning functions, including course administration, documentation, tracking, reporting, and delivery. Many instructors who choose a provider-offered platform use a learning management system (LMS), a software application that gives faculty members a central hub, which is a place in which to post content, facilitate discussion, and assess learning. (In the United Kingdom these systems are referred to as virtual learning environments, or VLEs). Some of the most frequently used learning management systems are Blackboard,[14] Desire2Learn,[15] Moodle,[16] and Canvas.[17] Moodle and Canvas are open platforms, which means that they are free and that instructors who use them may adapt the platforms to their own ends.[18] What these systems offer instructors and students is a single space in which they can interact. They also provide a relatively high level of confidentiality for course participants.

In addition, companies developing xMOOCs (Coursera,[19] EdX,[20] Udacity,[21] and Venture Lab[22]) offer their own specialized and uniquely tailored platforms that serve as a central hub. This kind of platform provides an environment that is in the open, rather than the traditionally closed system of the LMS, and it offers features such as code execution and automatic grading. The emergence of the xMOOC platform has led some LMSs to provide their own open features, and LMSs, in turn, have features that may well lead MOOCs to offer more opportunities for course design; in short, these two currently different kinds of systems may soon become more aligned.

A do-it-yourself (DIY) approach involves drawing elements together from many existing media to design your own platform. Many individuals who choose a DIY approach in creating a learning platform for online courses use social media, such

Why Use Social Media to Teach Online?

HOWARD RHEINGOLD
Critic, writer, teacher, and founder
Rheingold University, US

I've been using social media in teaching and learning for many years, both in hybrid courses that mix face-to-face and online interactions and in purely online courses. I found that the use of these media influenced me to change my style of teaching, because (together with my attitude) these technologies enable students to communicate with me and with one another in ways that traditional classrooms don't allow. They make use of the cornucopia of informational and human resources available through online networks, and (with my encouragement) make it easier for students to learn collaboratively (working on projects together) and cooperatively (taking responsibility for each other as co-learners). The tool itself doesn't magically make these changes happen or guarantee that they will work out. The critical factor is in knowing how to use the technology. It isn't that complicated, but it's new—and to those who have explored the possibilities of forums, blogs, wikis, videos, and other forms of online communication, it is more richly nuanced than the hype about "automating education" would have us believe. To me, the real magic in using social media in learning is not the ability to scale traditional teaching-as-knowledge-delivery (Paulo Freire's "banking model" of learning[1]), but the ability to inquire together, to seek understanding and construct knowledge together, and to reflect personally on the learning process itself. The critical uncertainty is know-how. The tools don't teach you how to learn. But the best practices for social learning online are not secret.

Note

1. Freire (1970, 1973) discusses the "banking model" of education.

as blogs (WordPress,[23] EduBlogs,[24] Blogger[25]), microblogs (Twitter,[26] Tumblr[27]), social network sites (Facebook, Google+), wiki (e.g., Wikipedia), and video-sharing sites (e.g., YouTube). Many faculty combine several of these applications to form a learning environment for an online course. What these media offer is the opportunity to employ tools that individuals often use in their everyday lives, providing a native environment for learning. They also allow for easy sharing of a variety of media, whether text, pictures, audio, video, or a combination of them. Howard Rheingold, a cultural critic and author of several books (including his recent *Net smart*[28]) as well as the founder of Rheingold University, describes why he uses social media.

Another form of social media is an immersive world,[29] such as Second Life,[30] Activeworlds,[31] or OpenSimulator.[32] Instructors and students typically take up an avatar (a graphic representation of the user) within a virtual space and interact with each other, so they have proximity to other individuals within the same virtual space at the same time. Immersive worlds give students the sense of "being there" even when they are unable to be present physically. While such courses differ widely from each other, what they share is mirroring some of the positive aspects of an onsite course, such as physical proximity, simultaneous interactions amongst participants, and some semblance of physical markers and identifiers from which participants can derive meaning about themselves and others.[33]

PATHWAY

A learning pathway is another structural element of online courses, an element that is receiving increased attention with the growth of DIY open courses. An online course may have a centralized, decentralized, or distributed learning pathway, each of which is illustrated in figure 4.1.

In a course with a centralized pathway, all of the students interact with the course content in the same way. They join the course and find the content and each other; the learning forms the center of the course network. The instructor chooses, organizes, and controls the content / information flow. Learners receive the same information at the same time, participate in the same activities, complete the same assignments, and so forth. There is a central and structured pathway to learning that all students follow. Students may communicate with each other, but this communication may be minimal. The focus is on the instructor and the course content. Such a course can feel organized and manageable, and faculty can ensure student exposure to certain bodies of knowledge. This type of course can also feel rigid

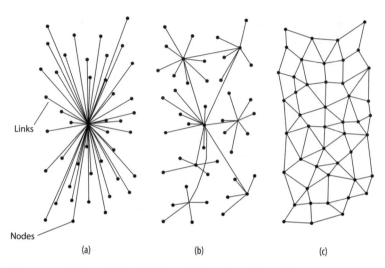

Figure 4.1. Online structural elements: (a) centralized (star);
(b) decentralized (tree); (c) distributed (mesh). These are adapted from
Baran's (1962) famous report. Baran is widely considered as one of the
founding fathers of the Internet and a pioneer in computer networking.

and unchanging, however, for both students and faculty, as well as overly direc-
tive of students.

In a course with a decentralized pathway, there is still a course center, but students can interact with it or each other and the course content in different ways.
The instructor provides central support, and students, in various clusters, take on
similar tasks. Within these clusters, students may form communities of interest
or communities of practice. Information flow and content are generated by the
communities. Information is shared within the community and published across
the network.[34] The focus is on groups. In this kind of course, a center exists, providing students with some stability and an assurance that they are getting and doing what it is they are supposed to do. There is also some flexibility, in that students
can branch out and pursue their own interests. Such courses can be more difficult
to organize than centralized ones, however, and it also may be harder to ensure
that students have adequate exposure to core concepts and skills. Online tools may
include email, discussion boards, and interactive websites. The courses may also
make use of social media, which are a group of Internet-based applications that allow people to create, share, exchange, and comment on the contents in virtual communities and networks.

In a course where the learning pathway is distributed, there is no center. Students interact with each other and with the instructor at different times as they proceed through the course at various paces and in multiple ways. That is, course communication and activities may happen in different spaces, and there may be more than one pathway that a learner can take to fulfill course and personal goals. The network is fluid and groups can form, reconstitute, and dissolve at will. The focus is on people. In such courses, students have high levels of freedom and the flexibility to pursue their own interests. Distributed courses also have an authentic feel to them, so students may well have the impression that they are participating in something worthwhile. Students can feel lost, however, without a center or grounding. They also can feel like they are missing important parts of the learning process in the course if they are not connected to the network at appropriate junctures and times.[35] Many faculty who teach decentralized courses tend to make extensive use of social media.

Case Studies of Online Instructional Practices

In the accompanying sidebars, which begin on page 88, five faculty members who have taken different approaches to teaching online share information, in their own words, about their courses and their experiences in teaching them. First, Lisa Lane describes a history course. Second, Patrick Biddix discusses a course offering in higher education. Third, Cris Crissman recounts aspects of her young-adult literature course. Fourth, Alan Levine depicts a computer science course on digital storytelling. Fifth, David Evans reports on a computer science course on search engines. These authors have different goals for teaching online and varying perceptions about the processes. And their classes stand as evidence of several types of online courses.

Strategies for Structuring Online Courses

Online learning is not one specific thing. Rather, the possibilities for different combinations of the core elements of online courses are myriad. I offer the following strategies for selecting the structure of online courses.

STRATEGY #1: LOOK TO INSTITUTIONS FOR CLUES

Certain institutions, departments, and programs have set standards regarding what are acceptable course structures, although they can vary by institutions and, at times, departments and programs. Some institutions may not be as excited about offering open courses as others, and anyone hoping to develop an open course

(Photo credit: CC A-NC-SA
Lisa M. Lane)

A Mature, Asynchronous Course

LISA LANE
Instructor
History
MiraCosta Community College, US

Course Classification for Modern Western Civilization

Enrollment: closed
Amount: online
Timing: asynchronous
Platform: provider-offered
Pathway: centralized

The course I teach is a community-college-level class that covers Western civilization from 1648 to the present. It is intended to be offered as a one-semester general education course, emphasizing the humanities. Students come from diverse backgrounds—some have never had a college class, or are concurrently enrolled in high school, or are returning to school after being in the workforce. Their ages and levels of preparation vary widely. I teach the class using the Moodle learning management system, although the lecture and multimedia files are stored on a separate server and linked from within the system.

The Moodle system allows the main page of the course to be organized like a syllabus, with blocks for each week's activities and smaller information blocks on each side of the screen. I structure the arrangement visually. Communication blocks(e.g., instant messaging to the instructor, a participant's list, and Moodle messaging features) are placed on the left. Information blocks (e.g., the calendar, course information, and the grading scheme) are on the right. The center column lists all tasks by week.

My pedagogy is balanced between presentation and interactivity. Each week consists of context readings (often from Wikipedia) and lectures. My lectures are detailed and contain audio sections (with me reading the lecture), images, video clips, and links to primary-source documents. A multiple-choice quiz is assigned to check the students' comprehension of the content of the presentation portion.

Interactivity occurs primarily in the discussion forums, although I do not use them for discussion per se. Rather, at the beginning of each week, students must post a primary source for that era, complete with full citation information. They are encouraged to post visual sources, although excerpts from text documents are also common. My frequently asked questions (FAQ) section provides all instructions for embedding media in Moodle.

I am present throughout the class in various places in the site. Every week or two, I use an information block on the main page to post a Voki (animated character with my voice)[1] or a talking-head video clip of me discussing that week's tasks. My voice is in every lecture, reading my own writing. My forum posts are clearly in my own writing style.

In the forums, which are organized as one nested page, I post the initial primary source. Students have until Wednesday night each week to reply with their own primary source. On Thursday I create an extensive post, commenting on their sources and providing guidance for what to do for the rest of the week. Usually my post highlights their written work from the week before and provides instructions on writing their second post. This second post from students each week encourages them to practice writing a historical thesis, supported by some of the primary sources posted in the forum. They develop their own theses, based on their interests. Although they must support their theses only with sources that have been posted by the class, they may always add sources to any forum throughout the course.

Community is not an articulated goal for the class; nonetheless, their forum work encourages interaction. The initial forum invites the class members to get to know each other, and each week's work often includes a request to comment on someone else's writing, either adding context, or posting an additional source, or evaluating a peer's thesis. Since I create a different post each Thursday, I can encourage more peer interactivity at appropriate times for what we are doing that week.

(continued)

In terms of my instructional time, a great deal is spent setting up the class. When I first offered it, many hours were devoted to creating the lectures. All of the readings, the links to lectures, and the forums are set up in advance each semester, and I frequently make revisions. During the class, most of my time is spent grading, reading student work in the forums, and posting guidance for each week. I also have instant messaging (IM) open to talk with students in real time. IM time is unscheduled, but I use Plupper[2] to indicate when I am online and available—the status indicator is embedded in a communication block so they can see if I'm accessible whenever they're logged in to the class.

My goals for this course not only are to introduce the events and sources of Western civilization from 1648 to the present, but also to encourage students to participate in what historians actually do, rather than simply reading and recalling facts. I am interested in them learning higher-order thinking skills and developing their writing, gradually and with guidance. I create an environment and materials that are designed to lead them from an emphasis on facts to the creation of their own interpretations and the discovery of larger themes. I am particularly gratified that my forum activities fulfill these goals by having the students practice each week and engage in more complex tasks as the semester continues. Students comment on how much they enjoy the opportunity to research their own interests and shape their own interpretations and themes.

This class is a mature online course, having been developed over a period of many years. I began teaching online in 1998, before the advent of course-management systems and with little guidance. My first class was modeled after a philosophy class being offered by a colleague who had only begun teaching online the semester before. I then got an *HTML for dummies* guide and taught myself how to make web pages.[3] Discussion took place through a program called WebBoard, a threaded forum that was similar to Blackboard's forums today. When my college adopted Blackboard, I used that system but was frustrated with threaded discussions, so I changed to Moodle solely to use the simple forum that lets you see all the posts nested on one page, like a real conversation. It would be very difficult to see forty primary sources all at once in a threaded forum, where each post must be opened individually. I have offered the class as a hybrid in WordPress, however, and that technology works very well for creating a format similar to the one that I use in Moodle.

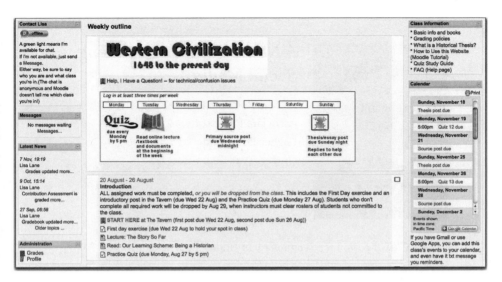

Modern Western Civilization main page screenshot. (Photo credit: CC A-NC-SA Lisa M. Lane)

Overall, I consider it a successful course, because students both are engaged and demonstrate skills as they learn. They receive frequent feedback and other communications, which prevent isolation and encourage participation. I am also happy with the materials I have created, though I am continually updating them. The use of multiple forms of presentation (audio, video, text) and multiple modes for learning (reading, listening, searching, writing, posting, analyzing, synthesizing) creates a rich experience for both the instructor and the students.

Notes

1. Information about Voki is available at www.voki.com.
2. Information about Plupper is available at www.plupper.com.
3. HTML stands for hypertext markup language.

A New Online Course Using Social Media

J. PATRICK BIDDIX
Associate Professor
Higher Education
University of Tennessee, US

Course Classification for Technology in Higher Education
Enrollment: closed
Amount: online
Timing: asynchronous
Platform: DIY
Pathway: decentralized

Tech595 was the unofficial name for ELPS 595 (Special Topics: Technology in Higher Education), a graduate-level, 100% online, asynchronous course I developed and taught over a four-week period in summer 2012. The course had two core purposes. The first was to introduce current, significant discussion surrounding the use of technology in higher education. The second was to expose students to technology that enables them to work in higher education institutions. Course objectives related to these purposes included "Identify the influence of ICT in governance and administration of higher education institutions" and "Evaluate the potential for online learning to provide greater access to higher education."

The idea for this course came to me after I read about Kraken, one of the supercomputers maintained on our campus. Up to that point, I thought I was pretty current on campus technology. Learning that one of the world's fastest supercomputers resided on campus reminded me that I knew much less than I thought about the breadth of technology at a major research institution. As a faculty member responsible for both preparing future administrators and introducing current professionals to new research, theory, and application, I came to believe that exposing students to campus technology and contemporary developments was critical to their understanding of how a major aspect of higher education works. My revelation also had me thinking about where and how administrators stay up to date on technology. I had essentially created a course I needed as much as one I wanted to teach. A social-learning approach seemed a natural fit.

Conceptually, the content of the course was a good match for the needs of my students. Unfortunately, the timing of the course and the availability of students in the summer, which was when I could offer it, created two significant challenges. First, the online teaching and learning infrastructure at my institution is unwieldy and unintuitive for new online learners. Second, my recently discovered lack of knowledge about campus technology could make developing and teaching the course problematic.

I addressed the first challenge by adopting technology already familiar to me: social media. I began with the assumption that most of my students had some experience with blogs as consumers, producers, or both; if not, I thought they were familiar enough with other forms of participatory social media to learn quickly. After some deliberation, I chose Blogger to run the course, a site that allows features I deemed essential to online teaching and learning, such as privacy, multiple contributors, social-media widgets, and the capability for hosting discussions. I loaded the site with familiar course elements (e.g., syllabus, readings) and added a detailed "Start Here" page, an updatable calendar, and RSS and Twitter feeds for new-content alerts.

Once the structure for the course was in place, I developed a task schedule for managing the three types of assignments (discussion, presentation, analysis) and kept it updated with a calendar widget from my mobile phone. The four-week course had twelve routinized discussion assignments due each Monday, Wednesday, and Friday, with corresponding readings. Since students got to choose when to submit one of the two major assignments, an online presentation, I gave them access to the calendar to add their preferred date and topic. This structure helped the students fall into a routine for keeping up with the fast-paced course. The second major assignment was a reflective analysis, in which students answered one of three culminating questions as a blog post. Students were required to provide evidence for their analysis with hyperlinked citations

(continued)

to reference material. All student work was evaluated on three basic criteria: (1) following assignment instructions, (2) creating clear and concise posts and comments, and (3) completing assignments in a timely manner.

I addressed the second challenge by adopting social media. This allowed me to moderate my lack of specific content knowledge by capitalizing on the peer expertise of my students. As the instructor and course designer, I would create the infrastructure and run discussion prompts, but I would leave some content specifics to the experts—students who used the technology in their work settings. I thought that much of what they used daily was unique to their setting and unfamiliar to the rest of us, and I was correct. In addition to scheduled discussion assignments (e.g., "Explore a course or module in Coursera or Khan Academy and post about your experience/s."), students created a detailed overview of a technology they used as a review post on the blog (i.e., the presentation assignment). They were also required to employ some form of media beyond text for their presentation. Some students chose Prezi,[1] others created custom videos of the technology in use, and still others interviewed users or technicians. The topics they chose ranged from housing room-assignment software to campus alert systems.

For me, the two core purposes of exposing students to technology and conducting a discussion on its use in higher education were easily met. The frequent discussions allowed me to direct students to where to find

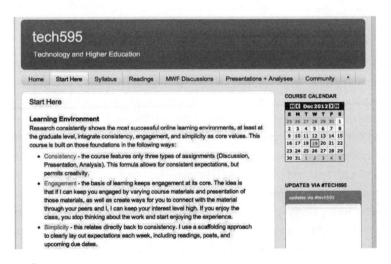

Tech595 start page

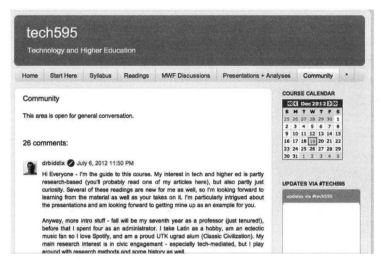

Tech595 community forum

the latest material related to technology and keep up with it (e.g., Wired Campus,[2] EDUCAUSE[3]). The discussions also facilitated debates about the merits and use of technological trends, such as the explosion of MOOCs in higher education. Students took the discussions seriously and frequently used links to outside material to substantiate their perspectives or point out a related trend.

The technology-review posts exceeded my expectations. The class indicated to me that online social learning may offer new ways to connect the collective knowledge of students into a highly efficient and effective learning environment.

Notes

1. Prezi is a presentation software. More information is available at http://prezi.com.

2. Wired Campus (http://chronicle.com/blogs/wiredcampus/) is a technology-related blog of the *Chronicle of Higher Education*.

3. EDUCAUSE (www.educause.edu) is an organization whose membership is interested in issues related to technology in higher education.

An Open Online Course

CRIS CRISSMAN
Adjunct Assistant Professor
College of Education
North Carolina State University, US

(Photo credit: Bill Lovin)

Course Classification for Teaching Literature for Young Adults

Enrollment: open

Amount: online

Timing: synchronous and asynchronous

Platform: DIY

Pathway: decentralized

ECI 521 is an open online course—open to creative explorations of pedagogy, open to innovative uses of digital technologies, and open to anyone interested in the teaching of literature for young adults. It is in this environment of openness that I have come the closest yet to being the mentor for my students that I want to be.

My students are pre- and in-service teachers who want to learn about the latest trends and methods for teaching literature to middle and high school students. I include a strong young-adult (YA) literature component because I find that many students are not familiar with this category of literature and have no idea of its potential for both engaging young-adult readers and helping them come to know themselves and the world for which they will be responsible. Teaching for social responsibility and justice is an integral part of both the course and our College of Education's mission.

The course design breaks the standard online course mold, and I pay for that with a longer-than-usual buy-in period. Most students do not expect to have weekly class meetings in an online course. And to meet in an online virtual space, the Bookhenge in Second Life, asks for a suspension of disbelief, a willingness to be open to change, and a playful, creative spirit—all valuable attributes for a twenty-first-century teacher.

Here is one student's response to the course in a 2012 fall-semester midterm survey:

> This is the biggest shocker of the course. I'm open to lots of technology, but I entered the course thinking that having a class in Second Life was the STUPIDEST thing I'd ever heard of. What can I say? I'm a complete convert. It's sheer brilliance.

A typical week is built around an inquiry into a question/issue related to teaching literature. Students review resources, construct responses (we use blogs for text, audio, or video responses and, occasionally, a collaborative VoiceThread[1]), extend the conversation by commenting on each others' contributions, and then come to class to engage in small-group work and a whole-class seminar. My students also choose YA books during various genre studies and meet in the Bookhenge to participate in book clubs and plan collaborative responses that include digital storytelling.

An asset of meeting in our virtual space is that we can invite the world. Open-course participants are invited to join us in real-time classes

(continued)

Bookhenge screenshot. (Photo credit: Bill Lovin)

that often feature conversations with guests, including award-winning YA authors.

Buy-in may take a while but, once achieved, reflects the openness that is the model for the course. As Christine, a fall 2012 pre-service teacher, reflected in her blog:

> All of this technology would have been daunting just a few short weeks ago, but I'm starting to realize now why we're pushed to get out of our comfort zone and try it. My students are definitely going to benefit from this knowledge. . . . Try new things. You never know—what you learn could change your life.

Finally, I would like to give special recognition to DELTA (Distance Education and Learning Technology Applications) at North Carolina State University, and, in particular, to Cathi Phillips, instructional designer, for always encouraging me to try new things and giving me the support to make them happen.

Note

1. VoiceThread is an application that allows users to leave a video or audio comment. More information is available at http://voicethread.com.

(Photo credit: Jonathan North)

An Open Course (and Community) in Digital Storytelling

ALAN LEVINE
Consultant
Educational Technology
CogDog IT (http://cogdogblog.com), US

Course Classification for Computer Science 106: Digital Storytelling
Enrollment: open
Amount: online

Timing: asynchronous
Platform: DIY
Pathway: distributed

The open course ds106 (http://ds106.us), originating at the University of
Mary Washington (UMW) in Fredericksburg, Virginia, experiments with
convention, even by its very name. The actual course, located in the Computer Science Department, is CPSC 106. I have been part of ds106 as an
open participant, a teacher of a face-to-face section, and, most recently,
the instructor for a fully online class.

Digital-storytelling courses typically focus on personal narratives as
digital videos. In ds106, however, students not only use the web as a platform for publishing stories, but also as a genre of storytelling itself, as well
as a source of content for new forms of digital creations. As a process that
questions the very concept of what a story can be, ds106 explores Internet
culture and related issues of identity, representation, and the notion of
originality.

As first conceived by Jim Groom in 2010, a cornerstone of ds106 is that
students publish creative work in their own Internet domain and Word-
Press blog; they manage their own personal cyber-infrastructure. Students explore the concept of story via visual, design, audio, web, video,
and remix modes. Beyond using their personal publishing space to share
what they create, students reflectively write about their work and their
processes of creation .

The course runs in the open-source WordPress platform, and add-on
software makes ds106 a syndication hub that aggregates and reorganizes
the distributed content that is self-published by participants. The site currently subscribes to over 620 individual blogs.

In January 2011, the early age of massive online open courses
(MOOCs), ds106 was made available to the Internet community as an
open course. Open participants register their own sites, which can be
hosted on any blogging service that provides an RSS feed. Much of the
community interaction happens in Twitter, shared via the #ds106 hashtag
(https://twitter.com/search/realtime?q=%23ds106).

Since then, classes at other institutions (Temple University in Japan,
York College, Kansas State University, Kennesaw State University, State

(continued)

University of New York–Cortland, Jacksonville State University) connected students doing similar kinds of work into ds106. Thus the course
has become an overlapping community of students from these places as
well as UMW, plus people who joined out of general interest. Between
UMW and these other institutions, more than five hundred students have

ds106 screenshot

ds106 assignments page

participated in ds106 since January 2011; our database indicates that more than nine hundred individuals have participated in ds106 by publishing content syndicated into the main site.

The online UMW sections of ds106 have no lectures; weekly posts outline the materials and assignments for each section. Among the key developments of ds106 are regular challenges from the Daily Create (http://tdc .ds106.us/); from a web-based radio station (http://ds106.us/ds106-radio); and from the Assignment Bank (http://assignments.ds106.us/), a collection of over four hundred creative activities designed by the ds106 community. The latter provides much of the work students must complete. Rather than being given, say, a specific audio assignment, they have to finish fifteen stars' worth of Audio Assignments (each one is rated for difficulty by ds106 participants).

We do not prescribe or teach the nuts and bolts of the digital tools the students use; in addition to employing software they may have access to, we recommend choosing open-source or web-based options. Students learn how to use the web and how to acquire information from each other as a means of learning about the software.

The summer online versions of ds106 push the boundaries of the class itself as a participatory narrative. The 2011 Summer of Oblivion (http:// ds106.us/summer-of-oblivion/) included the disappearance of an eccentric professor who banished students, resulting in a class "rebellion." The following year, Camp Magic Macguffin (http://magicmacguffin.info/) deployed a happy summer-camp metaphor—where things were not exactly what they seemed.

More than three hundred UMW students have taken ds106, and the most common feedback on class evaluations is along the lines of "I cannot believe how much work this was for a 100-level class . . . but I have learned so much in useful skills." Former students often return to continue participating in ds106. They learn to understand the tweeted statement, "#ds106 is #4life."

(Photo credit: Cole Geddy)

An Open Introductory Computer Science Course

DAVID EVANS
Professor
Computer Science
University of Virginia, US

Course Classification for Udacity CS101: Introduction to Computer Science—Building a Search Engine

Enrollment: open
Amount: online
Timing: asynchronous
Platform: provider-offered
Pathway: centralized

Udacity CS101 (https://udacity.com/course/cs101/) is an introductory computer science course, targeted to students with no previous background in computing who want to understand the foundations of computer science and learn how to program.[1] Enrollment is free, and the class is open to anyone on the Internet.

The course was designed from the ground up as an open online course, rather than attempting to move an existing course online. Our goal was to teach computer science and provide students with a solid foundation to develop as programmers in an engaging, effective, and enjoyable way. This led to two main decisions for the course: (1) focus the course around a motivating project that would be used as a vehicle for introducing the computing concepts throughout the course; and (2) designing the lectures to be primarily centered on exercises students would do and for which they would receive automated feedback, on rather than long, non-interactive lectures.

For the motivating project, we selected building a web search engine. This is something nearly everyone uses every day, but to most people, search engines such as Google seem like magical oracles. Thus we hoped understanding how a search engine works would be a compelling motivation for a broad range of students to take the class. From a technical perspective, a search engine conveniently fit nearly all of the key ideas in computing we wanted to cover in an introductory course. The task of extracting a single link from a web page could motivate the first unit, and it could be completed using a few introductory concepts. The need to extract all links from a page motivates learning about conditions and loops. Maintaining a list of pages to crawl requires understanding simple data structures. Later units use the problem of looking up a keyword to motivate understanding how to measure cost and use more-advanced data structures. The technique Google invented for ranking pages by popularity provides an interesting way to introduce recursive definitions.

The course was first offered in February 2012 as a scheduled seven-week course. Each week involved a lecture unit, consisting of about ninety minutes of recorded video. The video was divided into short segments, typically one to three minutes in length, followed by interactive quizzes. A quiz could be a multiple-choice question, a many-choice question (select any number of items that apply), a request to enter a number or a text, or a programming quiz. For programming quizzes, the video player transformed into an in-browser programming environment that could be pre-loaded with code and comments. Students could submit quizzes as many times as they wanted, and they received feedback when their answers were incorrect. In addition to the lecture unit, each week included a homework assignment with a set of more open-ended problems that reinforced and measured the student's understanding of the unit. The lecture videos for the final unit were a series of field trips and interviews showing the past, present, and future of computing, followed by a comprehensive final exam.

Online discussion forums were an essential component of the class. They provided a very active environment, with over 88,000 discussion questions posted, most of which received at least a few answers. Because of the diverse group of students in the class, nearly every question is quickly answered by another student, although the course staff (primarily the assistant instructor, Peter Chapman) monitored the discussion forum closely and contributed additional answers and comments when useful. As well as the online text discussion, we recorded weekly video "office

(continued)

hours" where we would select questions from the forums, based on student votes and interest, and post a video discussion.

The first offering attracted over 94,000 enrolled students, ranging from eight-year-olds to eighty-eight-year-olds, residing over one hundred countries, with occupations covering the gamut from truck drivers to neurosurgeons to software professionals to educators. Of these, 25,757 attempted the first homework assignment, and 9,723 completed the full course at a level sufficient to earn a certificate (over 4,000 were at the highest-distinction level, which required answering all problems correctly, including the starred challenge problems).

After the first offering was completed, the course was relaunched in an open format, where students can complete the course at their own pace, with no deadlines, and then take a final exam to receive a certificate. The open course has enrolled over 159,000 new students. The unscheduled format makes the discussion forum less coherent, since students are at various units in the course, but enough students are active in each of the different parts that most questions still obtain good answers within an hour or less.

Teaching open online courses is a tremendous opportunity, and today's computing and networking technologies make it possible to deliver inter-

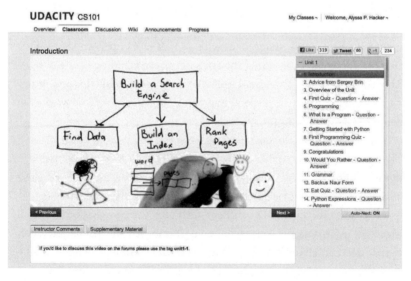

CS101 screenshot

active classes to students around the world at a significantly low cost. We are in the very early stages of learning how to teach well online, and rapid innovation and experimentation is needed. Some aspects of in-person teaching cannot be replicated online, but for many students, online courses can be a rewarding and meaningful experience, as well as an effective way to learn challenging material.

Note

1. The *Chronicle of Higher Education* has highlighted Evans's course on several occasions. See Gose (2012), Mangan (2012), and Young (2012).

---

would be wise to consult with chairs, deans, and distance-learning personnel before proceeding. Other institutions have specifications about which environment might be used, and some require a certain LMS. In one research study, the authors identified three institutional approaches to course structure:[36]

1. *The fully autonomous approach.* The institution leaves all structural decisions up to the instructor. There may be "encouraged" or "suggested" guidelines or tools, but without a formal policy, the instructor makes all final decisions autonomously.
2. *The basic-guidelines approach.* The institution provides basic, or general, guidelines for instructors to follow. In this case, the institution has minimal design and structural expectations that instructors are supposed to use.
3. *The highly specified approach.* The institution has an extensive set of components and standards that each online instructor must adhere to when designing and developing courses.

Moreover, some institutions develop a course with no input from the instructor; instead, faculty are responsible for teaching courses that others had previously designed and developed. Because of this, being aware of the type of approach institutions favor and the specific structural requirements they have (and the degree of autonomy they afford faculty for designing and teaching online courses) are important when choosing a course structure.

STRATEGY #2: EXAMINE SAMPLE COURSES TO UNDERSTAND
DIFFERENT STRUCTURAL ELEMENTS

A given course may be considered to have a type, as determined through the classification chain, since the parts create a new, unified whole. For example, one course might have the following chain: closed, managed, centralized, asynchronous, and blended. Another might be classified in a chain that is nearly the direct opposite: open, social, decentralized, synchronous, and online. A third might mix classifications to create a different chain: LMS and social media, centralized with some decentralized modules, asynchronous with some synchronous components, blended, and open access with limited enrollment for credit. Examining sample courses can help faculty gain a sense of how the elements work together to create a unique whole.

The sidebars included in this chapter not only highlight courses from multiple disciplines, but also structural features that cross these disciplines and combine in various ways, documenting each as a specific type of online course. Table 4.2 offers a comparison of the different structural elements of the courses featured in the sidebars.

The faculty involved describe their reasons for making structural decisions. They discuss their decisions about the pattern of enrollment as an effort to best provide course content and activities to students, to best meet their goals for the course, and to best answer student needs. A closed and central location offers students a safe and secure place within which to interact privately, and two of the five faculty

Table 4.2   Comparison of the different courses in case studies

	History (Lane)	Technology (Biddix)	Young-adult lit (Crissman)	Digital storytelling (Levine)	Computer science (Evans)
Enrollment	closed	closed	open	open	open
Amount	online	online	online	online	online
Timing	asynchronous	asynchronous	asynchronous and synchronous	asynchronous	asynchronous
Platform	provider-offered	DIY	DIY	DIY	provider-offered
Pathway	centralized	decentralized	decentralized	distributed	centralized

members chose to offer courses through this format. Opening a course enables it to cover a broad range of knowledge and experience, and three of the faculty believe this approach was most appropriate for the specific groups of students in their courses. While open courses are receiving a great deal of attention currently—with good reason, because they can provide greater access to higher education to a wider number of participants—there are also situations in which having some degree of privacy can be an asset. The faculty describing their experiences here considered a range of issues when making a decision about enrollment: the level of the course, the knowledge to be gained, and the level and experience of students.

In large part, these five faculty decided to offer courses through similar formats, and they chose a similar course timing. All of them offered courses that were fully online. They had several reasons for making the choice to teach a fully online rather than a blended course, from having an interest in the technology, to serving student needs, to teaching an already-existing online course. Most selected an asynchronous approach to timing. Some of them did so based on the needs of students, while others made their choice because the course was structured in that way, either previously or because of the technologists who were helping faculty develop the courses. One of the faculty members discusses the use of instant messaging for answering questions with students, based on her desire to seem present and available. Only one mentions offering significant portions of the class in a synchronous format, and she discusses the initial challenges to student buy-in because of this timing decision.

The five featured faculty describe their choice of a particular platform as being closely tied to the technology available at the time the course was developed. Their determination of which platform to use was based on their technological skills and the tools with which they were most familiar. In addition, several of the faculty augmented their primary learning platforms with different technological applications, in order to enhance them. These faculty seemed to gauge their own

Table 4.3 Sample structural plan

Core structure	Decision
Access	closed
Timing	mixed: asynchronous and synchronous
Amount	blended
Platform	LMS
Learning path	centralized

level of knowledge about technologies and about their motivation for and interest in learning new technologies. Finally, many of the faculty seem to have enjoyed experimenting with and adding on different technologies that have a specific purpose, which played a supporting role in their teaching. These faculty talk about the pathway for student learning indirectly, perhaps because, in some ways, the network is closely connected to the learning platform that they choose. With an LMS, centrality is a built-in feature. With social media, the course is already relatively decentralized. It is possible to achieve some degree of decentralization in an LMS, however, particularly with adding in features of social media. It is also just as feasible to maintain centrality with social media, as some of the faculty indicate.

STRATEGY #3: DEVELOP A STRUCTURAL PLAN FOR NEW COURSES

When developing new courses or reconsidering existing ones, faculty members may develop a structural plan for them, based on the structural elements reviewed in this chapter and the classification chain in table 4.1. Doing so can encourage additional intentionality during the design and development processes for the course. Table 4.3 depicts a sample online course structural plan.

Conclusion

Online learning has become a regular and accepted way in which we offer instruction in higher education. Today, however, online teaching is not a single, monolithic method. Rather, technology has advanced to the point where there are myriad ways in which instructors can and do choose how to teach online. Understanding the contextual nature of online courses can help faculty leverage the multiple possibilities available through the Internet. When examining, developing, or revising courses, working through the various structures of online courses can be a useful activity. Doing so can supply additional layers of understanding and intentionality that can permit faculty to make good decisions in devising or revising their courses.

Chapter Five

Course Planning

Spontaneity is one of the joys of existence, especially if you prepare for it in advance.

—ALAN DEAN FOSTER

The work of teachers is incredibly complex, and in order to create instructional experiences that can best facilitate learning, we engage in significant planning prior to the start of any given course. We set goals and objectives. We think about the potential learners and what their strengths and weaknesses might be. We consider which instructional methods and materials we will use and develop assessments that will help us determine what students have accomplished. Planning courses is hard work, particularly as we move from ideas to action. We typically navigate through the layers of complexity within this task with little guidance and even less formal training. Teaching online, however, involves us in a new set of experiences during the course-planning phase, and even fewer of us have had any formal training on how to go about it.

About Course Planning

Many instructional-design models provide benchmarks for key moments involved in course planning. While many different models of the process exist—such as the analysis, design, development, implementation, evaluation (ADDIE) model; John Keller's attention, relevance, confidence, satisfaction (ARCS) model; and Grant Wiggins and Jay McTighe's concept of backward design[1]—many of these have fairly common elements that typically involve some variation of guiding faculty through the elements in the process: goals and objectives of the course, a priori learner assessment, instructional methods, learning outcome, and assessments of student achievements. While these models can help faculty identify the kinds of activities that go into course creation, many of the design models are prescriptive and, at times, formulaic; they often follow only individualist models of learning. Most of the models arise from a particular theoretical position: cognitivism.[2] Moreover, these models may run counter to the structures and norms of our disciplines. One aspect is particularly problematic for online instructors: few of these design models deal directly with planning online courses and thus offer little guidance into the kinds of changes that accompany this process.

Changes to the Course-Planning Process When Teaching Online

There are many key changes that attend the course-planning process when teaching online. They range from deciding who will be involved in decision making, to determining what students will learn and how they will learn it, to considering what will demonstrate that students have learned it.

WORKING WITH OTHERS

At certain institutions some of the decisions about onsite courses have been made by groups of faculty members working together to develop some commonality across courses, but many times individual instructors are the sole planners of the courses that we teach. We often work in isolation from our peers, only occasionally chatting with colleagues about what we are doing. Oftentimes we alone identify and set the goals and objectives for the course.[3] Similarly, as individual faculty members, we often decide what content students will be exposed to in a given course, perhaps consulting syllabi from other, similar courses in making our decisions. Even if departments have already identified a course's goals and content, most of us make the sole decision about the pedagogical approaches that we will use to help students understand the content and reach the goals and objectives of the course. Moreover, many of us are solely responsible for determining the assessment and evaluation techniques for a given course, which ultimately are how we arrive at students' grades. In short, many of us have a great deal of ownership and authority in planning the onsite courses we teach.

When teaching online, increasingly we are not always the only ones involved in the course-planning process. We may be participants in teams of planners, consisting of other faculty members, instructional designers, videographers, artists, teaching assistants, and so forth.[4] Many institutions have instructional-development and design centers where faculty can find assistance with course planning and development, and many new companies also offer such services. Some of us may even teach courses that other faculty members, as individuals or as teams, had previously designed, thus reducing the extent of our course planning. These represent dramatic shifts in the course-planning process. While such a change can challenge our sense of who traditionally "owns" the course and thus can have attendant issues related to intellectual property,[5] it can also bring a wide array of talent together for planning high-quality courses.

SETTING LEARNING GOALS AND OBJECTIVES

When we teach onsite, most of us develop a set of goals and objectives that we hope students will achieve, whether we formally articulate all of them or not.[6] These have a purpose and a function in the teaching process. They help us determine what the core of the course is, in order to focus on its main issues and points. They help us stay on track, determine what students should already know, evaluate the effectiveness of our teaching methods, construct tests, and give feedback to students. They can also help students break the course into manageable sections, evaluate their own progress in the course, develop guidelines for studying, and feel confident in the evaluation criteria. Moreover, a series of objectives can help the students become competent in the key concepts, definitions, and skills they should know after completing the course.

When we teach online, we still have these goals and objectives. Very likely, they are similar or equivalent to those we have when we teach onsite. At the same time, they are different. If an instructor has a goal of helping students improve their communication skills, its meaning may not be the same onsite and online. In an onsite course this objective may well refer to oral and interpersonal communication, with considerations such as facial expressions, tone, intonation, and so forth. Unless the online course has synchronous video sessions, written communication may be more important. Even written communication, however, means different things onsite and online, since writing for a printed scholarly paper is not the same as writing for the web. Thus we have to rethink our goals and objectives and build these differences into the course-planning process.

ASSESSING POTENTIAL LEARNERS

When we plan an onsite course, we typically consider the potential students' readiness to learn the course's content and its particular skills. We attempt to gauge what the students know and what they do not, as well as what they can and cannot do. We may do so formally, through preliminary exams or assessments, or we may do so informally, either by asking students to self-assess or simply by coming to know the general degree of student preparation from working with similar student populations over time. We need such information to determine the most effective ways to teach students and to come to terms with how best to meet them at the level where they are.

When we teach online, we also do this type of assessment, but with an added layer of complexity. We also gauge the students' readiness to learn in an online environment. This typically is not an easy task, since there are many different factors associated with an individual's preparedness for online learning. Several surveys and tools exist for learner self-assessment, however.[7] These suggest that, in general, we need to have some sense of their experience with technology. Do they have the basic computer, email, and Internet skills that are required in order to succeed? We also need to know whether students will have regular and good access to adequate hardware and software. Many of the assessment tools also ask students about their study habits, their lifestyles, and their motivation for success in online courses; these are intended to help determine whether students are likely to be independent workers who want to succeed. In addition, some instruments ask about a student's learning styles or preferences. While there is not yet strong evidence that matching the type of instruction to a learning style improves outcomes, preference for a specific kind of learning may ultimately influence motivation and, therefore, the student's likelihood of success. When we teach online, these factors—particularly the technological ones—are important for assessing student readiness, and we should be ready to meet students at their level of preparedness. Thus this issue becomes a new part of the planning process.

CHOOSING ASSESSMENTS

When we assess learning outcomes, we typically attempt to document (in measurable terms) the knowledge, skills, and attitudes that students have gained as a direct result of the instruction. Assessments are generally linked to educational objectives, since their purpose is to demonstrate that these objectives have been attained. Faculty have a long history of judging students' achievement of the course objectives in onsite courses, and we have used a range of measures to do so, from formal multiple-choice testing to informal classroom-assessment techniques.[8]

Few faculty have experience in gauging learning in an online environment, yet the way in which we conceptualize this important element necessarily changes when we teach online. A primary difference is the form that our assessment takes.[9] A multiple-choice test onsite may be graded relatively quickly and then returned in the next class session; online, the same assessment may provide immediate feedback, with a response after each student answer. A written assignment for an onsite course is typically just that: written. The same assignment done online may well be written, but it may also contain links to sources. A musical performance

(Photo credit: MiraCosta College)

Matching Objectives and Assessments

LAURA PACIOREK
Instructor
Child Development
MiraCosta College and San Diego
Miramar College, US

My college provides an official course outline to follow for each class. The outline contains broad student-learning outcomes as well as course objectives that build into the student-learning outcomes. These guide the entire course.

I break the course down into learning modules when I teach online. Each learning module is an individual lesson. When I develop my plan for the learning module, I make sure that the lesson has its own objectives, which may be specific, compared with the general course goals and objectives. Assessment at the lesson level may be no or low-stakes at first, with the stakes becoming higher as the course progresses. For example, if students must eventually write a philosophy statement at the course level, analyzing various philosophies may be done at the lesson level. A sizeable assignment further along in the class may be to create their own philosophy statement, which is then turned in for peer feedback and, later, used for an assessment.

I like to articulate all of this in a conversational way through a welcome message in my learning modules, which are in text and audio format. Sometimes these are short, closed-captioned videos where students can see my face and hear me speaking to them.

It can become easy to simply focus on the presentation of information in an online class. In a face-to-face class, I would have students do activities that use the skills and apply the knowledge in the module. With some creativity, I can still do this in online classes. For example, if I want to be sure students can do something, I have them do that "something" and

(continued)

videotape it or take a photo of it—anything that might help them demonstrate the skill. I want the assessment to truly reflect their abilities. Giving choices for how students present their work may also be an option, as it can tap into the students' strengths and allow them to demonstrate their understanding. The ultimate goal is student success.

---

may be done in the moment when onsite; online, it probably will be recorded in some way and thus be more durable. These changes should be built into our planning processes. Laura Paciorek describes how she links objectives and assessments, and she notes how her form of assessment is different online (see p. 113).

DEVELOPING LEARNING MATERIALS

Material development is a key component in course planning, which changes when we teach online. A syllabus is one such example.[10] In the 1960s, a professor probably sat down at a typewriter and pecked out a first draft of a syllabus for a course, and then perhaps edited and retyped it. Regardless of the number of drafts, the final product was a fixed manuscript. It had permanence and authority. Now that we have computers, planning involves different activities, more than just substituting a computer screen and keyboard for the typewriter. That difference signals a substantial change in the planning process, which now is much less linear. The text of a syllabus can grow rhizomatically: it can start in the middle, at the end, or at the beginning.[11] We can draft a few ideas, waiting for inspiration and planning to bridge the gaps later. With the delete key, we can easily remedy mistakes, and we are freer to change our minds. Writing and editing, which at one time were separate stages, now occur simultaneously. Thus a syllabus is always tentative and subject to revision.[12]

When teaching online, technology mediates course planning even further. In the case of a syllabus, when we design one for the Internet, we no longer need to create a fixed, permanent document; rather, it exists online. No longer must we rely only on what we can fit into the space we have designated for the document; we can also embed links to other sources of information. Moreover, we do not have to be limited to text; instead, we can embed sound and images. A syllabus, once a static document, today can be a dynamic text, open for revision and change. It can even serve as the backbone, or structure, of the course itself. The planning processes and, ultimately, the course products are changed in several key ways.

SELECTING INSTRUCTIONAL ACTIVITIES

Faculty today have a range of instructional activities at our disposal, whether teaching onsite or online. We can lecture, lead discussions, use educational games, ask students to work in pairs, have students work in small groups, have students solve problems, have students engage in service to the community, have students do original research; the list goes on. We have a range of pedagogical possibilities at our disposal; when we are planning a course, our selections are restricted only by the spaces in which we work and by our bodies, as pedagogical instruments.

When we choose a tool as part of our instructional methods, the methods themselves are altered. For example, an onsite lecture is different from a video lecture. In the former, an instructor can react to nonverbal signals and change direction, based on what is going on in the class. For better or worse, a video is often thought of as a more finished product, rather than an event in progress. Does this really change the students' experience? Most likely. In a lecture, students are in the moment; it is an event, one which conveys meaning. On the other hand, when they watch a lecture in a video, it has already happened; the event is over. They can replay and rewatch the lecture, however, which allows them to self-monitor their progress. The lecture activity changes for both the instructor and the student, and one format may not necessarily or clearly be better. Nonetheless, they do differ, and, consciously or unconsciously, we consider these differences when planning our activities in online courses.

CHOOSING TOOLS

When we teach onsite, we have decisions to make about the tools we will use. We can choose whether we will use audiovisuals, for example, or whether we will wear microphones. The tools, however, typically support decisions we have already made. These devices serve as a background and as an extension of us and our intentions, in much the same way that lighting is background to our onsite teaching, and the projection of a slide substitutes for writing on a chalkboard.

When we teach online, the decision about the tool we will use necessarily is a more intentional part of the planning process than when we teach onsite. It is part and parcel of the decision-making process. In a blog post, history instructor Lisa Lane makes a similar argument, intimating that the chosen technological tool suggests what we may or may not do with it; in so doing, it, in turn, drives our plans. As illustration, she cites three platforms instructors can use when teaching online:

1. *Blackboard* is like the Lego kits you get, the ones that make a particular object using precisely the quantity of the parts inside the box. You can, of course, make other things out of the pieces, but you have to ignore the instructions and exercise a bit of creativity. Most people, however, buy a Lego kit in the first place because they want to make exactly what's shown in the picture on the box.

2. *Moodle* is like the boxes of Legos you get containing a certain number of each kind of brick. There is no set plan, except that you can only use as many bricks as are in the box, unless you buy more. There are a certain number of single-peg bricks, and a certain number of blue ones. You can build whatever you want, but it's limited by the number of bricks of each size and color that you have.

3. *Web 2.0* is like buying a bunch of Legos at a garage sale. You don't know what you'll get to start with, but it'll be fun discovering what's in there and figuring out how to use it. You imagine as you build and try out different things. Sometimes you think two pieces don't go together, and they do. Since you don't know what's there as you look into the box, you are open to possibilities. You plan ahead, but mostly to make sure you don't run out of the bricks you might want to use, and you can always go to another garage sale and get more.

The analogy is useful, as it provides us with information about what we can do with the various media, tools, and levels of freedom for planning that each of these offers to faculty members, with some technologies driving our decisions more than others. The differences matter. Many of us want to have as much freedom and as few restrictions as possible on our abilities to plan courses and instructional approaches. At the same time—unlike an onsite course, where we might not have a choice of tools, as they may simply come with the assigned room and be difficult to alter—many of us have some choice in deciding what technologies to use, which is also a form of freedom. That is, if we are able to choose our environment and if we are careful in our selection of tools, we exercise control. We can elect to follow the picture on the Lego box, or we can choose to piece together the Legos that we find. We may decide to substitute less freedom for the ease of use that an LMS offers us and for its central location for students, or we may choose to rage against the machine and go in our own direction with a DIY approach. The decision often rests with us.[13] Rose Marra, an expert in learning technologies, offers her perspectives about online course planning.

Planning
In and Out of the Box

ROSE MARRA
Professor
Learning Technologies, College of Education
University of Missouri–Columbia, US

Planning online courses can be challenging, for many of the reasons discussed in this chapter. When I teach a course on Designing Online Courses (which, naturally, is taught online), I posit that using a standard LMS, like Blackboard, in combination with Web 2.0 tools can allow course planners to effectively address a wide range of instructional objectives.

You might think of this as sort of an inside the box / outside the box approach. Inside the box, you get the functionality of a structured LMS; outside the box, you get the greatly expanded functionality of the vast array of Web 2.0 tools that are available. Lisa Lane has described these classes of tools using a Lego analogy. This brief sidebar explains how the different types of Lego sets can be used together.

But before I discuss these ideas a bit further, let's go back. Even with the approach I suggest, the first thing you need is to decide on the objectives you have for your learners. That is, what is it you want them to be able to do after they finish your course, or a particular lesson? I would argue that whether you are teaching face-to-face or online, you will want to try to stick to the same objectives.

Having said that, it is absolutely true that the kind of instruction you develop to help your learners accomplish those same objectives—and to support them during their learning processes—may be very different in an online setting.

This is where the inside the box / outside the box approach can be very useful. You get one set of tools with a standard LMS like Blackboard

(continued)

Tool	Types of learning objectives supported
VoiceThread (www.voicethread.com)—a tool for creating asynchronous conversations around media (documents, videos, pictures)	• building community • co-constructing knowledge
ConvinceMe (www.convinceme.net)—an online "debating" website. Supports and scaffolds learners in creating and visually representing an initial premise or challenge and then allows community members to add evidence for or against and "argue"	• ability to persuade others • analysis and synthesis • knowledge representation • communication skills
MindMeister (www.Mindmeister.com)—an online concept-mapping tool. Best used with learners constructing their own maps of knowledge domains and labeling links between nodes[1]	• knowledge representation • co-constructing knowledge through the sharing and collaborative building of maps

1. Jonassen (2006) discusses concept maps and "mindtools" more fully.

(e.g., a threaded discussion forum, a grade book, built-in email, a course roster, announcements), but by expanding outside the box to Web 2.0 you get a much more extensive set of possible tools. Here are some examples of the types of tools I, or my students, have found on the web and incorporated into their online instruction, as well as the types of learning objectives they can support.

Incorporating interactive web tools into your online instruction has certain requirements and tradeoffs. First, you have to build your instruction around these tools. This is really no different than using the tools offered in an LMS like Blackboard. In Blackboard, you have access to a threaded discussion-board tool. As an instructor, you have to build meaningful lessons that use that discussion forum. Similarly, if you were to use MindMeister, you would need to construct a meaningful task using that tool to support your intended learning objectives. When I teach the course on Designing Online Courses, I ask learners to collaboratively build maps that represent the relationships between the instructional design process in general and how it applies to developing a specific online learning product that each student is working on individually.

You also have to be prepared to teach the students how to use the course tool(s) that are located on the web. Tools embedded in an LMS like Blackboard have readily available documentation to help your learners use them. Not so with web-based tools. You may be able to locate some "how-to" materials via the tool's website, or perhaps from a third party (e.g., YouTube videos), but you need to be prepared to vet these materials for your learning audience, and/or create your own. Additionally, after the students learn to use the tool, you have to be prepared to support students using that tool during the lessons (i.e., you are the "help desk").

Another requirement when using web-based tools is that as both a designer and instructor, you have to keep current on changes to that tool, checking to make sure it still is available and functioning! We all know how volatile things are on the web. You may find something that seems very useful, but it may disappear—or it may not be reliable. This is a risk you take with using web-based tools.

The tradeoffs you are facing is that by incorporating these outside-the-box tools, you get an expanded tool arsenal that can provide more ways to support your learning objectives and potentially appeal to more learning styles, but you take on the added responsibility of supporting your students as they learn the mechanics of that tool and then use it in their learning.

CREATING THE LEARNING ENVIRONMENT

When we teach onsite, we often are assigned the classroom in which we will teach. Someone else designed this room and has already made key decisions about this space. The classroom has a fixed ceiling height, a set number of windows (if we are lucky), a particular kind of lighting, and so forth. Moreover, someone had previously chosen the wall colors, floor coverings, tables and chairs (or desks), and the general placement of the furniture. They typically have also made a decision about how the instructor will be positioned in the room, often at the front of the class, with seats facing them. Occasionally instructors are positioned near boards or screens and, at times, are (curiously) positioned away from them. As instructors, we may have some ability to control the design of the classroom, such as rearranging tables and chairs or desks, but typically the environment is fairly fixed and stable, and we operate within it as best we can.

When we teach online, designing the environment becomes an additional part of the instructional planning process. Some learning management systems have preset features, such as core components, layout, colors, fonts, and so forth. We should first decide whether to accept these or "hack" (modify) them to create something different. If we will be teaching with social media, such as blogs, we have to make those basic decisions, plus some new ones. How will we link media together? How will we lay out text, including how much white space to have, how much space between the lines, how many inches for the margins? We also have decisions to make about the text itself. What kinds of headings and subheadings will we use, what kind and size of font, how much text should be included? Then we make decisions about color. How much contrast should there be between the text and the background? Alternately, we make decisions about existing themes that we can apply to our blogs, since there are many to choose from. Another aspect is graphics. What will we use them for, how many we should use, should we animate them?[14] These choices represent shifts in the instructional planning process, as they add a layer of complexity to what we should consider and do.

Strategies for Planning Online Courses

Because of the shifts in the ways we plan courses, when we teach online we need to engage in purposeful planning. We need to intentionally select goals, pedagogies, assessments, tools, and environments. We can go about this deliberate planning in several ways.

STRATEGY #1: CONSIDER WHAT AN ONLINE COURSE IS

Is the course to be a seminar? A conversation? A discourse? An event? A text? Something else? As individual teachers, most likely we have different perspectives about the answer, but our individual responses will drive much of our planning. Our conceptions of what the course is will influence what goals and objectives we have as well as how we will enable students to accomplish them. If we see the course as a seminar, we might ask students to do original research on learning theories; if we conceive of a course as an event, we might design (or suggest) meet-ups, during which students can exchange ideas with others and situate them within the broader context of the course's content. As faculty, our conception of what a course is will also influence how we see our roles in it. If we see it as a seminar, we might view ourselves as experts, guiding novices through the process of doing original research, although, if we envision it as an event, we might see ourselves as event coordinators, bringing the students into the course and designing activities for them to participate in. These are important philosophical considerations, and our answers to such questions will necessarily provide some structure to our work.

STRATEGY #2: INTERROGATE PERSONAL PHILOSOPHIES
AND IDEALS BEFORE PLANNING

Our philosophies and ideals should guide our plans, rather than the other way around. A good beginning is for us to clearly articulate our teaching beliefs,[15] so we can intentionally embed those beliefs in our teaching. Developing a written teaching-philosophy statement is something that can help us identify and embed our beliefs about instruction more fully.[16] Developing a statement about our online teaching philosophy can allow us to consider our beliefs about teaching within a different medium; while a philosophy statement on onsite teaching and one on teaching online probably would be related, they are also likely to have some important differences, as this book suggests, and we, as faculty, would do well to articulate them.

STRATEGY #3: KEEP THE GOAL OF STUDENT LEARNING IN SIGHT

At times, planning an online course can feel like a daunting task. It is all too easy to get caught up in the tasks of teaching, such as choosing instructional activities, planning materials, designing assessments, and so forth. If teaching does not ultimately result in student learning, however, the effort has been for naught. For this reason, it is imperative to keep the primary goal—student learning—in sight. Wendy Drexler encourages new teachers to focus on the learner and the learning, rather than on teaching per se (see p. 122).

STRATEGY #4: FOLLOW A NATURAL, RATHER
THAN A PRESCRIBED, PROCESS

We can accomplish this strategy by asking ourselves important questions. First, we can acknowledge and look for inspiration.[17] That is, ideas for how to go about teaching and learning come from somewhere; we do not really begin the planning process by sitting down and writing a goal or an objective. Rather, our minds are stimulated by the special act that is involved in creating a course. There is a sense of waiting for epiphany, or an "aha" moment, but there is also a sense of asking the right questions. What is important in the world? What content is worth knowing? What forms might that content take? Who are our students? What should they and what might they want to know? What should they or what might they want to do at the end of a course? How will they demonstrate their learning? How will

Learning Instead of Teaching

WENDY DREXLER
Chief Innovation Officer
ISTE Leadership Team
International Society for Technology
in Innovation, US

Remember the student. This is the primary advice I gave to new online instructors when I was the director of online development at Brown University. Focus on learning, rather than teaching. The most significant transition is the paradigm shift from the familiar classroom experience to a virtual environment that includes new ways of navigating, communicating, sharing knowledge, and assessing learning. Technical issues, concepts of time, and instructional-design challenges further complicate the transition. Ultimately, the goal is to reach students and help them learn.

Student needs are easily dwarfed in the cognitive dissonance experienced by a new online instructor. Yet students who are new to online learning experience a similar cognitive challenge. Most have learned in a traditional classroom setting: show up, listen, take notes, discuss. Well-designed online learning environments require the student to take more control of the learning process: collect information outside the classroom walls; seek out experts beyond the instructor; build on prior knowledge, and then synthesize and share it with others in the course. This approach, combined with a flexible learning schedule, requires greater self-regulation. A student's ability to take more control is further influenced by motivation, confidence, and his or her own paradigm of learning. With all this discomfort and confusion, one might wonder how learning takes place at all. Yet the deepest learning happens in an environment where sense making and discovery are paramount.

The challenge for online instructors is to create a learning experience that scaffolds this process for students and guides them toward autonomy and independence. Structure is important and comforting, especially at the start. The art in online instruction is finding a proper balance between teacher control and student autonomy, and this balance may need to change over time. Getting it right is an iterative process; thus good instructional design and flexibility are critical. It's really a learning process for both teacher and student.

---

they receive feedback? And why? Next, we can begin the process of ideation, or the creative means of generating and communicating new ideas, which can be visual, concrete, or abstract. We can go about this process in several ways, from brainstorming early ideas, to concept-mapping our navigation of the course, to storyboarding our plan for the course, to making sketches of what the course environment might look like. We can also ask ourselves questions. What is the best way to help students accomplish the course's goals? How can I know if they have met these objectives? How can I make this course a meaningful learning experience? Finally, we can move toward implementation, in which we develop the course. In this phase, we can try out things for ourselves, and we can have others, whether peers or a small group of students, review the course and provide feedback. We can also ask ourselves questions. How does this idea really work in practice? What challenges do learners encounter? What might make their experiences more positive? In short, planning really begins when we ask the important questions.

STRATEGY #5: USE VISUAL PRACTICES WHEN PLANNING COURSES

Trying to see things from a different perspective has the potential to inspire creativity. Doing so can allow someone to see how ideas might fit together in different ways. Looking for new connections between ideas can enhance creativity in our planning, as can reading broadly in multiple fields and working on several topics at once. Another way to look at things in a new way is through visual practice, as described by Giulia Forsythe (see p. 124).

STRATEGY #6: DO NOT JUST SUBSTITUTE, TRANSFORM

When teaching online, we have an opportunity to do more than simply use technology to accomplish what we were doing previously. The substitution, augmentation, modification, redefinition (SAMR) model (figure 5.1; see p. 125), developed by consultant Ruben Puentedura, argues that we should use technology to "teach above the line."[18] Charles Miller and Aaron Doering offer suggestions about how to plan for transformation, a goal of the SAMR model (see p. 126).

Adding Visual Practice to Your Online Course

GIULIA FORSYTHE
Special Projects Facilitator
Centre for Teaching, Learning &
    Educational Technologies
Brock University, CA

(Photo credit: Alan Levine)

Research shows that memory can be aided and intentions can be realized through visualization techniques.[1] Visual notes can be used for brainstorming, as a way of externalizing thought.[2] Instructors can use various techniques that employ drawings rather than text to plan and make connections in course outlines.[3] Learners can use sketch-noting skills to maintain their focus.[4] Visualization enhances engagement on both sides of the teaching and learning relationship, whether in taking notes or being used in presentations.[5]

As Temple Grandin says, "the world needs all kinds of minds," and some of those minds "think in pictures."[6] Doodling and sketch noting is a form of external thought that allows you to physically present the connections you are making while thinking. In the conscious mind, doodling can assist your concentration and focus, but even in the unconscious mind, doodling and daydreaming elicit mental connections. Digital tools make it increasingly easier to take visual notes electronically and share them quickly.

More formally, elements of creativity and play can be added to online interactions, allowing a departure from the usual text- or video-based work, which tends to be linear in format. Sometimes presenting information in a mind map can help highlight connections that were not obvious beforehand. A mind map also models different ways of thinking for learners. Encouraging students to take notes while reading or watching videos or listening to audio in an online course can help improve both their engagement and their retention of the material.

By sharing my thinking through visual means, my most important connections have been to people—giving my perceptions of their ideas, presentations, and words back to them.

Notes

1. Ainsworth, Prain, & Tytler (2011) describe visualization techniques.

2. Sachse, Hacker, & Leinert (2004) describe the use of visual techniques for brainstorming.

3. Biktimirov & Nilson (2003) describe using visual techniques for planning.

4. Andrade (2010) discusses the use of sketchnoting.

5. K. Wilson & Korn (2007) describe the ways in which visualization can increase engagement.

6. See Grandin's (2010) TED talk or her written work (Grandin, 1996).

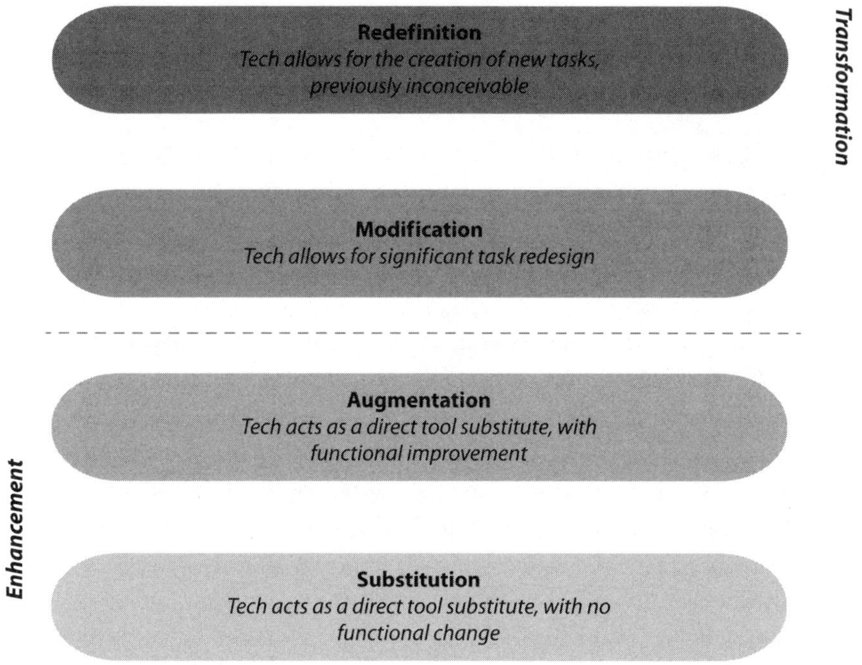

Figure 5.1. The SAMR model

Exploring Opportunities for Thoughtful Technology Transformation

CHARLES MILLER AND AARON DOERING
Associate Professors and Codirectors of the LT Media Lab
College of Education and Human Development
University of Minnesota, US

In the Learning Technologies program at the University of Minnesota, our MA and PhD-level courses are focused on the collaborative areas of online learning, the interaction of design and development, and the integration of K–12 technology. The expanding portfolio of courses we offer each semester is evenly divided across face-to-face (F2F), hybrid, and fully online offerings, providing our faculty with a diverse group of students collaborating throughout each unique course section and delivery method. Regardless of the course structure, the pedagogical and epistemological beliefs of the instructor, or the technologies integrated within the course, our primary focus is always on creating opportunities for students to have a transformative learning experience.

Although the learner's experience in a given semester or a day (whether online or face to face) is complex,[1] we need to understand how to design learning experiences that afford transformation.[2] In current research in the fields of instructional design and learning sciences, the term "transformative" has become pervasive.[3] The goal of transformation is impressive, but in the current educational climate, a close look at transformation and transformative learning experiences is necessary. We no longer can continue suggesting that we must promote "transformative learning" without providing insight into what transformation means and how we can offer educational opportunities to support such an endeavor. Although the literature in these areas urges educators to provide transformative experiences, pragmatic approaches to designing and creating opportunities for these experiences in F2F, hybrid, and online learning are seldom acknowledged. To expand the discussion, we crafted a collection of principles to foster transformative opportunities in F2F, hybrid, and online courses. The following is not an inclusive list of guidelines, but rather a framework to spark future exploration, design, integration, and research.

Principles for Technology Transformation:

- *Experiences, not products.* When designing an environment for learners, the environment and the tasks should reflect an opportunity for engagement, not completion.
- *Trust and inspiration.* Learning environments must establish and build a sense of trust and inspiration. The roles have changed in online learning, with the learner's first experience being with the learning environment rather than the instructor.
- *Learners as designers.* Students must be given an opportunity to learn by using the technology, so they can construct their own knowledge base while being active learners.
- *Learners as experts.* Many times, learners possess facets of expert knowledge. When this knowledge is elicited, learners are empowered and become the center of the discussion, ultimately increasing their motivation and engagement.
- *Collaboration and discourse.* Collaboration must move beyond the bulletin board of the 1990s to a blending interactions that allow learners to feel as if they are physically present with their colleagues, without a technology barrier.
- *Aesthetics.* With respect to the design and development of online learning environments, we define aesthetics as the symbiosis of thoughtfully orchestrated elements in an interactive design that enhance and heighten the learner's experience, as opposed to elements formulated merely to satisfy the pedagogical or technical needs of the instructional objectives. In other words, aesthetics is design

(continued)

going beyond the notion of "done"; the essence of the design process continues after completion of the pedagogical and technical requirements.

- *Self-narrative.* One of the most transformative outcomes of an instructional experience is when the experience itself becomes part of the learner's or instructor's self-narrative.
- *TPACK.* Learning environments should encompass the ability for all instructors to see themselves at the center of the TPACK model, where they meld all technological, pedagogical, and content-knowledge domains.
- *Innovative pedagogy.* Designers should strive to incorporate innovative pedagogy within their designs.
- *Instructor as learner.* When designing a learning environment, it is imperative to reflect on whether you would want to learn with and from the environment you have developed. Would it motivate you to learn, engage with others, and make a personal difference?

Based on the above guidelines, we believe it is the *structure* of our courses, as opposed to the content, that creates opportunities for transformative learning. For example, a fundamental difference between our courses and others is the learning environment we use, regardless of delivery method. We have used Ning for several years, rather than WebCT, Moodle, and other university-led endeavors, as it contains a critical element that the other learning management systems leave out: social presence.[4] Based on a social network, Ning allows our students to have individual portfolios and personal pages, create unique groups based on the class or an informal need, and connect with one another even before the course formally begins. In addition, we value and integrate problem-based learning for all of our projects; incorporate timely readings throughout the semester (not just limited to academic articles but also to technology journals, magazines, and online case studies); and involve collaboration in all course activities, small and large (as we believe authentic learning does not exist in a vacuum). We also focus on theoretical debates (as opposed to foundational discussions), and we establish trust, continued social presence, and engagement throughout all facets of the course (i.e., learning should always be fun, even in challenging or demanding contexts).

Finally, as an example of integrating tools into our courses, we ask students to reflect on and share their beliefs before each class session, through the use of our Flipgrid environment.[5] Designed and developed by the LT Media Lab, Flipgrid is an online environment where students respond to short teacher-created questions, enhancing a sense of community and social presence in their online, hybrid, or F2F classrooms. In our courses we focus each question on an open-ended topic relevant to each week's readings, discussion, or project. Once the students record their individual responses on video, these can be embedded in and displayed on our Ning website (we typically feature one or two of the most thoughtful reflections each week) or shared through Twitter, Facebook, and email among their peers. We have found that Flipgrid has enhanced social presence in our hybrid classrooms and ultimately seeds the opening discussion in our next F2F meeting. Moreover, the integration of this technology and the course content provides transformative opportunities for those students who are less vocal in class: they now have an equal voice, essentially moving from the back row to the front row.

(continued)

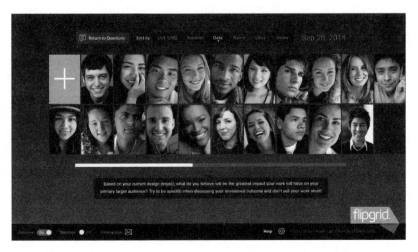

Students respond through webcam videos to teacher-generated questions each week in the Flipgrid online environment (www.flipgrid.com/cehd)

As a collective field of teachers, designers, and researchers, we must move beyond such surface-level qualities and questions as "Does the learning environment work for my learners?" and ask the more difficult query, "Does the learning environment *work well* for my learners?" In order to address this challenge, we must focus on designing opportunities for transformative experiences in our learning environments, as opposed to completing a development checklist focused primarily on content, usability, and feature sets. By reflecting on the collection of principles outlined above and using these principles as a discussion point earlier, rather than later, in course development, we believe that teachers and designers will create new insights into what it means for their students to have transformative experiences, ultimately defining and pioneering a new era of transformation in education.

Notes

1. Parrish (2008) describes learning complexity.
2. Doering et al. (2009) and Doering, Miller, & Veletsianos (2008) further describe learning transformation.
3. Parrish (2008) and Garrison & Kanuka (2004) also describe learning transformation.
4. More information about Ning is available at www.ning.com.
5. More information about Flipgrid is available at www.flipgrid.com.

Conclusion

Teaching online requires new ways of planning instruction. We have different decisions to make regarding old questions, and we have new questions to consider. As teachers in an online environment, we have to engage with a method that allows us to plan ahead and mediate technology into the teaching and learning process. What we do and how we do it matters. When we reconsider how students can accomplish course goals and objectives, these are fundamentally altered. Likewise, shifts in the forms of assessment that we use can lead to changes in student learning as well as to student development. Shifts in pedagogy mean alterations in the ways in which students experience it. We have a duty to stay vigilant in ensuring that the technology is not driving our work, and that we are staying true to our philosophies and our goals. Alternately, we need to ensure that we are harnessing technology in ways that allow us to develop new and different philosophies and goals that will better serve our students. Such work is not for the faint of heart.

Chapter Six

Intellectual Property

The instinct of ownership is fundamental in man's nature.
—WILLIAM JAMES

The professoriate, on the whole, is a creative group, and many of us belong to it because we enjoy engaging in high-level mental processes that have tangible results. As academics, we generally like to challenge traditional ideals and relationships, come up with new methods, discover additional knowledge, interpret information, and so forth. We like to see concrete results from these processes; thus many of us like to make things, such as books, articles, plays, paintings, music, software, formulas, chemicals, tools, devices, programs, and so forth. We often are drawn to our profession, then, because of the potential it offers for intellectual engagement and its outlets for creative expression. Being a thinker and a maker is a natural part of faculty work. One thing many of us "make" is courses, and when we teach online, we develop a wide range of products that represent our intellectual property.

About Intellectual Property

Our right of ownership of our intellectual property is known as copyright,[1] which is the ability to "reproduce the copyrighted work in any format; to prepare derivative works; to distribute copies of copyrighted work to the public by sale, rent, lease or gift; to perform the copyrighted work publicly; and to display the copyrighted work publicly."[2] We are considered to own the work at its creation, once such works are "fixed in any tangible medium of expression, now known or later developed, from which they can be perceived, reproduced, or otherwise communicated, either directly or with the aid of a machine or device."[3] We can sell or rent this right to others, and we can receive compensation for that use (i.e., an author might assign copyright to a publisher in exchange for royalties). Others, however, cannot take our original expressions without permission, nor can we take theirs, as doing so would be copyright infringement, which is a legal violation of a copyright holder's exclusive rights.[4] Copyright violations can take many forms, from making and distributing unauthorized copies of another's work to borrowing significant portions of another person's work in the creation of a new work.

Even before the advent of early forms of communications technology, access to creative expression was limited, and ownership of that expression was relatively clear. To have access to a story, one had to hear it from the storyteller, while the story was being spun. To hear music, one had to listen to the person making it in the moment. To see art, one had to watch it being made or to see it being displayed in a physical location. Internet technology, in particular, has provided us with access to many kinds of media through which to disseminate creative expression. It has made art, music, and literature much more accessible and ubiquitous. Today, such artistic products are everywhere, and they are being consumed to a greater extent than ever before, which, in a sense, makes them a little less rare and sacred. It has also removed us from the source of the creative expression. Sole ownership is much less clear. In consequence, it is more difficult for copyright holders whose works can be distributed electronically to enforce their copyrights.

Changes to Faculty Experience with Intellectual Property When Teaching Online

Most faculty are both consumers and owners of copyrighted materials. When teaching onsite, we have privileges, because our functions as educators allow us to use copyrighted materials under certain circumstances. We own our ideas, which are not always in a tangible form, and we share them with students as we deem appropriate. We exert our ownership over most of the instructional processes and products. When we teach online, however, it is no longer necessary for students to participate in the act of teaching in the moment and at the site in which it occurs; they no longer experience the creative expression directly during the process of its creation. Our online teaching materials, products, and processes necessarily are more explicit, more tangible, and more removed from the source, that is, from us. Online learning technologies have "shaken the very foundations of copyright and patent law and . . . promise to affect notions of intellectual-property ownership altogether."[5] These changes have implications for our roles and responsibilities as teachers.

USE OF EXISTING COPYRIGHTED MATERIALS

Almost all faculty members use someone else's copyrighted materials when teaching a class. We use newspaper clippings, scholarly articles, essays, photographs, and so forth. At times, we create course readers or course packs.[6] We are allowed to use works from others in our own teaching under the doctrine known as fair use. Fair use is part of copyright law and is intended to provide flexibility in extending other people's work to users and new creators. For our purposes, fair use grants an exception to copyright infringement for materials for educational use.[7] It does not grant a blanket exception, however, and whether such usage is protected is based on four statutory factors:[8]

1. *The purpose and character of the use.* Purposes that lend themselves to falling under fair use include educational, research, scholarly, critical, and nonprofit purposes.

2. *The nature of the copyrighted work.* In particular, this factor relates to whether the work is published or not. Published works tend to come under the designation of fair use (although it is possible for unpublished works to fall into this category). Likewise, borrowing from factual works is more likely to be considered fair use then borrowing from creative works.

3. *The amount and sustainability of the portion used in relation to the copyrighted work as a whole.* Using a smaller amount of a source work is more likely to fall under fair use than using a larger amount; but the amount is proportional. Thus three hundred words from a scholarly article may be more likely to be deemed fair use than three hundred words from a poem. While it is possible to use all of a source work, a lesser quantity is more likely to fall under fair use.

4. *The effect of the use on the potential market for or value of the copyrighted work.* While this factor can be challenging (or even impossible) to weigh, a good rule of thumb is to consider whether the use would substitute for the sale of the product. If so, it probably argues against fair use.

These factors provide us with some guidance, but they are flexible. While flexibility can be an asset, it can also be a challenge to those of us seeking to determine whether our proposed use of source material will or will not fall under fair use. The law is unpredictable on this issue. Anyone who attempts to determine whether something falls within the guidelines of fair use is simply making an educated guess, although clearly some guesses are more educated than others (e.g., a university lawyer would be a good contact for questions). Fortunately, copyright holders to date have been relatively tolerant of the limited use of their copyrighted materials without prior permission or payment of royalties, at least to the extent a faculty member deems necessary for teaching a class. Few copyright holders have taken issue with faculty using copyrighted material in onsite courses, perhaps due to the fact that copyright infringements that take place in a traditional classroom are exceedingly difficult to prove.

Nonetheless, fair use becomes an even murkier concept for those of us who choose to teach online. When we make copies available in an online environment (i.e., over the Internet), we do not have the same capacity to control the distribution of these materials. It is much easier and cheaper to disseminate information to large audiences over the Internet, particularly as student participation in online courses has grown. A real consideration is what counts as fair use in MOOCs, and many instructors for these courses are choosing to use open resources. In addition, online learning is much more visible, so copyright infringement is easier to identify. We may have large audiences for our online courses, which makes sharing copyrighted material simpler, and most students are able to copy and print these items in their own homes, making the issue even more problematic. Because of this, students, or, in the case of open courses, other individuals, can access as much (or as little) of a course—and, therefore, its copyrighted materials—as they want.[9] Thus the conditions of fair use are challenged in myriad ways in an online teaching environment.

The Copyright Act, which governs the fair use of materials when teaching onsite, is somewhat limited in setting forth what is permissible when technology allows greater access to and use of copyrighted items. For that reason, in 1996 CONFU (Conference on Fair Use)—a group of educators, attorneys, publishers, librarians, and others convened by the Clinton administration—developed a set of fair-use guidelines for educational multimedia, suggesting that faculty and students may use approximately 10% of another's works for educational use.[10] In addition, the Technology, Education, and Copyright Harmonization (TEACH) Act was established in 2002 as an amendment to section 110(2) of the Copyright Act. It has sought to expand educators' rights to use works in online learning, striving to make these rights more congruent with onsite teaching. The TEACH Act has been controversial, however, as some educators have suggested that it still leaves a considerable gap between onsite and online teaching, is overly complicated, and is difficult to interpret. Moreover, this act has been deemed to be more restrictive than the fair-use principle. Will Cross provides useful and accessible information about the TEACH Act.

Making Space for the Giants
Copyright, Technology, and Online Instruction

WILLIAM M. CROSS
Director
Copyright and Digital Scholarship Center
North Carolina State University
    Libraries, US

As Isaac Newton stated, "If I have seen further it is by standing on the shoulders of giants." No one understands Newton's famous axiom better than an instructor. For faculty members working in the classroom, instruction would be impossible without making reference to works that came before. From general-education requirements to graduate seminars, the daily work of teaching is built around the giants of the past. Foundational works are introduced, recent scholarship is evaluated, and this morning's news is presented to spark class discussion.

When copyright threatens an instructor's ability to share the text, the journal, and the newspaper, however, this spark could be extinguished. Negotiating copyright permission can be time-consuming and costly, and it would be perverse indeed if copyright, designed to "promote the progress of science and the useful arts" (Article I of the US Constitution), shut down the very instruction that encourages learning and creation.

To alleviate this tension between copyright and classroom instruction, US copyright law has traditionally carved out space for the use of works in the classroom without explicit permission. For example, the established practice of displaying images, performing plays, and showing films in the classroom is protected by the face-to-face teaching exception embodied in section 110(1) of the Copyright Act. Teaching activities, including "making multiple copies for classroom use," are similarly privileged by fair use, a broad copyright exception for socially valuable instances such as instruction.

(continued)

Taking Instruction to New Heights:
The TEACH Act and Online Instruction

The principle that instructors are free to incorporate copyrighted works into their classroom instruction without seeking permission was translated to the digital-classroom context by Congress with the passage of the Technology, Education, and Copyright Harmonization (TEACH) Act of 2002. Although the TEACH Act reflects this principle, it also includes several additional rules designed to replicate the classroom context in the online environment. It accomplishes this with two sets of specific responsibilities: one aimed at instructors, and one at the institutions where they teach.

THE INSTITUTION'S RESPONSIBILITIES

First, the TEACH Act specifies the types of institutions to which it applies and the way these institutions must behave to qualify for this copyright exception. Unlike many general copyright exceptions, such as fair use, TEACH is limited to "government bodies or accredited nonprofit educational institutions."

Institutions are also required to provide significant information about copyright to their stakeholders. This includes generating a written policy on copyright for distance education; providing information that promotes compliance by students, faculty, and staff; and including written notice to students that the works being shared via TEACH are protected by copyright.

To qualify for TEACH, institutions must also provide several technological safeguards that limit sharing to the virtual classroom. To the extent "technologically feasible," institutions must restrict access exclusively to enrolled students through password protection or similar measures. Institutions must also establish controls on the retention of course materials and their further dissemination beyond the end of the class session. As with limiting access, these controls need not be airtight; they must only "reasonably prevent" retention and further dissemination of copyrighted items.

Checklist—Institutions Must:

✓ Be a government body or accredited nonprofit educational institution
✓ Provide a copyright policy

✓ Provide copyright information and a copyright notice to users
✓ Limit access to enrolled students
✓ Use technological controls on retention and further dissemination

THE INSTRUCTOR'S RESPONSIBILITIES

Along with these institutional requirements, the TEACH Act also requires individual instructors who rely on this exception to behave in a manner that replicates their role in the physical classroom.

First, instructors relying on TEACH must provide supervision of and oversight for all materials shared. Performances and displays must be "made by, at the direction of, or under the actual supervision" of the instructor for the course. Similarly, the materials must be "an integral part of the class session offered as a regular part of the systematic mediated instructional activities" and be "directly related and of material assistance to the teaching content of the transmission." Further, all materials must be used to directly support the pedagogical work of the instructor, not simply for the entertainment of the students.

TEACH also specifies what materials may and may not be used. All nondramatic literary and musical works qualify for this exception, but the use of dramatic and audiovisual works must not exceed "reasonable and limited portions." TEACH does not define what a "reasonable" portion is, but in general the reasonableness will be evaluated in light of the instructor's pedagogical purpose. In other words, how much does the instructor reasonably need to use in order to make a point or introduce the concept to the students? Regardless of the type of work, instructors are permitted to display work in an amount comparable to that which is typically displayed during a live classroom session.

Instructors are prohibited from using materials that were unlawfully acquired, or materials that were produced or marketed primarily for performance or display, as part of the mediated instructional activities transmitted via digital networks.

Checklist—Instructors Must:
✓ Make, direct, or supervise all performances or displays
✓ Ensure that all materials are an integral part of systematic mediated instruction

(continued)

✓ Ensure that all materials are directly related and of material assistance to a course

✓ Use only nondramatic works or "reasonable" portions of dramatic and audiovisual works

✓ Avoid unlawful copies and work designed or sold specifically for online instruction

Stretching beyond the Shoulders: The Limits of TEACH and the Importance of Fair Use

The TEACH Act is an important component of online instruction, but it has several significant limitations. First, where many copyright exceptions concisely describe a general principle, TEACH is complex, technical, and rigid. It is more than five times as long as the text of the equivalent face-to-face teaching exception discussed above. It also introduces several limitations that go beyond merely recreating the confines of the classroom, such as the act's requirement for using just "reasonable, limited portions" of copyrighted materials and its application only to accredited institutions.

Second, TEACH is designed to support performance and display, but the exception does not encompass related instructional practices, such as electronic reserves or the creation of online teaching tools and resources. An instructor working online must be familiar with TEACH but should also be comfortable with related copyright exceptions—particularly fair use—that may apply to all aspects of course design, lectures, class projects, and related works. Resources such as the "Fair use codes & best practices" web page, hosted by American University's Center for Media & Social Impact, provide excellent guidance for instructors as they design and present online courses.

Finally, copyright exceptions like those in TEACH stand on the shoulders of related exceptions that support instruction. Copyright scholars have written about the way that particular statutes such as TEACH exert a "gravitational pull" on a court's evaluation of good-faith behavior. Engaging in the activities that TEACH is designed to support strengthens related exceptions, such as fair use, when instruction is done in good faith. An instructor does not have to choose which exception he or she relies on; the entire panoply of copyright exceptions work in harmony to make space for the socially valuable work that instructors do.

TEACH is an important part of the picture, but in a world of MOOCs, streaming media, and online universities, the 2002 law is best understood as one part of the infrastructure supporting teachers and their students as they reach toward the horizons of online instruction.

Further Reading

American University, Center for Media & Social Impact. Fair use codes & best practices, available at www.cmsimpact.org/fair-use/best-practices/fair-use-codes-best-practices.

Crews, K. (2012). *Copyright law for librarians and educators* (3rd edition). Chicago: American Library Association.

Duke University. TEACH Act guidelines, available at http://blogs.library.duke.edu/scholcomm/files/2007/12/copyright-review-flow-chart-v3x.pdf.

Hobbs, R. (2010). *Copyright clarity: How fair use supports digital learning.* Thousand Oaks, CA: Corwin.

North Carolina State University, Copyright and Digital Scholarship Center. CDSC tools for authors and instructors, available at www.lib.ncsu.edu/cdsc/resources/tools.

PATTERNS OF OWNERSHIP

In addition to using items from others when teaching courses, we also create our own materials. When we teach onsite, many of our products and processes are not subject to copyright. Lectures or group activities typically are not in a tangible form and thus are not copyrightable. We may, however, create materials that fall under this category. In most cases, the person who develops the work and fixes it in a tangible medium is the owner of the material, and copyright is thought to convey who conceived of the work.

The 1976 Copyright Act, however, provides an ownership exception for those individuals working within a company or an institution. If the work is developed by an employee during the regular scope of his or her employment, that person's employer is deemed the author and thus the copyright owner. The product is considered work-for-hire,[11] and the employer therefore owns the work. What this means is that many faculty members are subject to work-for-hire agreements. In short, when full-time faculty members develop work at a university as part of their employment, it could be considered the university's property.

This ownership exception does not always apply, however. Some institutions allow a "teacher exception" to work-for-hire. Moreover, there are factors that determine whether the works that were created would be deemed work-for-hire. In particular, in *Community for Creative Non-Violence v. Reid*, which was decided in 1989, the US Supreme Court identified factors that make up an employer/employee relationship:[12]

1. *Control by the employer over the work.* For example, the employer determines how the work is done, has the work done at the employer's location, and provides equipment or other means to create the work.
2. *Control by the employer over the employee.* For example, the employer controls the employee's schedule in creating the work, has the right to have the employee perform other assignments, determines the method of payment, or has the right to hire the employee's assistants.
3. *Status and conduct of the employer.* For example, the employer is in business to produce such works, provides the employee with benefits, or withholds tax from the employee's payment.

Most of us do work that is not under the direct control of our employers. We do it off the clock, and we do it on our own equipment. Thus our products often fall into a grey area.

In addition, under the Copyright Act, faculty may retain ownership of "commissioned" works if the work is done through additional or outside compensation and does not take place during normal employment hours; it is then considered "independently contracted" and the employee may still be deemed to own the copyright. Part-time employees are not generally subject to work-for-hire strictures and thereby tend to own their own creative work.[13]

In an exception to the exception, however, if an employee is deemed an independent contractor, the employing organization often specifies that it holds the copyright to the materials being created. In addition, in some for-profit institutions, faculty are employed under work-for-hire agreements, which means that the institution controls the course content and any new content that may be developed belongs to the institution.

In yet another twist, even if we as teachers fall under work-for-hire, an institution may choose to share the copyright for a work produced by a faculty member with that person.[14] While owning copyright as individuals is the clearest form of ownership, it is possible to hold joint ownership, which is what occurs when two or more authors contribute copyrightable materials that may be combined into a single work. In this situation, each contributor shares ownership to the entire work, not just to what he or she created, which, in turn, means that each contributor can exercise any of the rights of copyright, such as transferring or licensing the work.

There is wide variety in how they go about having joint copyright ownership, from licensing the whole of the work to the institution, or only part to the institution, or all to the faculty member.

CLEAR. AS. MUD.

Fortunately, even for the course products we develop teaching onsite that fall into this technically copyrightable category, there are few instances of universities taking action in order to assert ownership of such properties, very likely because they are deemed to have little value. Unfortunately, when we teach online, the game changes. Many of our recorded creative activities and outlets, such course materials and presentations,[15] multimedia, video, photos, and music, are products that may be copyrighted.[16] Lectures that once were intangible are now recorded and thus become tangible. Moreover, there is an increasing sense that this intellectual property may have some monetary value. Another issue is that faculty who teach online often work with educational technologists to create online courses. The creation of course materials and processes becomes a joint endeavor, and such products subject to joint ownership, which complicates the copyright. In addition, when an institution has invested significant financial resources to develop a course, they have more of a stake in it. For instance, faculty who are participating in MOOCs often work in teams with other faculty, research assistants, graphic designers, web designers, and so forth. Anyone involved in the creation of the course may have an ownership claim for it. There is also the accompanying issue of what stake MOOC providers have in course products or processes. Questions about the ownership of online courses are only beginning to be asked, and faculty who create original materials for them are facing a new frontier. Neal Hutchens describes some of the implications of faculty ownership of intellectual property in online courses under different ownership policies (see p. 142).

AVAILABILITY OF OUR PRODUCTS

When we teach onsite, we control the dissemination of our tangible course products. We determine what to release, when to release it, and to whom to release it. In short, we exercise a substantial degree of authority over our course materials and who sees them. While there have been some threats to faculty ownership of the materials we create and use during onsite teaching, such as companies that send in employees posing as students who take lecture notes and then sell them, for the most part our materials are not readily accessible to others. Thus we do not risk

Who Owns Online Course Materials?

NEAL H. HUTCHENS
Associate Professor, Higher Education
    Program
Senior Research Associate, Center for the
    Study of Higher Education
Pennsylvania State University, US

Variation characterizes the ownership standards adopted by colleges and universities regarding the intellectual property (e.g., syllabi) developed for online courses.[1] Some institutions designate copyright for online course materials as residing with faculty. Others assert ownership over such materials, adhering to the work-for-hire doctrine. A college or university may lack a clear policy, leaving the issue of ownership unclear. Even within the same institution, particular factors may affect ownership, such as one's status as faculty or staff or whether a person received additional compensation or resources to develop a course. This sidebar considers two different intellectual-property policies and the resulting implications regarding the ownership of online course materials.

Teacher or Academic Exception to Work-for-Hire

Legal ambiguity exists over whether the 1976 Copyright Act eliminated a judicially recognized teacher exception to the work-for-hire doctrine.[2] Previously, the courts had largely viewed faculty as possessing copyright over the intellectual property they produced. Despite the legal ambiguity under current copyright law, a number of colleges and universities have policies in place that recognize the traditional teacher or academic exception to work-for-hire.

The University of Minnesota's copyright policy and its accompanying guidance illustrate how this university maintains the traditional teacher or academic exception to work-for-hire, including in relation to online courses.[3] Under the institution's copyright standards, the format for a course (i.e., meeting online or in a physical setting) does not determine ownership. Whatever the instructional context, the university recognizes an exception to work-for-hire for its faculty members. In many instances the institution permits intellectual-property rights for academic work, including course materials, to reside with faculty instead of with the university.

While faculty members at the University of Minnesota own much of the intellectual property they produce, the university reserves the right to assert institutional ownership for course materials created under certain conditions. According to university policy, a faculty member does not hold copyright in "directed works." To qualify as a directed work, (1) the university must make a specific request for a faculty member to produce the materials, (2) a project must involve the use of substantial resources beyond those usually afforded to faculty, and (3) an agreement must exist regarding the directed status of the work. As these standards show, the particular circumstances surrounding the development of online course materials may affect ownership, even if an institution recognizes a teacher exception to work-for-hire.

Unlike the situation for its faculty members, and in alignment with usual copyright standards under work-for-hire, the University of Minnesota retains ownership of intellectual property, including course materials, produced by nonfaculty employees.

Joint Ownership of Online Course Materials

In contrast to what the University of Minnesota does, the intellectual property policy of the University of Louisiana System illustrates an alternative approach, that of joint ownership.[4] This system-wide policy gives a faculty member's home institution a nonexclusive, permanent, royalty-free license for materials developed for any courses, including online ones. Under the policy, universities in the system retain the right to use these materials, even if a faculty member leaves an institution. While not adhering to work-for-hire, the system's policy demonstrates a deviation from the teacher or academic exception for faculty.

Ownership Considerations with Online Course Materials

Several points come to mind when considering the ownership question in relation to online course materials:

(continued)

- Given the differences in institutional policies, familiarize yourself with the copyright standards specific to your college or university before developing a course.
- If a college or university lacks a clear policy or standards, a written agreement between the instructor and the institution can specify ownership rights.
- Remember that one's employment status can affect ownership. Even if you work at an institution that recognizes a teacher or academic exception to work-for-hire, these standards may not apply to clinical faculty or individuals with administrative appointments.
- Employees covered by a teacher or academic exception to work-for-hire may still not possess sole ownership rights to online course materials in all instances. Especially if a faculty member receives either additional compensation or substantial institutional assistance beyond that normally provided for course development, then a college or university may claim sole or joint copyright.

Notes
1. See Blanchard (2010).
2. See *Hays v. Sony Corporation of America* (1988).
3. See University of Minnesota (2007, 2008).
4. See University of Louisiana System (2012).

---

much in the way of losing intellectual property rights for our onsite teaching materials. When we teach online, however, the situation changes, particularly if we teach a course that is open or has open components. Others can access and use our materials at any time. If they do so without attribution, they may have committed plagiarism. If they use large amounts of our content, they may have infringed on our copyright.[17]

Strategies for Being Mindful of Intellectual Property Issues

Many ownership issues accompany teaching online, from using materials that others have developed, to owning our own materials, to making our materials available for others to use. Chad Tindol, director of risk management for the University of Alabama System, provides some general advice for online college teachers regarding questions of intellectual property.

Advice for Navigating Ownership Issues

CHAD TINDOL

Director of Risk Management and Deputy
    General Counsel
University of Alabama System, US

(Photo credit: Zachary Riggins,
University Relations,
University of Alabama)

With so many legal issues, what is an instructor to do? As a basic premise, do not expect an easy answer to most legal questions. Notwithstanding attorneys' fondness for sports analogies, the law rarely declares a clear winner, at least before a full contest. Instead, the law balances the interests at stake—creators versus users. A few good basics may be of more benefit than a futile search for the "right" answer:

- *Respect the concept.* A college or university is a place where knowledgeable folks are paid, usually from taxes or tuition, to share intellectual property (IP). It may be our IP, or it may belong to others. It may even belong to the public. Faculty should respect these rights.
- *Know the key sources.* Most IP law is federal, with a basis in the US Constitution. Patent law protects inventions, trademark law identifies goods, and copyright law protects creative works. Look to federal websites for a primer: www.uspto.gov and www.copyright.gov.
- *Know the vocabulary.* IP terms sometime sound common, but they can be loaded with legal meaning. "Fair use" is a great example. Understanding the major terms—including fair use, public domain, the face-to-face exemption—and the TEACH Act is worth the effort. These are the tests that balance owners' rights against legal use.
- *Do not be intimidated by technology.* Fallacies about the effects of a technology on the law are common. The basic legal principles

(continued)

should not be affected by the media at issue. The rights of an author to a digital work should be no less, or no more, than those of an author who applies quill to parchment. Moreover, just because something is technologically possible does not mean that it is legal.

- *Be careful with sources.* When looking for IP answers, be aware that there are advocates on both sides. Some believe the world is full of pirates. Others argue that owners are stealing the public's culture via overprotection.
- *Seek help.* At your school, there is probably a legal department, perhaps a copyright office, or a librarian who can help with answers. Many schools have a written copyright and patent policy. Do not be afraid to ask questions of your experts.

IP law deserves consideration as you plan and teach online courses. You should not allow anxiety over the law to overwhelm your goals and plans for your course. Without a basic understanding and some early work, however, you may invite trouble to pay you a later visit.

Beyond these general suggestions, there are several things that faculty should consider when negotiating intellectual property issues that accompany online teaching.

STRATEGY #1: STICK TO THE GUIDELINES

For those who decide to use previously available copyrighted materials, these guidelines may be helpful:[18]

- *Limit the amount.* Avoid offing the full content of copyrighted materials, but instead seek to use excerpts when possible.
- *Limit the time.* Avoid having the materials available for the full semester; rather, limit the time period when the materials are accessible for student use.
- *Limit access.* Make materials available only to students enrolled in the course, and protect the contents with a password.[19]

STRATEGY #2: USE OPEN EDUCATION RESOURCES WHEN POSSIBLE

Open Education Resources (OER) are free materials that are available under terms that allow sharing, reproduction, and (at times) repurposing. OER content includes full courses, content modules, course materials, software, and so forth. Using freely available materials may be particularly important for faculty who choose to allow open enrollment and open access to their courses. Moreover, many of the materials we would choose to have students use are free and readily accessible. Having students download these items provides them with useful life skills; using these resources reflects sound economic and pedagogical decisions.[20]

STRATEGY #3: CHECK OUT INSTITUTIONAL POLICIES

We need to know both whether our institutions consider our products as work-for-hire and what policies they have to govern how copyright is perceived. Learning whether our institutions have specified whether they own our copyrighted materials or whether they share them with us is a first step in understanding our rights.

STRATEGY #4: MAKE CONSCIOUS DECISIONS
WHEN LICENSING OUR OWN WORK

While we may choose to follow a traditional copyright route, there are other options. In particular, Creative Commons (CC), founded in 2002 by legal scholar and political activist Larry Lessig, is a nonprofit organization that seeks to build a richer public domain through alternatives to copyright (CC licensing), where the creator can choose which rights to reserve.[21] In short, authors can make their work more

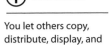 **Attribution**	**Share Alike**	**Noncommercial**	**No Derivative Works**
You let others copy, distribute, display, and perform your copyrighted work — and derivative works based upon it — but only if they give credit the way you request.	You allow others to distribute derivative works only under a license identical to the license that governs your work.	You let others copy, distribute, display, and perform your work — and derivative works based upon it — but for noncommercial purposes only.	You let others copy, distribute, display, and perform only verbatim copies of your work, not derivative works based upon it.

Figure 6.1. Creative Commons common licensing terms

 Figure 6.2. The Copyleft symbol

accessible through CC while retaining some rights we (as the authors) deem appropriate. CC offers an alternative to a conventional copyright and thus has the potential to provide faculty with sources that are freely available for use.[22] Figure 6.1 lists the CC licensing terms.[23]

A licensing term similar to CC's Share Alike is Copyleft (figure 6.2). By using the Copyleft symbol, creators agrees to give up rights to their creations, and anyone using these creations in their own work also agrees to give up their rights.

Whether we choose a traditional copyright, Creative Commons licensing, or Copyleft, it is important to protect our rights to our online materials. We should clearly display which licensing agreement we have selected, which will indicate the terms and conditions of the chosen agreement.

Conclusion

Faculty who are teaching online are facing new issues and questions when it comes to intellectual property, created in part from the fact that technology mediates between humans and their products. While protecting ownership of our intellectual property is important, we still should keep in mind that the goal is to provide students with useful materials to help them experience new ideas and receive new information. We should avoid becoming so concerned with protecting our products that we lose sight of the students and the value these creative expressions have for them and their learning.

Chapter Seven

Instructional Time

Time is an illusion. Lunchtime doubly so.
—DOUGLAS ADAMS

There is a certain rhythm to onsite teaching in higher education. We often work within semesters, quarters, or sessions that last a set number of weeks. There are breaks between sessions that allow renewal and regeneration, and a fresh start when the next one rolls around. Within a given term, we teach in chunks of time, with classes lasting fifty minutes, three hours, eight hours, or some other period. Courses are often designated by the number of credit hours they are worth, whether one semester-hour, three quarter-hours, or other. In short, our instructional work is bound by time. Teaching online, however, requires reconsidering these traditional notions of time.

About Time

As humans, we have an interesting relationship with time. We developed the concept of time to create meaning within our lives. Time provides us with relativity, or a point of reference, yet in some ways it is a limiting factor that creates segments of human experience from a greater whole. Time is not an objective category; rather, it is malleable. We have developed many different ways to measure time, count it, and keep track of it. As humans form and shape time, it, in turn, structures our understanding and the ways in which we experience life.

With the advent of technology, our relationship with time has changed. Humans once experienced time based on a natural rhythm of day and night, seasons, and years. Now, however, we experience it based on a new "electronic day" that has restructured time according to an artificial, technologically rationalized sequence.[1] We do not wake at dawn and go to sleep at dusk; we have electric lights that allow us to extend our wakeful periods. We do not plant only according to what the seasons allow; we have greenhouses and hydroponic systems that allow us to grow in the off-seasons and increase our yields. The change that technology allows in humans' relationship with time not only affect us temporally, but also in our relationships with our environment, with others, and even with ourselves.[2]

Changes to Faculty Experience of Instructional Time When Teaching Online

When we teach online, we find ourselves removed from naturally grounded notions of time. Our work is altered by the new electronic day. No longer does teaching have to occur synchronously, at a fixed time and location, during a class session. Rather, teaching and learning can, and often do, occur asynchronously, with individual students completing the class at different times and at varying rates. In a sense the online teaching environment stands outside time, ready to be grasped at any chosen moment.[3] The changes that technology allows reshape our experience of temporality. We may perceive time in different ways as the form and pattern of our work shifts, and this alters our relationships. When we teach online, we transcend traditional notions of time as a fixed ontological category of existence.

AMOUNT OF TIME

Scholars have asserted that the amount of time faculty spend teaching online is greater than that teaching onsite. In an American Council of Education Report,[4] Arthur Levine and Jeffrey Sun suggest that

> distance learning entails a host of teaching and learning practices that may be convenient for students but are far more labor intensive than traditional college practices. Creating courses, maintaining chat rooms, and responding to emails from students around the clock require far more time and energy from faculty than traditional courses. Additionally, distance learning comes with a new language and different expectations, including anytime, anyplace learning, 24/7 advising, and round-the-clock availability of instructors.

Educational technology consultants Rena Palloff and Keith Pratt posit that "faculty are afraid of feeling overwhelmed and overloaded when they enter the online arena."[5] These authors predict that "instructors in the online arena will find that the time needed to deliver this type of class is two to three times greater than to deliver an offline class."[6] After covering online instruction, Jeffrey Young, a reporter for the *Chronicle of Higher Education*, concluded that instructors' experiences confirm "what has become conventional wisdom at many campuses. It takes more time to teach in a virtual campus than in a regular one."[7]

Educational research supports the notion that faculty believe teaching online is more time-intensive than teaching onsite. Several surveys of faculty, ranging from studies that included more than ten thousand faculty members to smaller ones querying fewer than a hundred, suggest that most of the faculty who have taught online are of the same opinion.[8] Surveys of faculty also indicate that the additional teaching time may be a barrier to their adoption of online learning.[9] Several qualitative studies have documented faculty experiences with teaching online, including developing and teaching courses.[10] These individuals described the increase either in percentages or in hours per week.[11] Most of us who have been in the trenches understand these perceptions.

Data that document the time that faculty spend teaching online courses are in short supply, but a few studies have attempted to compare the quantity of time that faculty spend teaching online with that when they teach onsite.[12] Generally, these studies have used faculty time-logs as data, and they have collected information about the total amount of time faculty spend on various activities involved in teaching. The researchers tended to analyze these data on a time-spent-per-student basis. There is no agreement on the findings, with five studies documenting that faculty spend more time when teaching online,[13] three documenting equal time,[14] and one showing less time.[15] While a "vote count" of these studies might suggest that online teaching takes more time than teaching onsite, study limitations complicate the issue. It is noteworthy that many of the researchers were also the primary course instructors. While teacher research can be done to great effect, researcher bias can be an issue if precautions are not taken, and few of these study authors described their efforts to eliminate bias. There are also many critical differences among the studies, which make it hard to compare them. Some of the studies included only time spent on direct instruction in their analyses,[16] while others included pre-course design as well as delivery time.[17] Some researchers examined mature courses,[18] while others looked at new courses.[19] Additional differences that could have influenced the findings were pedagogical approach, instructor experience, class size, student variables (e.g., age/maturity), and institutional support for time spent teaching online. These differences make generalizations from the studies impossible.

Both quantitative and qualitative studies have documented the activities that could potentially expand the amount of time faculty spend on courses taught online. Continual contact with individual students, whether through emails or discussion postings, is most frequently noted by faculty as the cause of increased teaching time.[20] Another activity that appeared to contribute to this increase was course development and design,[21] although some research suggests that development time may decrease over multiple offerings.[22] Learning about and using new technology, as well as dealing with technological challenges, were other activities that increased faculty time,[23] as did the use of multiple technological tools and the inclusion of different pedagogies in the online environment.[24]

A common theme running across these studies, whether in surveys, qualitative studies, or quantitative efforts (and regardless of whether the researchers found that it took more, equal, or less time to teach online) is that, at the very least, teaching online *seems* to require more time than teaching onsite. There are several potential reasons why faculty feel online learning takes a greater amount of time than onsite learning, whether it actually does or not. When teaching online, both faculty and students experience time differently than when teaching onsite. That is, technology changes the way that faculty perceive time; in turn, this alters the way we engage with time.

SEPARATION BY TIME

When we teach onsite, instructors and students spend time together at a single location during a fixed time period. We share time and space and, in those mutual moments, we may share common experiences. These moments, whether specifically related to the course content or not, give rise to a common knowledge, a connected sense of both knowing information and knowing it *with* each other, as well as a common sense of belonging. We share first-day jitters of not being acquainted with each other or not perceiving how the course will go. We may share the experience of hearing an exciting guest speaker, discovering a new idea through debate and discussion, relating to a common joke, or responding to the surprise of a fire drill. We share the last day, the wrap-up session when we congratulate ourselves on our successes. These moments matter. They connect us in time and space. They link our experiences and give us a sense of unity and community. There is a depth and a richness to those experiences.

In an asynchronous online environment, instead of sharing time and space, we are separated by them, and our consciousness follows our own space/time. Time is divided by and among individuals. Participants in such courses may share a number of online experiences. They might comment on the same article, visit the same site, watch the same online lecture, or even work on the same group project. They may do the same things as learners in other courses, but, in an asynchronous environment, they do not do them at the same time. Individuals who participate in a course asynchronously necessarily experience it differently, creating their own histories in their own spaces/times. When this happens, we do not have the same kind of connection with each other as we do onsite. As teachers, we often have shared experiences with students as individuals, rather than with students as a group.

When teaching online, because we experience time differently, as do our students, professors necessarily seek new ways of allowing students to have shared experiences and, if possible, shared moments. This effort requires us to think more consciously about time and space than we do in onsite courses. Often we try to soften the sense of separation in time online through the use of communications technologies, to either improve synchronicity itself or, if this method is not possible, to otherwise demonstrate to students that they are sharing the same experiences.[25] In essence, we are seeking to recreate the sense of shared moments through a sense of shared experiences, even if they take place at a different time. These shared experiences may be equally rich as shared moments, but they are different.

FLEXIBILITY OF TIME

Given the capacity for both synchronous and asynchronous communication, time expands online.[26] During chats and instant messaging (IM), there are moments of delay to allow replies, a significantly longer delay than in real time. With email, blogs, and newsgroups, there are hours, days, or even weeks in which to respond. Thus the Internet creates a unique temporal space where participants' ongoing, interactive time together stretches out. This expansion of time provides a convenient "zone for reflection."[27] In other ways, however, Internet time is condensed. Change happens much more quickly online (software upgrades, shifts in the membership of online groups, etc.). Given that our subjective sense of time is linked to the rate of change in the world in which we live, the experience of time online can seem to accelerate.

FRAGMENTATION OF TIME

When we teach onsite, our teaching activities tend to occur in continuous blocks of time, and they do so by design. We may want long periods of time for reflection, since for many of us it takes a while to work up to a sufficiently high level of concentration and get to a point where we can really think through a complicated issue, even though we understand (at least theoretically) that we often are more creative when we can set the work aside for a while. We may have blocks time allocated for course preparation, for teaching, for office hours, or for responding to emails. These time periods seem linear, and they are often sequential. They are bounded and contained.

When we teach online, time is more fragmented, regardless of how hard we may try to make it otherwise.[28] We can work on course design for a while, fiddle with layout, add bits to content, and then take a break but come back later. For asynchronous course components, we do not teach at a set time; instead, we teach in what may feel more like bursts and fits. In particular, it seems as though online students need more frequent attention.[29] They also seem to expect attention at any hour of the day or night.[30] We may feel that we must respond to a student who needs an immediate response. (How can they *all* need immediate responses? Somehow, they all seem to.) That is, our work takes place in smaller and more frequent chunks of time.

These differences matter. They shift the workflow as well as the timing and pacing of the course itself. When we teach onsite, we might teach a single class session for a three-hour period per week, or two half-hour periods, or some other fixed configuration of time. Thus our teaching time is confined, say, to Monday evenings from 6:00 to 8:50. In teaching an online course in a given week, we might not be involved in direct instruction for three hours on Monday evening. Rather, the three or more hours could be spread over the week, in much smaller bursts of attention, as we update content, add links, respond to posts, and answer emails. Our teaching rhythm is altered, being less contained within time and space.

When we teach online in this way, our work is more fragmented.[31] The chunks, bursts, and fits break time apart. This sense of split time may lead to a greater feeling of cognitive overhead, the number of logical connections that our brains need to make in order to understand or contextualize our teaching. Perhaps we therefore devote more time to our teaching, which presumably should make it better, but the time we spend teaching online may be less-productive time; we may not have maximized our efforts. Occasionally we may feel as though we are stuck in stop-and-go traffic rather than making good progress on the highway. We may cover the same number of miles, but we may not get there as quickly. Progress may be slow but sure. This sense may well give rise to a feeling that teaching online requires more time and, ultimately, greater effort.[32] Our sense of time may be altered, and the challenge is to enjoy the change in pace for the different vantage point that it offers.

SIPHONING OF TIME

When teaching online, we may feel not only that time is increased—separated and separating, and more fragmented—but also that it exceeds any boundaries we try to give it.[33] The time we spend teaching online is not contained. Rather, the changes in time—short bursts over a greater period rather than concentrated attention over longer blocks—can take a toll on our other professional activities, such as research and writing.[34] When we teach online, we simply may not have as many extensive periods or blocks of time for high levels of concentration on these other professional activities; the chunked-time approach spills over into all our activities. If we let it, teaching online siphons time from our other professional activities. This sense of attrition can be particularly challenging for new faculty, who are on their own time-clocks for promotion and tenure and who may not be rewarded for such online work.

Moreover, since we can teach online anywhere and at any time, it is all too easy to take a few minutes in the evening to quickly check emails and see whether any of the students need anything. They often do, particularly since many online students work full time and thus do the bulk of their coursework at night and on weekends. It is also easy to check emails again first thing in the morning, before breakfast. This quick scan often extends into a lengthy response to a question. Such actions mean that teaching online ultimately siphons off our personal time.[35] It is easy in theory to recommend trying to contain this practice by putting limits on it, or deciding not to check email from home, but it is much harder to do so in practice. Because of this shift in the rhythms of teaching, it is easy to slip into the role of a professor on call 24/7. Doing so, however, can take personal and professional tolls. The constant dilemma is one of being there for students when they are doing the work and maintaining boundaries so we preserve time for our other professional and personal activities.

FREEDOM FROM TIME

While there are clearly some pitfalls to the amount of faculty time spent when teaching online, ones that we necessarily strive to manage, there also are some advantages to the ways in which time is reconfigured in an online environment. Clearly the shift in time provides access to courses for students who might not be able to take them because of job or family responsibilities, or simply because they are trying to take multiple classes in the same term. These students often have much to add to a discussion, and other students can learn from them. Not only do online students have freedom from time, but, in many ways, our time as faculty members is also freed up. While we may think teaching online could consume more of our time, we are in direct control of that time. We have more autonomy, more flexibility.[36] We can set our schedules and work during the hours we choose, even if they are irregular. In theory, we should be able to take advantage of this freedom to pursue other activities that are important to us. In practice, it takes great effort to manage our time when teaching online so we can pursue such alternatives.

EFFICIENCY AND TIME

Even among those who believe the time they spend with courses decreases when teaching online, many of them still think that the initial course design and the first few occasions when teaching that course require a significant outlay of time. They also believe a level of efficiency may eventually be reached. That is, after the initial outlay in designing and developing a course, faculty may be able to perform to the best of their ability with the least amount of wasted effort and energy. We may be able to design the best course content, the best visual space, the best assessments, and so forth, with (in theory) the result being more time for us to use in other areas. Alex Tabarrok offers his perspectives on this issue.

Strategies for Managing Time

Online teaching redefines a faculty member's work life, and managing one's time as an online teacher can be a challenge. For this reason, time management is essential. There are several important ways in which we can seek to apportion the time we spend when teaching online.

STRATEGY #1: PRIORITIZE WORK

Developing a to-do list can help with prioritization. When following a good to-do list, we can resist the urge to check email first. We can tackle the most important things early, which helps ensure that we get them done. Setting aside a specific period in which to work on the online course each day can help reduce the feeling of fragmented time. It can also diminish the sense of cognitive overhead. Being able to process information quickly, synthesize it, and turn it into actions is an important skill. When reading emails, if one of them can be answered with a simple yes or no, if something can be put on a meeting calendar, if the information can be scanned quickly, those things should be attended to once and only once. If something requires more than a quick decision, that can be put on a to-do list.

New Medium, New Message
Teaching Online and Time

ALEX TABARROK
Associate Professor
Economics
George Mason University and Marginal
    Revolution University (MRUniversity.com),
    US

Many of the early online forays into education were simply taped lectures: boring, flat, and worse than the same lecture delivered in person. To take full advantage of the online format, an online lecture should not replicate an in-class lecture. Different mediums demand different forms of messaging. Tyler Cowen and I have created a new online education platform, MRUniversity.com, short for Marginal Revolution University, after the name of our blog. In putting together our first course, Development Economics, we were surprised to discover that we could teach a full course online in less than half the lecture time of an offline course. A large part of the difference is that online lectures need not be repetitive.

Dale Carnegie's advice to "tell the audience what you're going to say, say it, then tell them what you've said" makes sense for a live audience. If 20% of your students are not following the lecture, it is natural to repeat some of the material to keep the whole audience involved, so everyone can follow your flow. But if you repeat something whenever 20% of the audience does not understand it, then 80% of the audience hears something twice that they only needed to hear once. Highly inefficient.

Carnegie's advice is dead wrong for an online audience. In an online lecture, it pays to be concise. Online, the student is in control and can choose when and what to repeat. The result is a big savings in time, as students proceed as fast as their capabilities can take them, repeating only what is necessary to further their individual understanding.

(continued)

Online education can also break the artificial length of fifty- to ninety-minute lectures. Many teaching experts say that an adult's attention span is ten to fifteen minutes in a lecture, with many suggesting that this attention span has declined in the Internet era. A good professor can refocus the attention of motivated students over longer periods. Nevertheless, it is clear that the standard lecture length has been determined not by optimal learning time but by the high fixed costs of traveling to school. Lower those fixed costs and the lectures will evolve to a more natural level, probably between five and twenty minutes in length. Perhaps not coincidentally, the natural length of a lecture probably is not that different from the length of a typical popular music track or television segment.

Online lectures also demand more from teachers. In producing videos for my Development Economics course, I estimate that every two to three minutes of video requires upward of an hour of work. It takes a lot of time to be concise! The potential audience for an online video is also much larger than that in any classroom, so it pays to be more precise. Students will find mistakes in a video that they can review at will, compared with a lecture that whizzes by at a pace not under their control.

Education in the online era will change much more rapidly than in previous millennia, because education has now become tied to rapid advances in the field of information technology. Moreover, the economies of scale in online education—teaching thousands or even millions of students in one course—will invite much larger investments than have been made in the past. Online education will also increase the amount of knowledge about education, because the online world is inherently data-rich. Every video watched, every link clicked, every question answered or not answered—all can easily be collected and analyzed. Randomized controlled trials, which are very expensive in the offline world, become very cheap in the online world. Online education will allow us to find out what works in education much more quickly than in the past.

When pressed for time, we can strive to be more linear about our work, progressing through the to-do list to get one task accomplished before taking up another. This allows us to see some progress and helps us avoid getting bogged down in too many details.

STRATEGY #2:. BUILD TIME MANAGEMENT INTO THE COURSE

Writing/authoring specifically for the web is an important way to manage time.[37] Doing so can save periods that might otherwise be spent later on responding to students' questions about confusing text. In writing for the web, part of being clear generally means using less text than when writing for print formats. A hierarchy of ideas is also critical, as is using descriptive headers and subheaders to highlight those ideas. Using lists, captions, and hyperlinks also helps maintain the students' focus.

STRATEGY #3: MANAGE COMMUNICATIONS WITH STUDENTS

Setting minimum or maximum participation requirements for discussion postings also can help manage student expectations by defining the amount of communication to which we will respond. Targeting communication to the group saves time spent on responding to individual emails. To target the group rather than an individual, a list of frequently asked questions posted on the course site can be effective. A related technique, adding a "what's new" section, let students know what they should check first.[38] Developing standardized responses to common student postings or questions can help regularize communications and save time that otherwise would be spent recrafting similar messages on multiple occasions.[39] Making the time period for communications clear to students is essential; telling students the portions of the day in which we typically will respond to questions helps manage their expectations. Similarly, setting regular virtual office hours can help with student expectations.[40]

STRATEGY #4: INVOLVE STUDENTS IN COURSE MANAGEMENT

Deborah Raines recommends creating an "ask the class" discussion area in each module/unit, in which students ask general questions and respond to each other.[41] It may be important to be explicit about the kinds of questions students can ask and answer and the kinds that are not permissible (e.g., stating that it is not acceptable to ask for answers to quizzes or tests, paralleling what happens with on-site exams).

Time Management for Online Instructors

MARILYN J. STAFFO
Director, Faculty Resource Center
Center for Instructional Technology
University of Alabama, US

(Photo credit: Teresa Golson)

When transitioning from onsite to online teaching, one of the changes you encounter will be how much time you will spend time preparing your course before it is taught. Both onsite and online courses are guided by the objectives and the list of topics and assessments found in the course syllabus, but in onsite teaching we can continually tweak the presentations and class activities up until the time we enter the classroom. Whether you are working with an instructional designer or developing an online course yourself, you will prepare most of the content delivery, activities, and assessments before the first student begins taking your class. Prior to your first course session, you will also spend time learning about the technologies available for use when teaching online.

Time is also a consideration when setting due dates for online activities and assessments. Although you do not have a regularly scheduled class meeting, as you would for an onsite class, it is still good practice to provide a consistent day of the week when assigning deadlines for the submission or completion of online activities. Tuesdays work well for online due dates, since they allow a margin for students who need to complete their work on weekends, while also accommodating those who are tied up on weekends and need to finish their online assignments on a weekday.

Having a consistent day of the week for due dates also helps you organize your online grading time. Unless the majority of your students work weekdays during normal business hours, it is better to have deadlines during those hours, when the most knowledgeable support personnel for online technologies are available. That way, if students encounter a technological problem as the deadline approaches, they are more likely to receive timely and helpful assistance.

The final time-management concern is setting reasonable expectations for your students regarding online communications and feedback. Letting your online students know that you will reply to messages within twenty-four or forty-eight hours, but that they should not expect replies to be within minutes of each message they send, is reasonable. Even though the technology is in place 24/7, it does not mean that you must be available to your online students 24/7.

STRATEGY #5: USE TECHNOLOGIES THAT CAN HELP WITH TIME WHEN TEACHING ONLINE

Tools like OER Commons, Connexions, Curriki, iTunes U, Academic Earth, and MIT's OpenCourseWare provide us with more free educational resources than we have ever had before. Moreover, there are many tools that can help us organize content and resources, such as bookmarking services and RSS feeds. These services permit us to compile information in one easily searchable and sharable place.[42]

STRATEGY #6: KEEP A WORK-LOG OF TIME SPENT

In some ways, maintaining a time-log adds to the workload for teaching online, but in others, it can help make us more aware of where our time is spent, which can then allow us to make changes in our actions. Moreover, for faculty interested in doing teacher research about online learning, this strategy can also help create useful data.

STRATEGY #7: USE TIME-MANAGEMENT STRATEGIES

There are several time-management strategies that online instructors can follow to improve their experiences with instructional time. Marilyn Staffo offers some useful suggestions.

Conclusion

Given the extant data, the answer to the question of whether teaching online takes more time than teaching onsite is a resounding maybe. While evidence is mounting that teaching online does take more time than teaching onsite, borne out in time-logs and qualitative studies, further research is needed to provide a definitive answer. Such findings should be considered in light of their potential for increased efficiency over time; thus longitudinal studies could improve our understanding of this important issue. At the very least, faculty perceive that teaching online takes more time, probably due to the shift in the ways in which faculty members experience time when teaching with online technology. A key challenge in such findings is that the difference in the amount of time faculty members devote to online courses, whether in total time spent or simply in a shifted rhythm, can detract from their other activities. For these reasons, faculty who teach online need to be particularly aware of time issues and carefully manage the challenges inherent in them.

Chapter Eight

Teacher Persona

Any teacher that can be replaced by a machine should be!
—ARTHUR C. CLARKE

At the beginning of each semester, whether we do it intentionally or unintentionally, those of us who teach necessarily put on our teaching faces, or our teacher personas, to prepare to meet the various groups of students we will be seeing during the semester.[1] How we go about this is a complicated issue, and some scholars have grappled with the idea of how we present ourselves as teachers.[2] James Lang, an English professor and *Chronicle of Higher Education* reporter, suggests that we intentionally create our teacher images: we choose a personality and a style to project.[3] We make decisions about the level of formality we will use, how we will dress, and so forth that signal our personalities in many ways. When we enter a physical classroom, we establish a presence, our professorial persona, based initially, at least, on our physical beings. We may choose to fine tune it or shift it, but it is built in; we wear it on our backs. We establish who we are by virtue of our age, height, weight, posture, and so forth. We also convey our personas by the choices we make, even prior to entering the classroom, through our decisions on what to wear, the number and size of the bags and carrying cases we have, and so forth. Whether we wish it or not, we are recognized as the center of the classroom, the teacher, the one who determines what to study, who keeps things moving and flowing in class sessions, and, perhaps most importantly to students, assigns grades. Our choices send a message to students about who we are as teachers and how they are to engage with us. We create these faces over time, and they may vary from course to course or semester to semester. Thus our teaching faces, our masks, are our personas. They are important because, as Lang argues, they have the potential to influence the student experience as well as student learning.[4]

About Persona

A persona is an aspect of identity that individuals apply in different situations. The term itself comes from a Greek word meaning "mask." A persona, then, is something we put on, a mask between us and society. It represents a compromise between the role that a given individual is willing to play and the role that society expects. We signal persona in a number of ways, from how we dress, to how we carry ourselves, to the ways in which we look at others. A persona not only can impose expectations, but also impose responsibilities for others, making them respond to it in a certain way. A persona intimates how an individual expects to be approached by others, which, in turn, suggests how they should approach that individual. We choose different masks in different situations—as parents, employees, teachers, friends, and so forth—so we always have multiple personas. Thus we construct and assume our personas as we interact with others. If these personas fit us well, they make our interactions with others feel smooth and natural.

Changes to Faculty Experience of Persona When Teaching Online

When we teach online, establishing a persona requires additional thought and effort. Since we no longer have physical markers, such as our appearance, dress, and nonverbal gestures, we have to find new ways of creating and communicating a persona. Therefore we construct the online, virtual person the students will know and respond to. We have to decide whether to display a picture of ourselves or use an avatar, and, in the latter case, which one. We necessarily choose which and how much information about ourselves we will make available. Thus the choices that we make seem in some ways even more intentional, and perhaps more pressing, than when we teach onsite. At the same time they may be more freeing, since they are not tempered by our physical presences. We may have to document and prove our existences, sometimes over and over again, but this, too, is a luxury, since teaching online provides us not only with the challenge but also the opportunity of creating our personas. There are both philosophical and practical choices we make when developing an online teaching persona, and these differ from the ones we create when we teach onsite.

AUTHENTICITY OF PERSONA

One of the key questions for us when we teach online, which we do not face when we teach onsite, is whether we should try to recreate in virtual space who we are in the real world. Should we try to make our online personas look, sound, feel, and act as much like our onsite teacher personas as we can? In other words, should we or can we construct a virtual doppelganger?[5] Or should we instead allow ourselves to present a more theatrical version of the flesh-and-blood professor that we intentionally project to onsite students? Should we try to look, sound, feel, and act differently, in a way that seems appropriate to an online environment? We might alter our physical appearance by using avatars, or shift our personalities by intentionally suppressing any regular use of sarcasm as a form of humor (which can be difficult to follow online anyway). Or we might make subtle changes, such as being either more or less reserved in the way we communicate in writing. Is the online environment fundamentally different, thus requiring an altered, virtual presentation of ourselves? The phenomenological question at issue here is what are our *real* personas? Are they the selves that we show to students when teaching onsite? Or is what we present our digital mask? And does that digital mask hide what we think and feel, or does it allow us more freedom to express those aspects of ourselves than we might otherwise? Is the virtual person we construct more real or less real than the actual person?[6] Thus we make decisions about whether to attempt to recreate our onsite selves in an online environment, or whether to appear as someone different, someone new, a decision that few of us have grappled with previously. Maggi Savin-Baden, an expert in learning in virtual worlds, reflects on this issue.

MANAGEMENT OF PERSONA

Online courses take place in an environment that requires constructing (or deconstructing) different aspects of selfhood and displaying them in segments, which ultimately demands paying attention to and continually managing this persona. When compared with onsite teaching, in an online course it is easier to present fewer aspects of ourselves. If we meet students face-to-face, they can see what we look like and how we move, detect our personality, and so forth, all in one space. Online, we choose which parts of ourselves to convey in a given situation, highlighting some and setting others aside for later. And we can decide when, where, and how to do that. We can decide whether we want students to see us, how we want them to see us, if we want them to hear our voices, and where we want them to do any or all of that. We do not have to mention our ages, hair colors, or heights to students, which, were we in front of them, many would be able to roughly gauge on their own in a single glance. Because of the control we have over information about ourselves, we are much better able to compartmentalize it and thus manage our various personas online. Bringing together the

Reflections on Identity in Virtual Worlds

MAGGI SAVIN-BADEN
Professor
Higher Education Research
Coventry University, UK

As someone who has been exploring virtual worlds since 2007, I still find myself intrigued about issues of identity in virtual worlds. Some of this stems from my interest in presence and immersion, but it also comes from the way in which people choose to dress and position themselves as avatars. For me, identity is not fixed, or static, but is something that shifts and changes at different stages of our lives. In real life we can only reinvent ourselves to some degree, so the opportunity to play with our identities in virtual worlds perhaps offers an occasion, whether as students or teachers, for those identities to reflect the shifting positions and perspectives in our lives at different times.

The bodily markers used to present ourselves in life—clothes, ethnicity, gender, and speech—may be re-presented (differently) in virtual worlds, but they also indicate choices about how we wish to be seen or the ways in which we might like to feel differently. This sense of an interruption of our real-world identities seems to me to bring with it a sense of both *ludos* (playing with a sense that there are some kinds of rules) and *paidea* (the sense of playing for pleasure). In a virtual world, there is a constant shift between the two. This dynamic of alternating between *ludos* and *paidea* when both teaching and learning can be troublesome for faculty, many of whom would prefer to control and manage the virtual world in ways that can become barriers to interesting and effective teaching.

This, in turn, brings to the fore not only questions about underlying pedagogies (and pedagogical possibilities), but also the assumptions that are made about issues of power and control in virtual worlds, a setting where avatars are representative of "someone else" as opposed to a representation of one's own identities. Yet this shifting of identities in learning spaces also seems to suggest that we can be changelings. Possibly the most well-known example is the changeling boy over whom Oberon and Titania fight in Shakespeare's *A Midsummer Night's Dream*, who exists at the borderlands of human- and fairykind. The play itself explores issues at the margins of where power and rules change and often break down. Perhaps identities in virtual worlds, like the changeling boy in the play, are seen as insubstantial components of learning in higher education. At the same time, they are sources of conflict and locations of indeterminacy for those who teach in these borderlands of virtual spaces, which remains an area addressed by few.

---

various components of our online and onsite identity, which John Suler, a psychologist, calls the integration principle,[7] is important. Managing multiple selves, however, can be a challenge. We have to ensure that we eventually present enough of ourselves to make it clear that we are really there. We have to remember what we have revealed, as well as when and where, to avoid too much duplication of information. We have to strive to avoid self-contradiction. Being successful requires us to efficiently juggle our presentation of these selves, but it simultaneously allows us to explore and develop aspects of our personas that we may not express onsite.

RELATIONSHIP TO ROLES

Our personas are evident in the teacher roles we adopt. We express our personas in our stances toward our degree of centrality in the teaching process, which may change when we teach online. Social research suggests that when we teach online, our views of our own centrality to the teaching process may well shift.[8] Many faculty who have participated in interviews about their experiences with online teaching roles have suggested that when teaching online, they can no longer be the "sage on the stage," but instead become facilitators of the learning experience.[9] Faculty also often articulate changes in their teaching stance, some citing a shift to a model, or mentor, of good thinking and others citing a shift toward a coaching role, asking and answering questions and guiding students' understanding. Our personas are reflected in the roles we adopt, and students read these roles for clues about us and who we really are.

A study by Peter Goodyear and his colleagues, in which many experts in online learning came together to consider the various responsibilities of an online instructor, provides a good description of the different tasks online instructors take up: designers, content facilitators, process facilitators, advisors/counselors, assessors, technologists, managers/administrators, and researchers.[10] These also provide a good illustration of how personas might be perceived. A designer who creates a welcome page may come across as friendly; one who focuses more on course rules may be seen as authoritative. The content facilitator who provides regular and in-depth feedback may be viewed as available and helpful; one who points to resources may be seen as a delegator. An advisor/counselor who is overly helpful may be perceived as touchy-feely; one who never offers encouragement may seem distant. The assessor who uses traditional tests may be viewed as challenging; one who bases an assessment on personal journals or digital storytelling may be thought of as more concerned with the individual than with the content. What is important is for faculty to think about their personas—who they are presenting themselves as in the classroom—and ensure that their chosen persona matches the way in which they carry out their roles, in order to provide the most authentic and consistent persona possible.

CONNECTION TO MEDIA

When we teach onsite, the media we select assist us in communicating our messages. If we use presentation software to support our lectures, it says something about who we are as faculty, as does the slide design we choose, the font we use, the images we include, and so forth. If we use PowerPoint, it may signal to students that we value text and linear thinking. If we choose a Comic Sans font instead of Times New Roman, it may indicate that we value humor and play. If we choose to use nothing but images instead of text, it may show that we value the visual, the pictorial. If we choose Prezi or another nonstandard software, it may say that we like to try new things or prefer to think outside of PowerPoint's literal box. If we choose not to use presentation software, that, too, communicates something about our personas, perhaps that we value direct communication among humans, a method not mediated by technology. On the other hand, depending on how we have presented ourselves in other ways, it could signal that we are luddites and do not try to keep up with technological advances. The media we choose, or do not choose, gives students a signal about who we are.

When we teach online, the media we choose do not simply support communication; they are part and parcel of communication. Thus what we select may well send an even greater signal about who we are. If we choose primarily text communications, we may be suggesting that the semantics of language—and perhaps linear, composed, rational, analytic discourse—are important to us. If we use graphics, we may imply that we value the symbolic, imagistic, holistic reasoning that is expressed via the creation of avatars and web graphics. Asynchronous communication suggests the importance of a thoughtful, reflective, measured style. Synchronous communication reflects the spontaneous, free-form, witty, temporally present self. Thus Marshall McLuhan's suggestion that "the medium is the message" has some weight.[11] It sends a clear signal about what a teacher values, which in turn indicates who we are, or at least who we want to be. Therefore we need to be conscious of the role our media play in asserting our personas. We should try to ensure that they do not drive how we present ourselves, but instead use them to present ourselves as we wish to be. Instructional-technology expert Bonnie Stewart offers her reflections on the intersection of media and persona (see p. 170).

Strategies for "Being Present"

In *The art of teaching*, Jay Parini argues that faculty members need to be conscious of and critical about their personas.[12] He asserts that we need to be deliberate in the choices we make when assuming a persona. In *Teaching literature*, Elaine Showalter recommends staying as natural as possible when developing a teaching persona and avoiding the artificial.[13] When we teach online, accomplishing such feats can be an even greater challenge than doing so onsite. How do we make deliberate choices when creating our personas? How can we be "natural" in a virtual environment? The remainder of this chapter suggests some steps that faculty can take to create a natural persona in representing themselves online.

STRATEGY #1: BE CONSCIOUS OF USERNAME CHOICE

The choice of a username may seem insignificant, but it is not. Decisions about whether to use a professional title, a first name, or an initial carry some significance for the student. A professor might consider whether to show up in the online course environment as Jane Brown; Dr. Jane Brown; Professor Brown; Jane Brown, PhD; jbrown; J. Brown; or some other variant. Alternatively, an instructor might select a username that looks good on the surface or pick one on a whim. Ultimately, this choice might reveal something about the teacher that may or may not be intentional. There could be some underlying symbolic meaning in the choice of a username that may communicate persona.[14] If the instructor chooses Professor Brown, is she signaling that she demands recognition of her

Hybrids and Subversives
The Cyborg as Teacher

BONNIE STEWART
Educator and writer
University of Prince Edward
Island, CA

I began teaching online in 1998, the same year I encountered Donna Haraway's Cyborg Manifesto for the first time.[1] Her cyborg—partial, ironic, always hybrid—offered a model for identity that helped me navigate in that new environment. The cyborg's emphasis on breaking down binaries enabled and encouraged me to approach some of the institutional and technocratic power relations that shaped our online learning context and grapple with them in ways that have continued to influence my understanding of my educational practices and research to this day.

The cyborg teacher is a hybrid, both an instrument of the schooling system and yet subversive to it: the cyborg teacher is a learner, too. Teaching from the cyborg point of view helped me frame my digital classroom not as "less" or "more" than conventional learning spaces, but instead as a site for building ties of curiosity and affinity. It helped me escape the concept of the virtual and approach my online work very much as real, as both human and technological.

Now, fifteen years down the road, I see the cyborg as a metaphor for networked identities. These are the kinds of selves cultivated when people integrate online social networks into their personal and professional practices, not just as consumers, but producers—when they blog, tweet, filter, curate, and share ideas within networks of joint interests.

At a time when our technological platforms are primarily corporate-owned and when even mundane daily practices like bankcard usage expose us to constant digital surveillance, the cyborg strikes me as a particularly important figure. A teacher, through example, collapses the binary distinctions about social technologies our media narratives are so eager to create; he or she calls into question both the utopianism and dystopianism that shape our cultural narratives about education and our futures.

The message of the cyborg, as I see it, is that we are complicit, a part of this digital world. But we are not necessarily subject to its terms. In an age in which human agency can seem dwarfed by the innumerable invisible digital systems we interact with, the cyborg—illegitimate offspring of the very things he or she subverts—stands for me as a figure of hope.[2]

Notes

1. See Haraway (1991).
2. For a video description of my experiences, see my blog at http://theory .cribchronicles.com/2013/02/27/hybrids-subversives-the-cyborg-as-teacher/.

---

status? If she uses Jane Brown, PhD, is she demanding recognition of her credentials? If she selects jbrown, does that indicate she is less central to the instructional process? The name we choose to represent us as teachers—along with other nomenclatural choices, from our online user identities, to our email signature lines, to our Twitter names—may indicate something about our personas. Attempts to work through our persona names thus requires a conscious grappling with the unconscious elements of our personality.[15] Being more aware of these issues can improve our decisions about how we present ourselves and allow us to better establish our online personas.

STRATEGY #2: MAKE INFORMATION ABOUT
YOURSELF AVAILABLE WITHIN THE COURSE

Many learning management systems offer the ability to create a profile. They provide ways to include the selected teacher name, a short biography, a description of interests, uploaded pictures, favorite links, and so forth. These features can be useful in allowing instructors to present information about ourselves to students. If an instructor is not using a course management system, it can be useful to create an electronic portfolio / personal website. Doing so can allow faculty to showcase what they believe is important as well as highlight their accomplishments.

STRATEGY #3: "MEET" THE STUDENTS, ALBEIT
VIRTUALLY, AND ALLOW THEM TO MEET YOU

Making introductions at the start of a given course can give students an idea that a real person is serving as an instructor and can help set the tone for the remainder of the term. Norm Friesen, a noted author in the area of online learning, provides some insights about these issues.

Establishing Persona Online

NORM FRIESEN
Associate Professor
Education
Boise State University, US

In my studies on the lived experiences of online education, I have come to see teacher and student as being connected in a particular kind of relationship: one with both personal and professional aspects, in which student and teacher gain some familiarity with each other's character or disposition. A teacher often has the first chance to suggest a persona online—sometimes through a short introductory video, but generally through writing. Creating a compelling persona online depends (in good measure) on one's skills and craft as a writer.[1] Letting students know that you are online while in your slippers, sitting with your iPad in your favorite easy-chair, creates quite a different impression than, say, copying and pasting your bio into an introductory message to your class.

I have also looked at the way in which a teacher's persona and disposition are closely connected to what, in phenomenological research (and in everyday language), is called "atmosphere." This is a kind of relational mood that can be shared in a classroom, at a party, or in a conversation. Teachers strive to cultivate a positive tone, or atmosphere, through their own dispositions and individual personas; in the classroom, this is about voice and tone, promptness and proximity, and myriad other details. Online, it's different. Would an online student joining a face-to-face class, entering a classroom via another's webcam and mic, be able to sense the atmosphere? The answer would probably be, "Well, maybe." One of the reasons for this ambivalent response is because this shared relational dimension becomes increasingly diffuse as it is mediated through camera and mic, or via avatar and written word. This makes it all the more important to be mindful of some of the experiences in online teaching, such as meaningful silence or hesitant uncertainty, that may very easily be lost in the data stream or somewhere between the lines.

Note

   1. See Friesen (2011).

STRATEGY #4: COMMUNICATE WITH STUDENTS
IN THE COURSE REGULARLY

Instructors have to make a conscious effort toward teacher presence, which is the visibility of the instructor as perceived by the learners. Students should sense that the instructor is "there"; they should be aware that the teacher is a real person. Instructor immediacy appears to be directly related to instructor behaviors, which are directly related to interactions, such as the amount of contact through emails, discussions, postings, or other forms of communication. Entering an online course regularly and communicating with students frequently is essential in establishing a sense of being there.

STRATEGY #5: USE SPECIFIC VERBAL STRATEGIES

When interacting with students, specific verbal strategies can help enhance an instructor's presence and immediacy. These include praising, acknowledging, and using self-disclosure.

STRATEGY #6: HOLD VIRTUAL OFFICE HOURS

Making connections with a faculty member through virtual office hours (or online or in-person chats) can help students understand that they are communicating with a real person and can make the interactions more personal. Virtual office hours can also help students feel more closely connected to faculty, which may help improve their objective course outcomes as well as their levels of satisfaction with the course.[16] As a bonus, this practice may ease time-management issues instructors may have (see chapter 7).

STRATEGY #7: USE SOCIAL MEDIA TO CREATE AN ONLINE PERSONA

New media or social tools can offer faculty an opportunity to develop an online presence beyond the confines of the course. This gives a sense of permanence to their personas and allows them to express themselves in different ways. There are several important tools that faculty can use:[17]

- *Blogging.* Creating a weekly or biweekly blog can help communicate that we are there, as well as let students see us and get a sense of what is on our minds. Weekly or biweekly blogging can add to the sense that we are out there and available. Faculty can create their own blogs through sites such as WordPress or Blogger; alternately, most course management systems have blogging-like capabilities.
- *Twitter.* We can create pseudonyms on Twitter, but most people use their own names and include a short biographical sketch. If we choose to write almost exclusively about our subject area, straying from this topic time to time (e.g., every fourth or fifth observation) can provide students with a personal glimpse of ourselves.
- *Facebook.* Most students today use Facebook, and it can be an effective way to stay in touch with them. On Facebook it is possible to create a community that is just for students. This tool can allow students to see the professional side of us in a medium with which most of them are familiar.
- *Social bookmarking.* Sites such as Delicious or Diigo provide a way for teachers to organize, store, and manage links. Sharing these links gives students information about the kinds of things that teachers believe are important.

These tools are ones with which many students are familiar and use as a regular part of their everyday lives. Employing them to support online courses can give students the sense that their instructor is a real person. Stephanie Blackmon, who has conducted research on faculty personas in virtual environments, provides a list of additional technologies for establishing a persona in an online environment.

Ten Technologies to Help Establish Teacher Persona in Online Courses

STEPHANIE BLACKMON
Assistant Professor
Adult and Higher Education
University of Oklahoma, US

Establishing a persona online can be a challenge, but, with the advent of social media, instructors have a range of tools at their service that can help them seem more "real" in the classroom. The following are among my favorites for this task.

1. *iTunesU*. The segment of iTunes known as iTunesU lets educational institutions share downloadable content, such as presentations and course lectures. Upload a presentation to iTunesU, and learners will have access to your work. They will have an opportunity to get to know you through your work, which will help you establish an online persona.[1]

2. *Instagram*. A social-networking site designed for photo sharing, Instagram lets you tell your story through pictures. Establish an online persona by creating a research-driven photo narrative about your work. For example, if your research area is botany, you can use Instagram to chronicle the interesting ecosystems you encountered on your trip to the rainforest. Followers can get a sense of your online persona and who you are as a teacher or researcher through the photos you share.[2]

3. *Pinterest*. The online bulletin board Pinterest is probably best known as the hub for home crafts and do-it-yourself projects. You can also use Pinterest, however, to establish an online persona. Share personal photos and videos to show elements of who you are outside of the classroom, or pin photos and videos related to a course or your research. For example, if you are teaching a service-learning course and want students to get an idea of what you and others experienced in the course last semester, post pictures and video footage to Pinterest. Followers can get to know you online and learn more about the course through your photos and videos.[3]

4. *Photo Story.* Photo Story is a free, downloadable, digital-story tool that allows users to create, customize, and share their digital stories. Use Photo Story to highlight a special topic or share more about yourself with your students. Upload your digital story to the "About me" section of a course blog or learning management system, and students will have un-limited opportunities to get to know you online. You could also have students upload digital stories, and everyone can get to know each other.[4]

5. *GoAnimate.* GoAnimate is an animation tool. Use GoAnimate to de-velop an animated story or presentation. Share these animated creations with your students, and they will instantly be exposed to the whimsical, humorous side of your online persona.[5]

6. *Second Life.* Second Life is a three-dimensional virtual environment. Establish an account in Second Life and create an avatar. Share who you are online by dressing your avatar in clothes that you choose, with a hairstyle and accessories you think are fitting. Then create a course or a university island where students can visit and interact with your avatar online.[6]

7. *Mediasite.* A live-stream and video-capture platform, Mediasite, among other things, allows you to stream a course live or post a recorded lecture to the learning management system of your choice. Establish your online persona by interacting with students through live streams or shar-ing recorded lectures. Students and others can get to know you through the videos and live sessions.[7]

8. *Google+.* Share photos, post videos, and create a sense of community online with the social-networking tool Google+. Use Google+ to hold con-ferences with students about papers or projects, or create a course com-munity for discussions and idea sharing. The time you spend interacting and sharing in Google+ will help you establish your online persona.[8]

9. *Edmodo.* An education-based social-networking tool, Edmodo is similar to Facebook. Create an Edmodo account for your class and post articles, start chats, or connect with other classes. Use the interactive tool to establish an online persona for yourself and a rapport with your students.[9]

10. *Gravatar.* With the avatar-creation tool Gravatar, you can design an avatar that follows you around the web. Each time you post to a blog or website, your avatar will appear beside your comment, which helps you

(continued)

establish an online persona. People will begin to recognize you based on your Gravatar.[10]

Notes

1. More information about ITunes U is available at www.apple.com/education /ipad/itunes-u/.

2. More information about Instagram is available at http://instagram.com.

3. More information about Pinterest is available at https://www.pinterest .com.

4. Photo Story is available for download at www.microsoft.com/en-us/search /DownloadResults.aspx?q=photostory.

5. More information about GoAnimate is available at http://goanimate.com.

6. The official Second Life site is at http://secondlife.com.

7. More information about Mediasite is available at www.sonicfoundry.com /mediasite/.

8. More information about Google+ is available at https://plus.google.com /+google/posts/.

9. Edmodo may be accessed through https://www.edmodo.com.

10. Information about creating a Gravatar is available at http://en.gravatar .com.

Conclusion

When we teach online, we can strive to be aware of and communicate our online personas to students, but it takes planning and considerable effort. Teachers tend to be most comfortable with online personas that match closely with their philosophical beliefs about teaching and learning, and they tend to stick with those with which students are familiar and appreciate. Thus identifying and conveying a persona requires grappling with our teaching goals as well as with who we believe we are as teachers. Once we have engaged with those issues, then we may feel more comfortable in our own virtual skins. Developing and maintaining a recognizable and consistent virtual persona is still not an easy task, however. It requires ongoing effort and attention in any given course. In short, we have to continually "be there" in order to establish and communicate persona.

Chapter Nine

Communication

The single biggest problem with communication is the illusion that it has taken place.

—GEORGE BERNARD SHAW

Teaching is an act of communication, involving the intentional design of an exchange between a knower and a learner. Even in prehistory, elders taught individuals by sharing their knowledge through storytelling and songs. About 2000 BC, Egyptian masters taught scribes through apprenticeships. Students who learned from Socrates around 300 BC responded to his series of increasingly complex questions. During the college era in colonial America, faculty—who were called "tutors," signaling in many ways their roles and responsibilities toward individual learners—taught students through formal readings and recitations. Over time, we have viewed a close physical proximity between the knower and the learner, along with an immediate communication of information and ideas, as critical components of the teaching and learning process, and we have designed our interactions accordingly. The act of communication is different in online courses, and our experiences of it are also not the same.

About Communication

The term "communication" is difficult to define, and there is significant scholarly disagreement about what it is exactly.[1] At a basic level, communication is an activity that involves an exchange of thoughts, ideas, or information through a variety of means. It is a social interaction in which two participating agents share a common set of signs and a common set of rules for understanding them. It needs a sender and a receiver of information, who are reciprocally linked. It also must contain a message, whether verbal or nonverbal.[2] The communication process between the two agents requires a set of skills in order for this understanding to occur: interpersonal and intrapersonal processing, listening, observing, speaking, analyzing questions, and evaluating. It crosses multiple sites: home, school, and community. Communication, then, is the process by which we assign and convey meaning in an attempt to create shared understanding. We consider communication to be effective only if the receiver understands the information or the idea the sender intended to transmit.

The processes of communication have changed with the development of technology. Writing, printing, telecommunications, and the Internet have allowed verbal communication to take place at a distance and over time.[3] With the emergence of writing, there was an accompanying shift away from forms of knowing and conveying knowledge in which meaning could be transmitted by tone, facial expressions, and body language, and in which meaning could be understood through sense perception and emotional perception. People moved instead to a form of communication that revolved around a new system of symbols representing the thought process; rather than requiring interpersonal knowing, this system instead required semantic and grammatical ways of communicating knowledge and a rational processing of these symbols. Information shifted from something acquired and shared in the same way, in many instances nonverbally, to something that could be gained and shared through reading and writing. The printing press and the subsequent mass distribution of writing changed ways of knowing from an exchange between individuals to an exchange with a community. It brought deductive reasoning, which had long been a form of knowing that belonged solely to the elite, to the masses. With the advent of this technology, ways of obtaining knowledge shifted toward perceiving reason and authority.

The Internet not only has provided greater access to information and quicker forms of knowledge transfer, but it also accompanied changes in ways of knowing. Communication has moved even further away from perception, making emotion more difficult to apprehend, and shifted language as a way of knowing from being verbal or written to multimodal (verbal, written, and graphic). Moreover, ways of knowing have changed from communicating knowledge to the masses through a clear and recognized source of authority to putting the production of knowledge and judgments about what is and is not useful or practical into the hands of users. Knowledge often develops through synthesis and evaluation as well as through pattern formation. Thus ways of knowing, developing, and communicating knowledge have coincided with technological developments.

Changes to Faculty Experience of Communication When Teaching Online

Discourse—and thus learning—in online courses typically occurs through Internet-based technologies.[4] In such courses, communication between and among instructors and students happens differently than it does in face-to-face courses or in correspondence courses.[5] These differences are important, since they affect not only student comfort, attitudes, and perceptions of course quality, but also student learning itself.[6] In some ways, the quality of the communication in an online course becomes the quality of the course itself. The differences in communication in online courses, including both the amounts and kinds of communication, require and ensure fundamental changes to the ways in which teaching and learning happen.

PATTERNS OF COMMUNICATION

The pattern of communication changes in online environments. It shifts from something that happens among a few individuals who must be present in the same space at the same time to communication with mass audiences having online access at any time and anywhere. In this way communication ceases being either one-to-one or one-to-a-few and instead moves to being either one-to-one or one-to-many. At times one-to-many can mean *very* many, given that some massively open online courses (MOOCs) have enrolled more than a hundred thousand students in a given semester.[7] These changes have produced a difference in the amounts and kinds of communication that occurs.

When teaching online, it can feel like the number of communication acts these courses require increases substantially. It is easy to have more one-to-one communications in online courses than in traditional ones. In particular, we may find that we have many more individual emails and messages to respond to when we teach online than when we teach onsite. There is a tradeoff, of course, because we are not as often in class, directing communications to a large group, but the participation patterns may alter how we feel about the number of times we are responding. This change can increase our senses of connectivity in the communication process and simultaneously makes us feel more disjointed. It may have the advantage, however, of students feeling like they have more direct access to us.

FORM OF COMMUNICATION

The Internet is, by design, a communication tool, a way of sharing information with others regardless of distance, time, hardware, or software.[8] Early online courses were heavily text driven initially, and many current online courses are largely text based. Text is a useful form of communication and a special form of conveying meaning. Text-based communication can be a powerful form of self-expression and interpersonal exchanges; it is a sophisticated and expressive art form. An individual's personality or even mood may be reflected in the writing style or the format of the text. The frequency of line breaks, size of paragraphs, insertion of quoted text, and so forth all signal emotion and a state of mind.[9] Abbreviations, symbols, and phrasings communicate meaning. The subject lines of emails add an important layer of meaning. Parenthetical expressions (behaviors or internal thoughts described as "asides" in parentheses) can further communicate ideas. Using emoticons, capital letters, and other text features can add creative expressiveness to a text message. At times, however, the structured nature of the Internet cannot capture nuances that are typical of face-to-face communication. It is difficult to express something, such as sarcasm, in a subtle way. Humor, particularly dry or deadpan humor, is also difficult to convey in text. Two studies have outlined several useful categories and indicators for gauging social presence, based on the kinds of communication students may exhibit online:[10]

- *Emotional expression / affective responses.* Expressing emotions, using humor, revealing oneself.
- *Open communication / interactive responses.* Continuing a thread, quoting from others' messages, referring explicitly to such messages; asking questions, complimenting, expressing appreciation, expressing agreement.
- *Group cohesion / cohesive responses.* Employing vocatives, addressing or referring to the group using inclusive pronouns, phatics, salutations.

Moreover, many online courses these days are breaking away from their text-driven origins and adopting a wide range of communication tools. Teaching online gives faculty and students unique opportunities for multimodal communication; that is, individuals can use a range of tools and strategies to communicate in different situations and with various communication partners. Voice over Internet Protocol (VoIP) allows instructors and students to communicate via video in real time, whether through a web-conferencing system offered through an LMS or through technologies such as Skype or Google Hangout. Internet-based technologies offer ease of communication, speed of communication, and multimodal communication, all of which are more synonymous with an onsite class than a text-based environment. Moreover, these systems can permit an easy and immediate sharing of sound, images, and text.

REFLECTION AND COMMUNICATION

There are many aspects of online communication that have the potential to encourage deeper and more expressive responses than can occur in face-to-face courses, particularly in ones that have at least some asynchronous components, as do most online courses today. People have more time to reflect on what they say prior to sending an email or posting a comment. This additional time for reflection can increase precision and give people a better opportunity to convey what they intend to say. It also gives them time to elaborate on a statement and provide details to support their argument, which they might be disinclined to do in onsite communication, where they could feel rushed to get to the point.[11] They also have time to compose more complex communications. This time for reflection is good for introverted and extroverted students, both of whom may need time to compose their thoughts before talking. Moreover, it can help equalize the levels of participation between these two groups. People also have more time to adjust to the pace of the others with whom they are communicating, so they can time their pacing and reach a similar level. Thus the rhythm of communication becomes a part of the meaning itself.

EXPECTATIONS FOR COMMUNICATION

Expectations for communication change in online courses. In such an environment, there is a sense that another person is always present and ready to receive a message. Thus individuals can express their thoughts in the moment, rather than having to wait to see someone with whom they might communicate. This may be one reason that students seem to expect an immediate response from instructors. In some senses, the instructor is always present. Issuing an instantaneous reply to a question reinforces this sense and establishes patterns of expectation for communicating; on the other hand, not responding quickly enough makes the instructor seem absent and unavailable. For these reasons, it is important to establish what the expectations for communication are.

There are also some psychological effects that influence the expressiveness of communication. Some individuals are less inhibited online. They may feel freer to express themselves for a number of reasons, including the a sense of anonymity. The nature of communication is often more asynchronous online, so students have more time to compose their thoughts before communicating, and they may believe that they are responding as characters rather than as themselves. This freedom can have a positive effect; research studies suggest that students who are typically more reticent may be more likely to participate in an online environment.[12] If they feel too free, however, they may engage in communicative acts that are not appropriate in an online course, including too much familiarity with others or inappropriate language. Moreover, some individuals believe they have less liberty to express themselves online; they are more guarded and more suspicious of people they cannot see.

SKILLS REQUIRED FOR COMMUNICATION

In an online environment, physical markers—such as facial expressions and body language—are often absent or minimized, and individuals have to interpret different kinds of information when trying to elicit meaning.[13] When online, the essence of being is established in the absence of concrete reality, deconstructed and reconstructed in the new medium. This re-creation occur through further changes in communication. Embodiment categories shift from observable markers of race, age, and gender to a space in which such markers are not fixed or known. Social relations move from occurring through face-to-face communication to appearing in the disembodied forms enabled by technology, and these require new skills and abilities beyond either talking or listening.[14] Some important aspects of a person may be obvious face-to-face but almost invisible online. Moreover, changes in voice and tone are not as easy to read in text as they are with in-person settings. While audio and visual conferencing, podcasting, and internet-phoning can add to the sensory experiences, seeing, hearing, and combining the two is still largely restricted. Lacking onsite cues, communication only through text can be limited, ambiguous, and an easy target for misunderstandings and projection. Thus individuals need a different set of skills to communicate in an online environment.[15]

What determines an individual's influence on others in an online environment is that person's communication skills, persistence, quality of ideas, and technical know-how. Online communication typically demands a greater reliance on intellective rather than interpersonal skills.[16] It needs a different type of writing ability, and it also requires alternate ways of comprehending received messages. People have different levels of skills and capabilities for expressing themselves in text. Some individuals are naturally good at it, and others have to learn to express themselves in writing. Some people are better able to understand the meaning and mood of text than others. Some individuals simply enjoy text-based communication more than others do. Some like the intellectual and linear nature of text, and those who have fewer onsite social skills prefer online communications and interactions. Moreover, people who have stronger writing skills may prefer online communication more than those who have stronger speaking skills. Those of us who teach online may enjoy writing and find communicating in online environments to be satisfying in many ways. We may prefer longer forms of communicating and thus may be happier in composing more extensive posts and responses, such as through discussion postings or emails, than we are in writing shorter and more frequent segments, such as texts. We may find that some students, however, respond better to the shorter and more frequent bursts of communication that take place through media such as instant messaging and microblogging.

The skills that an individual needs necessarily change the nature of communication in online courses. In many ways social relations are more abstract. At the same time, the different techniques we have to employ in online classes can allow closer connections to take place during moments of physical disconnection. When we teach onsite, we know students by sight. We know their names; have a general sense of their personalities and the ways in which they like to learn; and have a sense of who their friends are, based on who they sit near in class and whom they enter and exit with. We sometimes recognize their social or political affiliations by the logos on their clothing. Such visible signals help us get to know our students. Online, however, we do not have those clues. Instead, we rely on getting to know the students at an intellectual level. We learn their writing styles and voices. We can often tell when they are in good or bad moods, based on their communications. We may teach students online who then talk to us onsite; we may not recognize their faces, but on learning their names, we may feel like we know them better than some of the students in our onsite courses. It is a different way of relating, which can be either less personal or hyperpersonal, depending on the level of communications and interactions onsite.

DURABILITY OF COMMUNICATION

Most activities in online courses are recorded, including email correspondence, chat sessions, and web conferencing. Unlike real-world interactions, there is a sense of having a permanent record of what was said, to whom, and when. Some relationships can thus be documented in their entirety.[17] These records could be useful to faculty and students alike. Teaching onsite is frequently an isolated event that happens behind closed doors. It is transient, and often there is very little evidence that it took place. When teaching online, the teaching moments and artifacts (such as emails, discussions, chats, course content, and videos) are captured. There is a record of the events, which we may revisit and reflect on. Thus these records can allow someone to reexperience and reevaluate any portion of the exchanges. They also provide a ready source of text that individuals can quote as a reminder of the original argument or use to request clarification or elaboration. Text from several communicative acts occurring over time can let a person consult multiple layers of these communication simultaneously. Moreover, documentation of text in this way can help reduce errors of recall.

It is tempting to think that these recordings are objective, but, depending on how we feel when we read them, their meaning can change; thus in many ways they are subjective, providing only a snapshot of a moment in time. Documentation of this type can cause individuals to be more reflective, thoughtful, and careful as they compose responses.[18] On the other hand, these recorded formats can have some negative aspects, since they can create anxiety among faculty and students by knowing that their words are being tracked and recorded. If someone is examining or quoting a piece of writing, words can be taken out of context and, when juxtaposed with other quoted text, the meaning may be distorted.[19] What we say online does not take place behind closed doors, as it does in a traditional classroom. Students may even read what we write multiple times (of course, this may be wishful thinking). Thus we might employ an additional level of care in communicating online than we would in an onsite course, where what we say typically is more spontaneous. Communication online can be simultaneously more thoughtful and reflective, and less spontaneous and free.[20]

Many of our online interactions are durable in the moment, but others are interrupted. Although this has not always been the case, nowadays we expect our technology to work. That, unfortunately, does not always happen. Sometimes the software fails, and sometimes the hardware. Sometimes connections break. Sometimes noise intrudes. Reliability, dependability, and predictability issues also have psychological effects, such as frustration. The technological disruptions may influence our relationships if they interfere with communication and with our feelings about those with whom we seek to communicate. Courses may run without a single technological glitch, which is a rare and wonderful thing. The technology, however, may fail, sometimes miserably and often. When this happens, other forms of communication between us and the students may increase exponentially, and our back-and-forths with the technological support staff may increase in kind. At times such events simply cannot be helped, but it is always useful to be prepared and have an alternate plan to keep communication flowing during technological meltdowns.

Strategies for Managing Communication When Teaching Online

While students share the responsibility of establishing and maintaining communication, the vast majority of researchers in this area suggest that the instructor has the biggest role in ensuring strong communication (or a social presence) throughout the course.[21] Communication can be established in three key areas: course design, instructor-led communication, and student-led communication.[22]

STRATEGY #1: DESIGN COURSES WITH CLEAR COMMUNICATION

At a fundamental level, online courses are a form of communication. Most courses include at least some delivery of content, which, in itself, is a communicative act. Providing an online welcome message and asking students to do the same, requesting students to create profiles, and including opportunities for audio and visual conferencing, if possible, are all ways of designing social presence. From a pedagogical perspective, including collaborative learning activities online (such as group discussions, group assignments, group projects, debates, brainstorming, etc.) can lead to learner-to-learner social interactions.[23] Course design, then, is where the communication process begins. Susan Lucas discusses various aspects of "being present" online.

Being Present

SUSAN LUCAS
Academic Chair
Higher Education and Adult Learning
Kaplan University, US

Online communication is generally thought of in terms of the technologies available, or as the medium for the message: chat, texting, email, discussion boards, and the like. Current research, however, is pointing to presence—both of the instructor and the students—as being the most important aspect of communicating online. Communication, by its nature, is a social event, so "being there" has become key in terms of online communication. The medium and the message are no longer adequate to enhance the learning process. We now need to combat the inherent isolation of online education with the concept of presence. Just as in a face-to-face classroom, the instructor and the students need to be present in order for optimal learning to take place. Yet how can we "be there" in a world where a physical presence is impossible? Technology is important here; without it, online presence would be not exist. We need to start examining additional aspects, however—such as immediacy, visibility, and social interconnectedness—in order to accomplish this sense of presence.

Electronic communications are a here-and-now form of communication. We expect chat feedback in seconds, text-message responses in minutes, and email replies in hours. Without understanding this immediacy, an online instructor or student will not be successful. An instructor who takes longer than forty-eight hours to respond to a student will create frustration and distrust. One who takes longer than twenty-four hours to respond to a student will still be suspect. Immediacy is critical in online communication.

Invisible instructors create an environment of isolation, and isolation is detrimental to communication. Establishing your visibility requires a concentrated effort to be present in the virtual classroom. Contact with an online student once a week generates a sense of absence; contact three times a week fosters complacency; contact five or more times a week creates visibility.

Online communication isn't simply about disseminating information; it is about creating a social environment, a place where learning to take place. Communication is a two-way street between student and instructor and between student and student. For this to occur, students need to feel they are part of a whole community, connected to both the instructor and their fellow students.

STRATEGY #2: ENGAGE IN INSTRUCTOR-LED COMMUNICATION

There are many ways in which instructors communicate; being aware of these and planning for them can help faculty improve communications and create a deeper sense of social presence. Content-related communication can involve presenting lectures, describing assignments, providing clarifications, engaging in discussions, and—because instructors need not reply to each learner posting on a discussion board—summarizing discussions. Process-related communications can include providing information, sending assignments, posting syllabus information, and indicating how the class will work. Technologically related communication can involve providing tips about software, stating how to navigate the class platform, and indicating how to send attachments. Behaviorally related communication can include providing information about plagiarism, codes of conduct, and netiquette.[24] Instructors also tend to post answers to questions, particularly questions sent through email and instant messaging, and provide frequent feedback. André R. Denham describes the importance of instructor communications.

Instructor Communication and Feedback

ANDRÉ R. DENHAM
Assistant Professor
Department of Educational Leadership,
    Policy, and Technology Studies
University of Alabama, US

There are many techniques and approaches first-time online instructors can apply to create a satisfactory learning experience for their students. One of the most powerful tools is feedback.

Feedback is an important element within any learning environment. This is especially true in web-assisted courses, where face-to-face direct instruction does not take place. In my experience, detailed, timely, consistent feedback has been a reliable means of having a significant influence on student satisfaction and learning outcomes. First, feedback should go beyond a letter grade or saying "Good job." It provide details relevant to the students with regard to their academic progress and their areas of strength and weakness. It is also a means by which they can improve the quality of their work. Second, feedback should be given to students in a timely manner, so learners can make adjustments while it is still worthwhile for them to act on this information. By delaying feedback, you, as an instructor, are increasing the chances of this feedback not being applied by the students. In other words, delayed feedback can miss an opportunity for a teachable moment. Finally, feedback should be consistent. In this way, the learners become conditioned to receiving feedback relative to their academic progress and will be more likely to develop metacognitive strategies.

Due to the lack of direct, face-to-face contact in web-assisted online learning environments, providing detailed, timely, and consistent feedback should be a priority for instructors. A concerted effort to do so should result in improvements in student motivation, students' performances on learning outcomes, and overall student satisfaction.

STRATEGY #3: BE CLEAR ON EXPECTATIONS FOR COMMUNICATION

Tisha Bender, the author of a book on discussion-based online teaching,[25] offers practical suggestions for communicating in an online course.

(Photo credit: Jeremy Bender)

Suggestions for Effective Online Communication

TISHA BENDER
Online teacher trainer and writer
Rutgers University, US

I believe that optimal learning is accomplished through dialogue (from the root words *dia*, meaning "between," and *logos*, meaning "word"), since it is in the flow of words between teacher and student, and between the

(continued)

students themselves, that meaning is constructed and knowledge discovered. And when the class is held online, dialogue promoted by the Socratic method is of even greater importance. In the absence of student responses, how can the teacher know the students are there, or that the information is meaningful?

Before the course begins, instructors should state their expectations for how often the students should participate in online dialogue. Teachers should also be explicit regarding how often they themselves will be responding. Moreover, it is essential to convey not only the frequency of online responses but also their quality. Students should be warned against simplistic responses, such as "I agree with Susan," and encouraged to express themselves with enthusiasm, respect, and acceptance of any differences of opinion. It is often beneficial to involve students in drawing up a code of civility for the class, because if they are the ones democratically creating this code, they are more likely to conform to it.

Communicating online can potentially break down some constraints that occur in a traditional class. There can be freedom from temporal, spatial, and even cultural constraints, since the asynchronous online environment means no one interrupts anyone else: it eradicates the spatial advantage of front-row seats and even provides opportunities for students from different cultures to find their "voices" online. The online teacher should respond to all students by weaving together their responses and mentioning each person by name, so no student feels ignored.

That said, problematic situations can arise in online communication, especially if some students don't post any responses. I propose that students can be encouraged to participate if the teacher asks thought-provoking or evaluative questions. Clearly, asking a factual question like "When was the Battle of Waterloo?" is something to avoid, since as soon as the first student provides the correct answer there is nothing else to discuss. The teacher should also try to encourage students to write in a snappy, conversational style, which will attract responses from others, rather than writing in a long, essay-like fashion, which their fellow students might skim over or skip. Furthermore, the online discussion should continue to deepen and evolve as the teacher synthesizes responses and probes more intricately by asking follow-up questions. The teacher could also select students to lead the discussion, or play devil's advocate to intellectually stretch the students and make them see a topic from different perspectives.

If participation in the online discussions remains low, another strategy could be to incorporate Twitter, Blackboard, blogs, or Skype, since these new forms of digital media are likely to be more familiar to students than the discussion forums in an online class. If these tools are used, it is important for the students to still communicate in an informed, conversational style; the fact that this communication is within an academic setting takes precedence over the fact that these new digital media are being employed.

Very rarely, a discussion might become heated. The best approach to this is not for the teacher to delete the responses, but instead to allow cooling-off time by asking students not to respond for a day. Everyone can then have a period in which assess the points discussed, thereby coming up with a new interpretation. In this way a potentially difficult situation can be turned into a teachable moment.

Another problematic situation is if a student is late in joining a discussion. It is generally not only the teacher but also the students themselves who do not like latecomers to the dialogue, as it pulls conversation backward rather than letting everyone move forward to greater levels of understanding and sophistication. Latecomer students should be encouraged to join in with the most recent discussion and thereafter keep current, but they should be informed that it is too late to contribute to previous online discussions, and, of course, be reminded that there are penalties for not participating at the start.

If all goes well and the online discussion is vibrant, with full participation, it is important for the teacher not to feel overwhelmed by too many new responses. The best strategies would be for this teacher to establish priorities, not necessarily respond to every student at once, delegate responsibilities, or vary the learning activities, all of which can be beneficial to students.[1]

Note

1. Bender (2012) provides additional suggestions about communication in online teaching.

Conclusion

The Internet is a social medium that can bring people together, but, in so doing, it can simultaneously separate them.[26] Given that education is a social practice, when teaching online, professors have a responsibility to establish and maintain effective communications.[27] Communication is what makes or breaks an online course. Ensuring regular and high-quality communication, however, is a challenging aspect of being an online instructor. Making sure that communication actually happens requires careful planning and structuring, as well as maintaining a high level of effort throughout the course. Because of its importance to the educational process, faculty will need to find new ways to connect with students and help them connect to each other. The first step for any instructor is modeling how communication should happen.

Chapter Ten

Student Rights

To deny people their human rights is to challenge their very humanity.
—NELSON MANDELA

Students come to higher education with different abilities, skill sets, background experiences, learning goals, needs, and life circumstances that dictate their actions at a given moment. In our roles as instructors in institutions of higher education, it can be challenging to know where to begin working with such a diverse group of students. These learners have certain things in common, however, and one of them is that each individual has a guaranteed set of rights, not only as a citizen but also as a student. We can start by respecting and honoring the rights of all students as individuals. When we teach online, with our teaching accomplished through technology, we face new and different challenges in helping ensure that students retain their rights.

About Student Rights

Students who participate in higher education have a set of rights given to them as average citizens: civil, constitutional, contractual, and consumer rights. These include such rights as free speech, due process, equality, autonomy, safety, privacy, and accountability in contracts or advertising. They also have rights that are guaranteed to them specifically as students, so they can make use of their education. The effect is that these rights regulate the treatment of students by institutions as well as by instructors. While some countries have a bill of rights that lays out the primary laws that affect students, the United States does not. Instead, court precedents typically govern the way in which institutions of higher education respect student rights. Faculty, however, are not necessarily well versed in legal precedents.[1] Thus some ambiguity exists as to what instructors, at least those of us teaching in the United States, need to do to meet our shared responsibility of ensuring student rights.

Changes Related to How We Ensure Student Rights When Teaching Online

Ensuring that student rights are upheld becomes even more complicated when teaching online, as this form of instruction is so new that all of the issues have not yet been fully tested in a court of law. Precedents for ensuring student rights in online courses have not always been established. Moreover, when courts have made decisions on legal issues related to student rights in online courses, the results have not always been widely published. As a result, instructors do not always have the information they need to guide their actions with regard to the treatment of students.

The lack of clarity about student rights in online courses has caused some educators to consider the issues and propose potential guidelines. One such group convened in 2012 for the purpose of crafting a Bill of Rights and Principles for Learning in the Digital Age.[2] This group has come under some criticism for its processes, which have been called exclusive and top down. The ideas expressed in the document also been have subject to criticism: some educators have suggested that the rights and principles are ambiguous, and others have noted that some of the drafters do not adhere to their own suggestions.[3] Yet several of the rights they identified not only have a direct influence on the faculty experience of planning for and supporting student rights in online courses, but also have been decided on by courts. These are the right to access, privacy, and ownership of intellectual property.

ACCESS

Educational access is the provision of services and accommodations to ensure educational opportunities for all students, including individuals with special needs; the latter form a substantial proportion of the overall number of higher education students. According to a 2011 report on disability from the World Health Organization, 11% of postsecondary students report having a disability that could potentially interfere with their educational access.[4] These areas may include cognitive or learning disabilities, auditory disabilities, visual disabilities, motor disabilities, or invisible disabilities (such as mental-health ones).[5] Both state and federal laws protect this right to educational access:

- *The Reauthorized Rehabilitation Act of 1998.*[6] This act authorizes programs such as vocational rehabilitation, supported employment, independent living, and client assistance. It includes provisions focused on protections for individuals with disabilities, such as those indicated in sections 504 and 508.[7]

- ○ *Section 504* is an antidiscrimination measure focused on prohibiting discrimination in the admission or treatment of students (and in most employment practices) based on disability. Specifically, institutions that receive federal funding must accommodate individuals with special needs by providing equal access to learning facilities and materials.
- ○ *Section 508* mandates that institutions must provide resources that are accessible to everyone. Section 508 applies to most public college and universities, since they receive federal funding through Pell Grants or the Assistive Technology Act. It states that electronic and information technology purchased by institutions must be able to be accessed and used by individuals with disabilities. This section enumerates US federal accessibility standards for the Internet. It also provides enforceable standards that must be met when designing Internet-based materials.
- • *Americans with Disabilities Act (ADA).*[8] This act prohibits discrimination against individuals with disabilities. Both public and private schools are covered by this act.
  - ○ *Title II* prohibits discrimination based on disability by all local and state agencies, including schools.
  - ○ *Title III* specifies that no individuals may be discriminated against on the basis of disability and that they must be able to enjoy all goods, services, facilities, or accommodations in any place of public accommodation.

Educational access is thus guaranteed to all individuals, including those with disabilities.

When we teach onsite, we have at least a certain history of working with students with disabilities to ensure that they have educational access as well as accessible materials. Over time, we have developed a degree of knowledge about how to ensure students' rights to educational access, and we have some supports in place to do so. We typically have buildings with ramps, elevators, and other accommodations, such as accessible testing facilities. We often have an institutional Office of Disability Services that can provide classroom support for individuals, such as translations of lectures, note-takers, or other assistance. While we can do better and continue to improve, we have at least some practice at accommodation and at least certain procedures in place to ensure it.

Online learning has been hailed for its potential to increase student access to higher education. Unfortunately, the issue of access to online learning is also one of its biggest challenges. Students with disabilities may have difficulty using the tools they need to be able to work in an online environment. They may find chat rooms and videoconferencing challenging. They may have difficulty completing certain tasks that are typical of online courses, such as reading, listening, or typing. They may find a host of activities that make this new instructional form of higher education, one that is intended to provide increased access, less than accessible.[9] Yet individuals have rights to online as well as onsite instruction. As the group of individuals who drafted the Bill of Rights and Principles for Learning in the Digital Age put it:[10]

> Everyone should have the right to learn: traditional students, non-traditional students, adults, children, and teachers, independent of age, gender, race, social status, sexual orientation, economic status, national origin, bodily ability, and environment anywhere and everywhere in the world. To ensure the right to access, learning should be affordable and available, offered in myriad formats, to students located in a specific place and students working remotely, adapting itself to people's different lifestyles, mobility needs, and schedules.

Since the right to educational access extends to online learning, instructors often find themselves in the role of developing environments, instructional activities, and instructional materials that are accessible, often with little guidance and even less experience. When we create or choose learning environments, we have new decisions to make about which ones can best support students with different levels of ability, while in an onsite environment many such decisions have been made for us. We also have new questions and considerations, such as whether the learning management system we employ is accessible and thus compliant; the same applies when we choose to use social media. As we strive to select instructional activities that allow students maximum opportunities to participate, we at times grapple with new decisions about whether we should use video or text and, depending on the answer, how to make the format most useful to the students who might take the course. We need to consider materials in formats that can best be understood by people with disabilities (perhaps those with auditory difficulties, or those with visual ones) and choose modes of distribution that allow individuals to access and use these materials. Teaching online, then, changes the way faculty prepare and deliver accessible instruction to the students who wish to take advantage of it. In so doing, it changes our experiences as instructors, not only of what we need to know, but also of what we do with that knowledge.

PRIVACY

Privacy is one of the most frequently recognized student rights in higher education. As educators, we acknowledge that institutions should keep the personally identifiable information students give them private. We believe that students should feel safe and be confident that institutions will not wrongly disclose such information. We also believe that students should know about the data that institutions collect from them, as well as how such information will be used. Many sources of student information are protected, whether by laws, regulations, or institutional policies. Such sources may include social security numbers, ID numbers, password phrases, and security or access codes.

The Family Educational Rights and Privacy Act (FERPA) is the primary law that governs higher education students' privacy. The law applies to any school that receives funding from the US Department of Education. In general, FERPA protects the privacy of student records. In particular, it gives students (and the parents of minors) the right to access their educational records, to request that these records be amended if necessary, and to determine who has access to these records. The question of what counts as an "educational record" does not always have a clear answer; thus it may be defined broadly. Educational records, however, only include those records maintained by an institution that are related to students, past or present, and are personally identifiable. Educational records may include registration records, transcripts, papers, exams, email messages, and the like, and instructors may not disclose such information to others without a student's permission.

Students in online courses also have the right to privacy. As the authors of the Bill of Rights and Principles for Learning in the Digital Age, put it:[11]

> Student privacy is an inalienable right regardless of whether learning takes place in a brick-and-mortar institution or online. Students have a right to know how data collected about their participation in the online system will be used by the organization and made available to others. The provider should offer clear explanations of the privacy implications of students' choices.

When we teach onsite, it is relatively easy to maintain student privacy, since the main pieces of information we instructors must protect are those records that can reveal the names of students and their grades to others. Online classes are also covered by FERPA, so these student records must remain private, too. Because of students' right to privacy in online courses, it behooves instructors to be familiar with how we can strive to ensure it. In an online environment, as information becomes digital—and thus more tangible and portable—deciding what is and what is not acceptable can be a bit more challenging, however. When using an LMS, even if the issue of privacy is not crystal clear, there are a few extant examples that provide some guidance:[12]

- What information is revealed online.
  - *Acceptable.* Students enrolled in the same online course may see each other's names and email addresses as a part of a class roster in a learning management system (LMS).
  - *Unacceptable.* Instructors may not scan and upload official rosters that contain personal information, such as student ID numbers.
- How guest speakers may participate.
  - *Acceptable.* Instructors may bring in outside guest speakers to talk to the class through VoIP offered through an LMS.
  - *Unacceptable.* Instructors may not send guest speakers an advance copy of the class roster (without the permission of all the students in the course).
- How grades may be posted.
  - *Acceptable.* Each student may access and view his or her grades through a course site or LMS.
  - *Unacceptable.* An instructor may not post a list of grades, even using codes or other seemingly neutral identifiers (such as the last four digits of a student's social security number).

The issue of a student's right to privacy becomes murkier, however, when an instructor decides to use a form of social media, such as a website, a blog, Facebook, or Twitter, instead of a university-designated LMS. With these tools, what constitutes an educational record and what does not can be less obvious. Yet, for many instructors, activities that involve information sharing through social media represent an integral part of an online course. Thus we find that we need not only tools but also guidance on how to engage students in information sharing in an appropriate way.

While FERPA does not prohibit sharing information in online environments, at worst the act has been misunderstood as applying to any activity requiring the use of social-media tools, and, at best, it is not always clear what the act does or does not prohibit. We do know that FERPA does *not* prohibit instructors from having students use social-media tools for course activities. Moreover, we know that content created by students using such technological tools to fulfill course requirements (e.g., creating blogs on WordPress or posting videos to YouTube) does *not* constitute an educational record covered by FERPA.[13] These facts are reassuring, since assuming that FERPA applies to all social-media interaction could diminish the options instructors may believe they have.[14] One higher education lawyer, Justin Bathon, aptly describes the issue:[15]

> FERPA cannot be interpreted as building a total and complete wall between the school and the community. We would have really bad schools if that happened and very disengaged students. This is a good example of where the lawyers can't get in the way of the learning. Podcasting is a fabulous learning tool. Digital storytelling, amazing. I love VoiceThread, as do thousands of educators around the country. Sharing is an important part of learning and the ability to share has increased exponentially in the past couple decades. Some students right here in Kentucky are sharing with students in Brazil every day, for instance. FERPA cannot be extended to prohibit all of this sharing.

On the other hand, if an instructor keeps copies of these creations (such as YouTube videos or digital stories) in his or her own files, then these *do* constitute FERPA-protected student educational records. The line between what is and what is not acceptable is not always clear, particularly in the case of social media, and this uncertainty can influence our actions and our experiences.

OWNERSHIP

In some courses, students create content that is protectable by copyright law.[16] Many institutions have policies that suggest who owns those properties, and many of them grant the rights to the student, with some typical exceptions (e.g., if the student is also an employee at the institution or if the student is paid by the institution, in which situations the rights may transfer to the institution). The idea is that generally students should retain the rights to their own intellectual property.

The issue of student ownership of content created during onsite courses has been receiving some attention as of late, as in the case of a lawsuit brought by students concerned over submitting their papers through Turnitin (www.turnitin.com),[17] or the instance where students developed an iPhone app during a computer science course.[18] The issue of content created during online courses has received less attention, although arguably it poses more questions for faculty, due to the relatively tangible nature of student work products and the fact that they can be shared widely with the class (and even beyond). The authors of the Bill of Rights and Principles for Learning in the Digital Age argue that students should own the intellectual-property rights to any content they create when participating in online courses:[19]

> Students also have the right to create and own intellectual property and data associated with their participation in online courses. Online programs should encourage openness and sharing, while working to educate students about the various ways in which they can protect and license their data and creative work. Any changes in terms of service should be clearly communicated by the provider, and they should never erode the original terms of privacy or the intellectual property rights to which the student agreed.

One challenge to this ownership right in online courses arises when technology providers have terms of service, or terms of use, that claim rights to any of the content created and shared through the relevant technology.[20] For example, it is common for service providers to claim at least the right to copy, adapt, and share the content as needed.[21] Because of such claims, there is an extra wrinkle in ensuring that students retain ownership of their intellectual property. Instructors should be aware of these issues so they can make the best possible decisions about which tools to employ, as well as be prepared to share relevant information about intellectual-property ownership with their students.

Strategies for Ensuring Student Rights in Online Courses

Ensuring that student rights are recognized and respected in online courses involves new ways of thinking about the issues and new means of creating instructional environments, activities, and materials. I offer the following strategies for respecting and upholding student rights.

STRATEGY #1: FOLLOW STRATEGIES OF UNIVERSAL DESIGN

"Universal design" is a broad term intended to guide individuals as they create buildings, products, and environments that are inherently accessible to the greatest number of individuals. Some educators have begun applying the principles of universal design to educational environments. Creating courses while keeping universal-design principles in mind will benefit not only students with disabilities

Access for All

AMANDA E. BRUNSON
Research Assistant and ESL Instructor
Higher Education Administration Program
    and English Language Institute
University of Alabama, US

Universal design for instruction means that a course is accessible to a wide range of students, not just the average or typical student. Sally Scott, Joan McGuire, and Teresa Foley came up with nine principles that should guide universal design: equitable use, flexibility in use, simple and intuitive rules, perceptible information, tolerance for error, a minimal need for physical effort, sufficient site size and space for everyone to access it, a community of learners, and a supportive instructional climate.[1] While these were created with offline classes in mind, some of these principles also apply to online ones. Here are some examples of how instructors can use a few of these principles to make online courses accessible to a wide range of students.

Equitable use. Employing videos or audio files is great for many students, but it is important to have subtitles or a transcript available for students who are hearing impaired. Additionally, English-language learners benefit from having subtitles if their reading skills are better than their listening-comprehension skills or if the lecture includes much new vocabulary.

Flexibility in use. It is essential for online instructors to keep the cultural and religious backgrounds of their students in mind. As the world becomes more globalized, we encounter a greater degree of diversity among students in our classrooms. Online education increases the opportunity for students from all around the world to participate in a course. For that reason, those who teach online must be aware of the various cultures to which their students belong. Instructors should be ready to be flexible and accommodate students with different beliefs and values. For

(continued)

example, a woman from a culture where men and women are usually seg-regated may feel uncomfortable doing an assignment that requires her to collaborate with a male student, even in an online format. In this situa-tion, an instructor might allow the student to do another assignment on her own or only collaborate with other female students. Since this type of circumstance cannot always be anticipated by the teacher, however, the students need to take the initiative and inform the instructor early on in the term if they may require certain accommodations.

Simple and intuitive rules. It is always good practice to provide a clear list of expectations and grading rubrics so students know what is expected of them. When we teach online this is perhaps even more important be-cause we might have students who are unfamiliar with online classes or who are from a different culture and thus have assumptions that differ from our own. Provide precise, easy-to-understand goals and objectives so students know what they need to do to be successful in the course.

Tolerance for error. Students come from a variety of backgrounds and upbringings; as such, they have different levels of experience and accumu-lated knowledge. A student may have the aptitude to do well in a particu-lar class, but if the readings and assignments assume a certain back-ground knowledge that the student does not have, the class might be unnecessarily difficult for him or her. Optional introductory readings could be included as part of the course to provide additional information. Also, the course's writing prompts or other assignments could be kept broad enough so students can use their own level of expertise, personal knowledge, and experience to complete the task.

Supportive instructional climate. Making a class accessible does not mean lowering standards. Online instructors should still have high expecta-tions, but they should also keep in mind that their students potentially represent different cultures. The climate of the course should be open, inviting, and inclusive of all. By responding to students with respect and being willing to listen to their perspectives, those who teach online can create a positive instructional climate.

Note

1. See Scott, McGuire, & Foley (2001).

but also those with a number of other potentially inhibiting life circumstances. In online courses, the basic principles of universal design can help us create more accessible environments, activities, and materials. Amanda Brunson describes how such principles work in practice (see p. 201).

STRATEGY #2: IF YOU DESIGN YOUR OWN WEBSITE,
FOLLOW UNIVERSAL-DESIGN PRINCIPLES

Many faculty choose to create their own websites, whether they use them as the primary course sites or as ancillary resources. When we decide to use the DIY method, we should make every effort to ensure that these sites are accessible, and following universal-design principles can help us achieve this goal. In the spirit of

Table 10.1   Design elements for accessible websites

Issue	Suggestion
Format	Use a standard template predesigned by the technology provider (e.g., WordPress, Blogger)
Fonts	Use common or default fonts recommended for the Internet, particularly sans serif fonts. Use only one font type
Typeface	Limit the use of all caps, italics, and boldface text. Do not underline (because it can masquerade a link)
Background color	Use high contrast, with a light background and dark text, preferably black text on a white background. Avoid bright colors for background
Images	Use alternative descriptive text (alt tags) to describe the content or function of an image
Links	Use a descriptive anchor text, instead of "click here." Do not use images as links, because it can be difficult to tell if they are clickable
Audio/video	Provide time-synchronized text (close-captioning). Provide a textual version of content
Video	Include time-synchronized text (close-captioning) so students can read while watching
Graphics	Use alternative text (alt tags) so screen users can read what the image is

thinking about universal design and online course materials, in table 10.1 I offer suggestions for creating an accessible site.[22]

STRATEGY #3: EXERCISE CARE WHEN DECIDING TO USE NON-INSTRUCTIONALLY SUPPORTED TECHNOLOGY

Deciding to use social media gives faculty an opportunity for a DIY approach to online instruction. It can, however, also provide some additional challenges, as Ted Major describes. If you should decide to use social media, consider these suggestions:[23]

- Communicate your intent to use noninstitutional tools in the syllabus, so students can decide whether to remain in the course.
- Consider making the use of the tool optional for students and provide alternatives (e.g., recommend a WordPress blog, but allow students to use the blog function of the institutionally supported LMS instead).
- Consider tools that do not require students to give personal information (e.g., Facebook asks for real names, while it is a common and accepted practice to use an alias on Twitter).
- Encourage students to assume aliases and use avatars when creating accounts for noninstitutional tools.
- Avoid referring to students by their full names in social media.
- Teach students best practices for employing the tools used in the course and alert them to the issues and risks, in order to educate them about proper tool use.
- Advise students that their work may be read by others.
- Advise students to restrict their posts to the course content.
- Avoid making your comments about or grades for their work public (although peer-graded work can be made public under FERPA).
- Consider getting parental support for posting work publicly if students are under the age of eighteen (this is not clearly required by law, but it may be good practice).

STRATEGY #4: DON'T GIVE AWAY THE INTELLECTUAL PROPERTY OF OTHERS

If it is possible or desirable for students to own the intellectual-property rights to information they will create and share during the course of an online class,

Caution in Using Social Media

TED MAJOR
Instructor
Business
Shelton State University, US

Students come to institutions of higher education with a range of technological capabilities in terms of access, experiences, and perspectives. When students register for online classes, some may be depending on computers in college labs or at a branch of the local public library, while others in the same class may have the newest MacBook Pro and a fiber-optic Internet connection. Some will have very little knowledge of computer technology and how the Internet works, while others will be highly skilled in the use of both their own machines and a variety of online technologies. Likewise, they will have a range of attitudes toward such technology. Some students may avoid technology in their personal lives for various social and political reasons, from not wanting to leave a traceable footprint to not wanting to support a particular company or its policies. On the other hand, some may be regular bloggers, Tweeters, or Facebookers.

When we decide to require student to use technological tools such as social media, we not only expect them to have technological access (and competence!), but we also impose our own value systems on them. Because these expectations may or may not correspond with the realities of our students, we should approach such requirements with caution. That is, we should balance the educational benefit of the instructional activity against social-justice issues, such as access to technology; against potential obstacles to effective usage, such as technological knowledge and skills; and against student rights and preferences, such as the right to

(continued)

decide how much information to share with others. There's also the simple matter of user-account fatigue—at some point, we have so many user IDs and passwords that the thought of adding yet another one is daunting. For students who are Internet novices, the risk may be even greater. They may be more likely to recycle passwords, and asking them to create a new user account is adding one more zombie account that may lay dormant until it is compromised by poor security or a failed social-media startup. One slip by a third party, such as Target's recent security breach, could put your students' online identities at rick. When in doubt, think long and hard about requiring students to sign up for yet another user account just for your course.

When we require students to use social media in which they do not already participate, we are making them to sign up for yet another account, courting increased marketing from yet another company and risking identity theft. When we require them to use their established social-media identities for class, we risk putting them in the uncomfortable position of potentially having to interact with students whom they'd like to avoid (and maybe even with whom they've had bullying or abusive interactions) or of having to interact with faculty in an uncomfortable and awkward manner (sometimes known as the "creepy treehouse problem"). Platforms such as Facebook or Google+ that insist on the use of real names are especially problematic. Platforms such as Twitter or Tumblr that allow and even encourage pseudonyms are more amenable to letting students create throwaway accounts just for class usage. Throwaway accounts, however, then create operational security problems for students and risk information leakage between their personal identities/accounts and the class-specific accounts. Corporate public-relations departments regularly fall victim to embarrassment when their social-media staff accidentally post a personal update to the corporate account; students who use pseudonymous accounts are no less vulnerable to accidental cross-posting. When making a decision to use a given tool, we should be sensitive to the issues of identity and forced interaction that we may inadvertently and unknowingly create for students.

instructors should follow the suggestions below, particularly when using technology that is not supported institutionally:[24]

- Review the terms of service of any noninstitutionally supported technology. Ensure that the owner of the rights (whether the student or the institution) agrees to these terms.
- Inform students of the platform's terms of use, which may claim some rights to their content.
- Suggest that students place copyright notices on their work. The Creative Commons license generator can help students formulate simple copyright notices that allow others to copy and distribute their products but still require certain conditions, such as proper attribution.

It may also be helpful to inform students that they will not have access to the content when the course ends, if this is indeed the case.

STRATEGY #5: WHEN IN DOUBT, CONSULT LEGAL COUNSEL

When questions arise about how to ensure that student rights are upheld in online courses, it is always a good idea for instructors to contact an institutional representative, such as a legal counsel, for advice and assistance.

Conclusion

As comic-book author Stan Lee suggests, "with great power comes great responsibility," and the Internet can be a powerful medium for instruction. When we choose to teach with it, we have to employ new strategies to ensure that the rights of students in these courses are respected, such as providing accessible materials, maintaining student privacy, and ensuring that students own the intellectual property they create. Doing so alters our work as instructors, however. This shift can be challenging, as we may be left with uncertainties, but it also can be positive, as we recognize and honor the rights of a growing body of digital citizens.

Chapter Eleven

Student Engagement

Thinking is the hardest work there is, which is probably the reason
why so few engage in it.
—HENRY FORD

Many of us teaching at the college level today actively seek ways to encourage students' interest and involvement in learning course content and skills.
We see it as our jobs not only to help students learn, and help them learn to learn,
but also to inspire their learning. Our efforts toward this end can range in intensity from attempting to make classes interesting enough to convince students to
show up to endeavoring to devise activities and assignments that encourage
students to use higher-order thinking skills, such as critical thinking and problem
solving. In short, we seek various means to engage students in their own learning.
The way in which we understand and experience student engagement, however, is
different when we teach online, which further compounds an already complex
educational issue.[1]

About Student Engagement

Although the term "engagement" is bandied about regularly in higher education circles, student engagement is a difficult concept to nail down. Educators have
suggested that "an explicit consensus about what we actually mean by engagement
or why it is important is lacking,"[2] which illustrates the complexity of the idea.
There is some agreement—at a broad level—about what student engagement is,
however, and these characteristics provide an essential framework for understanding student engagement and seeing how it differs in onsite and online courses. In
general, student engagement is the students' willingness and desire to participate
and be successful in a learning process that leads them to higher-level thinking and
long-term understanding. Engagement requires a psychological investment on the
part of the learner as well as persistence in undertaking the learning task. Several

interrelated factors underpin the concept of engagement, including motivation, attention, involvement, and intellectual effort.

Motivation, the first factor in engagement, is the level of enthusiasm students have for learning.[3] It is curiosity about a subject combined with a drive to learn about that topic. Motivation may be intrinsic, something from within that drives an individual to succeed. Students may love a subject or have a desire to learn about something simply because they find it interesting or important. Motivation may also be extrinsic, with students inclined to do something because of an external factor, such as grades, scholarships, or potential job placement. Thus, while some motivation is inherent to the individual, instructors share the responsibility for motivation, and we play a particularly important role in supporting external motivation.

The second factor in student engagement is attention, the process of concentrating on one aspect of the environment while ignoring others or of focusing on just one of several possible stimuli. It is the selective narrowing of consciousness and receptivity, and it involves the allocation of processing resources.[4] An individual may be either more or less able to ignore non-task-related stimuli, depending on the amount of processing resources devoted to the primary task.

The third factor is involvement, which, to some extent, is how much time and energy students put forth toward their learning. Alexander Astin, who is well known for his work on the involvement of college students, describes the concept:[5]

> Involvement requires the investment of energy in academic activities, and the amount of energy invested will vary greatly depending on the student's interests and goals, as well as the student's other commitments. Time is critical then; the extent to which students can be involved in the[ir] educational development is tempered by how involved they are with family friends, jobs, and other outside activities.

When students are involved and invested in the work they are doing, they become wrapped up in it. Learning then becomes personal; it matters. Clearly there are challenges to a student's involvement in a given class, such as competing courses, the need to work in addition to going to school, and social activities. But teachers can have some influence over the amount of energy that students are willing to expend.

The fourth factor related to engagement in a college classroom is intellectual effort. To be truly engaged, students need to move beyond simply skimming the material to learning to actively grapple with the content or skills in question. Educational psychologists Ference Marton and Roger Säljö's work provides insight into the concept of intellectual effort.[6] They asked students to read materials from an academic text and then describe what they had read. The researchers identified evidence of qualitative differences in students' reading outcomes that, rather than being related to the amount of material students could remember, were instead related to the meaning the authors of the text tried to convey. That is, some students fully understood the argument and the evidence to support it, while others partly understood the message, and still others could only remember details. Marton and Säljö characterized the approaches in which students focused on what the authors of the selected text meant and connected that information to what they already knew as "deep-learning approaches." Approaches in which students aimed to memorize facts and focus on discrete elements in the chosen reading were referred to as "surface-learning approaches."[7] Säljö furthered this concept of deep learning when he asked adult learners what they understood about "learning" and made distinctions between different levels of their understandings.[8] Säljö categorized their answers in a hierarchical pattern, observing that each higher conception implied all that preceded it:

1. Learning is acquiring information, or "knowing a lot."
2. Learning is memorizing, or "storing" information.
3. Learning is acquiring facts and skills that can be used.
4. Learning is making sense, or "making meaning," of the various pieces of information.
5. Learning involves comprehending, or understanding, the world by reinterpreting knowledge.

Deep-learning approaches, then, are evident when students seek a greater degree of understanding rather than just acquiring information; according to Paul Ramsden, the latter rests lightly on the surface, inert and unassimilated.[9] Both Säljö and Ramsden suggest that some students come equipped with deep-learning approaches, but they note that instructors can help students develop or improve such approaches.

While the concepts of deep- and surface-learning approaches have been widely understood as a set of strategies that students have or do not have at their disposal, there is also an element of intellectual effort to the differences between the strategies they employ, which becomes clear when looking at instruments designed to measure deep- and surface-learning approaches. For example, the Study Process

Questionnaire uses a Likert-type scale and asks students to rate items such as "I see no point in learning material which is not likely to be in the examination" and "I test myself on important topics until I understand them completely."[10] Hilary Tait, Noel Entwistle, and Velda McCune's Approaches and Study Skills Inventory for Students (ASSIST) also uses a Likert-type scale to ask for ratings on items such as "I work steadily through the term or semester, rather than leave it all until the last minute."[11] Even in Marton and Säljö's original study, surface-level readers saw the task of reading and answering questions as an external imposition.[12] Some students, however, are not only more able to use deep-learning strategies, but are also more willing to exert the intellectual effort required to do so.

Given that student engagement entails student motivation, attention, involvement, and intellectual effort, it is little wonder that engagement is critical to student performance. Lee Shulman, an educational psychologist and former president of the Carnegie Foundation for the Advancement of Teaching, suggests that "learning begins with student engagement," and he sees engagement as the foundation of his taxonomy of learning.[13] After completing their voluminous and meticulous review of higher education research on student engagement, Ernest Pascarella and Patrick Terenzini reached the following conclusion: "Perhaps the strongest conclusion that can be made is the least surprising. Simply put, the greater the student's involvement or engagement in academic work or in the academic experience of college, the greater his or her level of knowledge acquisition and general cognitive development."[14] Thus student engagement is a prerequisite to learning.

Changes to Faculty Experience of Student Engagement When Teaching Online

When we teach online, technology is a mediator between us and the students. Because of this intervention, the way in which we understand and experience the phenomenon of student engagement changes. Moreover, the means through which we seek to promote and assess student engagement change as well.

CONTROL OF STUDENT ENGAGEMENT

When we enter a physical classroom, we typically have a bounded area that surrounds and contains teaching and learning, a physical space that closes in and closes out. We have the luxury of teaching an arguably captive audience, with well-established social norms that indicate students should pay attention to what is going on in that space. Our very proximity in time and space sets the expectations that we will be in the moment together as a group and will come together in the present to exchange information and ideas. If we sense that student engagement is faltering, as instructors we can take action to rectify this situation, for example by moving physically closer to the students. We can also minimize distractions for students, perhaps by setting rules about what technology they can and cannot use in class, or else by establishing guidelines for how such technologies may be used (e.g., employing them as a way of accomplishing a task rather than a distraction from it). While there are some things we cannot control (e.g., intrinsic motivation), when we teach onsite we have the potential to influence the level of student engagement, since we can help guide the students' attention to and involvement in the teaching and learning process.

When we teach online, we often do not have the same opportunities for direct control of student engagement, which can be a challenge to learning. When students work offsite and alone, they can face a maze of distractions, including technological ones such as radio, television, email, texts, tweets, and social-network sites. The self-paced work often associated with online learning requires additional self-direction, self-discipline, and time management on the part of the student. Students in online courses necessarily act as causal agents in their own learning, which implies that they have the capacity "to make choices and to act on these choices in ways that make a difference in their lives."[15] Students should self-regulate and control their own levels of engagement with the course content and skills. While some students possess strong abilities in this regard, certainly all students need additional strategies to be successful in online courses. In many ways, some of the control and authority of engagement shifts from teachers to students in online courses. In the wake of such a change, we may not know how to provide online students with activities that can best enable them to self-regulate and drive their own learning.

EVIDENCE OF ENGAGEMENT

When we teach onsite, we often directly associate certain observable cues with evidence of student engagement. Verbal cues include how students use words/language to signal their involvement, and nonverbal factors include student gestures. When teaching onsite, we use both of these to assess the level of student engagement. We may think of students who show up for class as being engaged. We may think of students who arrive early and sit up straight, in the front of the class, as being engaged. We may think of those students who make eye contact and nod in agreement as being engaged. We think of the students who raise their hands to ask or answer questions as being the most engaged. Thus many of the ways in which we identify engagement in onsite classes come from the behavioral cues we receive from students. We are not always correct in our assessments, however, since engaged students may sit in the back of the classroom or look away when asked a question, but, rightly or wrongly, we often perceive certain behaviors as offering evidence of engagement.

When we teach online, we do not always have the same kind of behavioral cues to provide us with evidence about student engagement, and we often miss the nonverbal ones. We cannot see whether students are leaning forward when reviewing course material. We cannot make eye contact with them. We cannot see if they are smiling at a response or frowning in thoughtfulness. Students could be distracted by folding clothes or vacuuming while watching a video lecture, and we would be none the wiser. Without the physical cues, it can seem more difficult to tell when students are disengaged or unenthusiastic.

When we teach online, we may seek information about student engagement that corresponds to that which we seek when teaching onsite courses. We may consider how early in the week it is when they post an assignment or comment in a discussion. We may also choose to examine how long students stay on a page. Much of the research on engagement online examines time spent on task, as indicated by the length of a page view or how many times a video is replayed. But even these cues have challenges when seen as indicators of engagement. Students may be solidly engaged in the course but have work or family obligations that mean they cannot be the first ones to post or respond. Some students may appear to stay on a page for a long time when they are really doing something else. Other students may choose to print out information to read later, and thus may spend only a short time on a given page, when actually they have devoted a good bit of time to the assignment. Thus on-task information is not always a satisfactory indicator of student engagement. When we teach online, we can be left feeling uncertain about how to gauge engagement, which, in turn, has implications for our pedagogical practices.

IMMEDIACY OF ENGAGEMENT

When we teach onsite, we experience student engagement directly, since we occupy the same space and timeframe with students. When in a physical classroom, we receive immediate feedback from students about how engaged they are through the verbal and nonverbal cues described above. Immediacy is the perceived distance between people, a sense we share with our students. As psychologist Albert Mehrabian, the developer of the "principle of immediacy," suggests, the feeling of immediacy can enhance individuals' sense of physical and psychological closeness to each other.[16] And immediacy with students is important to our experiences as teachers.[17] Liking encourages immediacy, which increases liking. Teachers who perceive of their nonverbal students as still being immediate have more positive responses to these students than teachers who see such behaviors as being less immediate.[18]

Opportunities for immediacy are increased by both physical and temporal proximity. Given that instructors are separated from their students in online classes, at least in asynchronous courses, opportunities for immediacy consequently can be reduced. When we teach online, we may experience less immediacy with our students and thus may feel further removed from any sense of engagement. If we are not careful in structuring and recognizing engagement, this sense of less immediacy can lead to feelings of reduced levels of engagement.

Strategies for Designing Engaging Activities

Given the changes to the ways in which we experience student engagement when we teach online, it can be important to work toward creating better and more recognizable opportunities for it. In his 2001 white paper, Russell Edgerton, a leader in undergraduate education who served in a number of high-profile positions, including as director of the Pew Charitable Trusts and director of the American Association of Higher Education, coined the term "pedagogies of engagement," stating that "learning 'about things' does not enable students to acquire the abilities and understanding they will need for the twenty-first century. We need new pedagogies of engagement that will turn out the[se] kinds of resourceful, engaged workers and citizens."[19] His assertion holds true for online courses. Pedagogies of engagement offer instructors sound opportunities for increasing visible levels of engagement when teaching online.

STRATEGY #1: USE STUDENT-LED PEDAGOGIES

Any instructional activity may be led by either an instructor or a student. In instructor-led pedagogies, the teachers are central to the process and exercise authority and control. Students, in turn, primarily function as consumers of content. In student-led pedagogies, faculty are less central and have less authority and control over students. Students, in turn, take up opportunities to be active agents in their own learning. Shifting toward student-led pedagogies provides greater opportunities for students to engage in and drive their learning. Table 11.1 highlights

Table 11.1   Characteristics of instructor- and learner-led methods

Instructor-led	Learner-led
Instructor talks; students listen	Students interact with each other and with instructors
Instructor chooses topics or assignments	Students have some choice of topics or assignments
Instructor monitors and corrects	Students work and interact without constant instructor monitoring
Instructor answers students' questions	Students answer each other's questions, using the instructor as an information resource; the instructor provides comments and suggestions when questions arise
Students consume knowledge	Students produce knowledge
Instructor evaluates student learning	Students evaluate their own learning; the instructor also evaluates

some important differences between instructor-led and learner-led methods, which provide important information about how to structure student-led pedagogy.

Pedagogies such as lectures and demonstrations tend to be instructor led, while pedagogies such as cooperative learning, team-based learning (TBL), and problem-based learning (PBL) tend to be learner led. Pedagogies in the latter group provide opportunities for students to take an agency role in their own learning and create products that stand as direct evidence of their engagement with the course.

STRATEGY #2: USE PEDAGOGIES THAT EMPOWER STUDENTS
IN THE PEDAGOGICAL PROCESS

In higher education, instructors have traditionally been the ones to determine the pedagogy used in a course. Pedagogy has been something that we have imposed on students, yet it need not be this way. We can involve students in the pedagogical process and in pedagogical decision making in a variety of ways, from asking them to contribute their goals to the course and then revising the syllabus, to providing them with opportunities to serve as the instructors at some point in a given course, such as through a microteaching assignment. Moreover, when we teach online and blended courses, involving students in discussions and decisions about technology can lead to higher levels of student engagement. This process also has

Participant Pedagogy

JESSE STOMMEL
Assistant Professor
Department of Liberal Studies and the Arts
University of Wisconsin–Madison, US

The term "participant pedagogy" suggests something more than just active learning. It suggests learning that is both active and reflective, lively, and voracious. In his chapter on "Participation power," Howard Rheingold writes: "In the world of digitally networked publics, online participation—if you know how to do it—can translate into real power. Participation, however, is a kind of power that only works if you share it with others."[1] Digital space allows (and even demands) a new level, and a new kind, of participation. There is no "head of the class" in an online learning environment, not even the illusion of one. Instead, students must construct many of their own strategies, without a recipe, in the moment. They should even be called on to help map the terrain in which that can happen.

We should not use systems that etch curricula into stone. This means eschewing stock courses in which the content is static and the students are mere receptacles. Active learning puts students at the center of the learning space. Participant pedagogy asks students to help create the space. For this type of pedagogy to flourish, participants have to become fully involved in their own learning. Participant pedagogy, however, is not only about students being pedagogues, but also about teachers coming to class as full participants.

A good syllabus is not a contract, because the syllabus should be broken by the end of a course. I work to make my syllabus a living document that gets revised as the term proceeds. Where possible, students should guide the curriculum and create course content. This means using or enabling tools that give students at least some measure of control over design. With a small group of students, this might mean making assignments "hackable" and building the course site together in a wiki or coauthored blog. With a larger group of students, embedding Google Docs or allowing comments on course pages can foster and facilitate student collaboration. In my courses, I've also replaced talking-head video lectures from me with videos created by students.

Educators at every level must begin by listening to and trusting students. This means building space in every course for students to reflect on the course's pedagogy—an ongoing meta-level discussion of learning with student voices at its center. Teachers stand to learn more from students about online learning than we could ever teach them. Many students come to an online or a hybrid class knowing full well how to learn online. It's often our failure to know how to learn online equally as well that leads to many of the design mistakes in this generation of online courses. Recognizing the problem demands a culture shift—it demands that we acknowledge the diverse expertise of students as tantamount to our own.[2]

Notes

    1. See Rheingold (2013, p. 112).
    2. This sidebar was adapted from several articles originally published at www .hybridpedagogy.com.

---

the potential to leave remnants that serve as evidence of their engagement. Jesse Stommel, an expert in digital humanities and hybrid pedagogy, describes how he involves students in such opportunities.

STRATEGY #3: USE PEDAGOGIES THAT ENABLE STUDENTS TO
CONNECT THEIR PERSONAL INTERESTS TO COURSE CONTENT

An adult-education theory advanced by Malcolm Knowles suggests that students are more likely to be interested in topics that involve them directly.[20] According to this widely recognized theory, dubbed "andragogy," adult learners are internally motivated and self-directed. They bring experiences and knowledge they wish to apply to their learning. They are practical and want learning to be relevant to their own experiences. In addition, adult learners want to be respected. Wanda Sullivan, who teaches an online art course, describes ways in which she attempts to cultivate student interest in her subject matter by making critical connections to their lives. In so doing, she captures student-developed products that document their engagement.

Making Learning Meaningful to the Individual Learner

WANDA SULLIVAN
Associate Professor
Art
Spring Hill College, US

I teach Contemporary Art History online. The majority of the students are not art majors, so I do not have a captive audience. As a newcomer to online teaching, my biggest challenge is engaging the students online. How can I, in this type of environment, get "civilians" to appreciate contemporary art and surmount the mainstream idea that it is pretentious and only for the elite? During each week of the course, I introduce that week's topic: a PowerPoint comprising images, a discussion thread, and my "Art of the Week" choice. I strive, as we say in the art world, for unity with variety.

First, I try to make it personal. I ask for an "art biography" from each student to break the ice, requesting them to describe their current level of art knowledge and tell me about their favorite type of art. I also tell them to be brutally honest, so I can get a feel for my audience. This is my way of connecting with each student individually, something that comes easily for me in a face-to-face class, but not always online.

Second, I employ humor as my secret weapon. "Now That's Weird!," "Now You Made Me Mad," and "That's Not a Rectangle!" are examples of some of my weekly topics. Besides drawing the students into a subject that they may find strange and unusual, humor keeps me engaged and entertained as well.

Third, I give weekly assignments, in an attempt to spark the students' interest and exploit their need for variety. I give these creative titles to make it fun, including "Art in the Wild," "I Hate It!," and "Mainstream Art." I frame these assignments like online scavenger hunts. The students are enthusiastic about this aspect of the class, and several even mention it in their evaluations. I vary the parameters to create enough variety to keep them interested. Some weeks they can find material online, but at other times they have to go out into the community to fulfill the assignment. They post their images and respond to their classmates' images. It makes for some lively threads.

STRATEGY #4: USE PEDAGOGIES THAT SIMULATE REALITY

Students tend to be more engaged in activities that feel real to them. Pedagogies based on realistic experiences for students can range from case-based learning, in which students strive to solve real-world problems presented in the form of case studies, to game-based learning, in which students participate in simulations and immersive games. Fil Arenas describes the US Air Force Squadron Officer College's exploration of virtual learning, including prototyping multiplayer educational role-playing games to engage their students in virtual 3D environments, and he discusses its implications for future learning models.

STRATEGY #5: USE PEDAGOGIES THAT HAVE STUDENTS CREATE AUTHENTIC PRODUCTS

When we consider the process and the product, we should also remember that approaches emphasizing knowledge production using meaningful products are more authentic, and thus more important, to students; hence learners will be more likely to engage with them. These are activities that are contextualized in real life, rather than decontextualized to the classroom. Such approaches make engagement, and ultimately learning, not only more visible, but also more real for the students. Educational technologists Thomas Reeves, Jan Herrington, and Ron Oliver discuss authentic activities,[21] which they believe

- have real-world relevance;
- are ill defined, requiring students to formulate the tasks and subtasks needed to complete the activity;
- contain complex tasks to be investigated by students over a sustained period of time;
- provide an opportunity for students to examine the task from different perspectives, using a variety of resources;
- provide an opportunity to collaborate;
- provide an opportunity to reflect;

Multiplayer Educational Role-Playing Games

FIL J. ARENAS
Associate Professor
Organizational Leadership Studies
Maxwell Air Force Base (Alabama), US

As educators, we are continuously challenged with providing relevant pedagogical methodologies with limited resources. It is incumbent on all educational institutions to seek creative solutions to meet these student-learning challenges. Over the past few years, those of us at the Squadron Officer College (SOC) have been exploring alternatives to costly state-of-the-art technology to support our curricula. Beginning with Flash-based avatar vignettes (scenarios) to bolster professional military-education requirements, we embarked on a quest to incorporate affordable multimedia into our courses. We now use Second Life, one of the leading virtual-world platforms, and have launched a series of prototype lessons that I refer to as MPERPGs (Multiplayer Educational Role-Playing Games), with the emphasis on education. The term "serious game" was first defined by Clark Abt,[1] before electronic gaming became the ubiquitous form of entertainment it is today. We support his original intent to consider the educational purpose in the instructional-design process over mere amusement.

Traditional teaching and learning methods typically focus on faculty members communicating new knowledge in a classroom setting, where students listen, discuss, and take notes as required. In this type of situation, students are in a passive learning mode and often participate minimally in the overall process. A constructivist learning approach places its emphasis on student involvement, requiring them to become more self-directed learners. At SOC, we continually explore methodologies to engage our students yet also provide more interactive means for them to further enhance their educational experiences. Technological innovations, which offer opportunities to apply a constructivist approach to the instructional-design process, can create unlimited possibilities. Constructivist learning requires students to find their own solutions to problems, based on their prior knowledge and experiences.[2]

Allowing our developing officers to share their military knowledge and experiences with other students while attending SOC courses has proven invaluable. Research has revealed that gaming and simulation environments support a learner-centered education, where students may actively work through problems while gaining knowledge through participation.[3] The combination of gaming and simulation offers compelling educational benefits while providing an immersive learning experience.

One advantage of learning in 3D over 2D environments is that it enables students to experience a sense of immersion, or engagement, during the learning activity. This immersion, taking the form of an embodied avatar, makes it possible for a learner to engage with others while also taking part in activities that promote comprehension and the application of formal learning objectives. The technology that supports learning in 3D helps create the spatial and temporal conditions for immersion and interactivity. It also utilizes course content in the performance of tasks that require the application of new knowledge and skills.[4] Thus offering experiential activities through immersive, 3D-integrated learning environments provides our students with innovative approaches to academic challenges. Moreover, the ability to process information into knowledge, share that knowledge, and then act on it to solve problems culminates in the development of agile and adaptive leaders with the skills necessary for the twenty-first century.

In addition to multiple distance-learning courses, SOC offers one residential program that has delivered professional military education for over sixty years: the Squadron Officer School (SOS). The goal of this eight-week course is to educate US Air Force officers by applying airpower leadership to effectively execute military missions. MPERPGs, in the form of elective lessons using Second Life, are optional prototypes offered during this residential program. SOC was selected as a 2013 Federal Virtual Worlds Challenge (FVWC) award winner for the "Compound" MPERPG. The FVWC is an open, global challenge to the world for the "best of the best implementations" within virtual environments. The FVWC is an

(continued)

"Compound" illustrates students rescuing POWs and navigating a minefield to safety. "Compound" received first place in the Critical Thinking / Adaptability category of the FVWC awards.

"Gen. MacArthur" allows students to attend the "Duty, Honor, Country" speech given on May 12, 1962, at West Point, New York

annual event led by the US Army Research Laboratory Simulation & Training Technology Center and is highlighted at the Defense GameTech Conference. The event explores innovative and interactive solutions in virtual environments, and the criteria are intentionally unbounded to encourage creative results.

Notes

1. Abt (1970) provides a more extensive discussion of serious games.
2. Cheney & Sanders (2011) describe the concept of constructivist learning.
3. Annetta et al. (2006) provide information about games and simulations.
4. Kapp & O'Driscoll (2010) offer useful descriptions of 3D technology.

- can be integrated and applied across different subject areas and lead beyond domain-specific outcomes;
- are seamlessly integrated with assessment; and
- create polished products valuable in their own right, rather than as preparation for something else.

In short, students become more engaged when working on assignments that lead to meaningful products having value beyond the course. Activities like book reviews, digital storytelling, surveys, data analyses, case studies, and so forth can allow students to approach a meaningful task and produce a real and enduring product that documents their learning in a tangible way. Moreover, teaching online offers us unique opportunities that allow students to create tangible and meaningful products, such as journals, videos, articles, or digital stories. Technology researcher, speaker, and futurist Bryan Alexander's discussion of digital storytelling is one example of the ways in which students engage in and document knowledge production.[22]

STRATEGY #6: USE MULTIPLE AND VARIED PEDAGOGIES THAT
REQUIRE DOCUMENTED STUDENT ACTION

The body of research regarding onsite lectures is clear about one thing: when you insert other elements into a lecture, whether through a short writing activity, a discussion question, or a quiz, student attention and engagement—and, subsequently, student learning—improve. Pedagogies that demand breaking up the traditional long lecture session with brief, active learning assignments, sometimes referred to as punctuated lectures, have a solid base of evidence to support their efficacy at improving student engagement and, ultimately, learning outcomes.[23] After all, humans have a limited attention span; we have to be active to reset it and optimize learning.

Students in onsite courses need breaks from content consumption to actively engage in their learning, as do students in online courses. There are many activities that instructors can use to ensure student activity, even when presenting

Digital Storytelling

BRYAN ALEXANDER
Consultant
Educational Technology
Bryan Alexander Consulting, US

One of digital storytelling's great strengths is its ability to elicit the creators' imaginativeness in communication. We see this in the mental process of reconsidering one's work and/or life in storytelling terms. One must reorganize one's thoughts in terms of a narrative arc, which can be a productive shock to a person's memory or professional knowledge. This requires formulating a new timeline, aimed at audience expectations. The creator also reconceives remembered persons as characters, representing them as figures with depth, desire, and transformation. Accomplishing these revisions means revisiting one's sense of storytelling itself.

Moreover, the selection of a digital media platform summons up different types of creativity in communication. Twitter requires condensed writing, akin to poetry or aphorisms. Blogging compels serial thinking, organizing content into discrete, sequential chunks. Podcasting, in contrast, focuses attention on the human voice and the use of other audio forms to create soundscapes. Basic multimedia tools like VoiceThread[1] or Cowbird[2] require us to think through the connections between media types, as well as the contents of individual media items. Arranging images in sequence without text, such as with Flickr's "Tell a Story in 5 Frames" project, drives a comic-book-style logic of thinking through images and the gaps between them. Each of these platforms is less complex than the full scope of digital video, with its multimedia capacity and 2D or 3D visual depth. Nonetheless, all of these platforms can develop students' social-media skills when presented through the web.

This combination of creativity-driven processes offers pedagogical strengths. Students rethink course materials in new ways while assembling them into narratives. Their choice of a media platform presents technical and formal challenges; overcoming them can draw forth creative resources. Instructors can facilitate students' imaginative growth during the digital-storytelling process through encouragement, personal engagement, small-group work, and curricular connections. Additionally, the broader world of cyberculture can play a role in the creative process, once it is engaged by storytelling through social media.[3]

Notes

1. Information about VoiceThread is available at www.VoiceThread.com.
2. Information about Cowbird is available at www.Cowbird.com.
3. Alexander (2011) provides an extensive introduction to and analysis of digital storytelling.

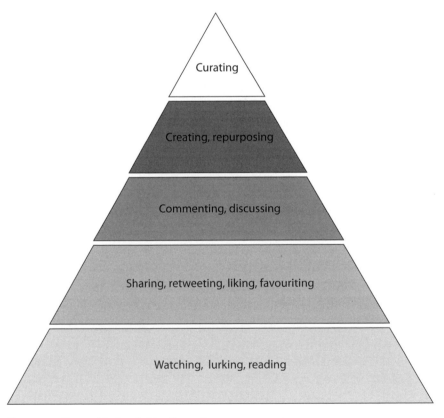

Figure 11.1. Pyramid of activities for online engagement

content. One option is to juxtapose short video lectures with active learning assignments, such as posting to a discussion board or uploading content. Some online instructors who have used longer videos have achieved success by frequently interspersing them with tests.[24] Written content may be mixed with links to assignments that invite activity, such as the opportunity to comment on a content post. We can ask students to engage in a range of activities where they act instead of watch or listen, such as accessing information, sharing information, contributing information, creating information, and curating information.[25] Steve Wheeler, an expert in learning, documents various levels of engagement. In figure 11.1, Wheeler portrays a wide range of activities to engage online students.[26] Students may work their way up from the bottom toward the top of the pyramid, demonstrating higher levels of engagement as they move along.

Conclusion

Engagement in the online classroom is an important step toward a positive learning experience that, in turn, can lead to positive learning outcomes. It requires effort from the teacher to motivate students, involve them in their own learning, and help them discover and use deep-learning strategies. Engagement in online courses is different from engagement in onsite ones in several significant ways, however, which are largely related to a direct experience of engagement versus a technological mediation of it. Using pedagogies of engagement in the online classroom can help faculty meet the unique challenges of designing activities that can promote and document student engagement in an online course.

Chapter Twelve

Community

What should young people do with their lives today? Many things, obviously. But the most daring thing is to create stable communities in which the terrible disease of loneliness can be cured.

—KURT VONNEGUT

Sometimes a group of students just seems to gel in a given class. They connect with each other, work well together, and encourage and support each other. They look out for each other. They generally seem to enjoy being in the course together as a group. Sometimes a group of students does *not* gel, however. They barely interact, and they do not work together. They may not discourage each other, but encouragement is not forthcoming, either. The difference between the two is sometimes referred to as community, a concept that can be particularly important in online courses, given the potential for students in such courses to feel isolated and alone. The ways in which we experience community with students differs when we teach online.

About Community

The term "community" has Latin origins and essentially means "to give or to make common among each other." The concept carries with it the intimation of shared ownership of something. At a fundamental level, communities are "collections of people who are bound together for some reason, and that reason defines the boundary of the community."[1] Community allows us to be around others who hold a common set of ideals and ideas and who can validate our own experiences and beliefs. It is what gives us a sense of identity and belonging. Community members share not only interests but also a desire to exchange ideas and information, to learn with and from each other. Communities allow us to gather and share knowledge. Thus communities enable a group of potential learners to meet common goals. In practice, community traditionally has been place centered, where individuals within the same physical space have identified with each other.

Countries, states, cities, and neighborhoods are examples of cultural or geographic communities; within such spatial boundaries, individuals may have many things in common, such as beliefs, goals, purposes, languages, symbols, and rituals. Over time, we have expanded our conception of the term to include a variety of groups, many of which are based on the interests of their members. Such communities may be either informal, such as when they form around the participants' interests in movies, old cars, a specific type of music, sports, and so forth. Alternately, they may be more formal, such as in communities of practice, where members share a craft, or communities of inquiry, composed of members of a scientific community who are involved in a certain type of inquiry into social problems.[2]

Our concept of community has evolved dramatically over the past couple of decades, alongside the emergence and development of many new communication technologies. These technologies allow us to extend and broaden our communities. We do not see our fellow members solely in supermarkets and local stores or at meetings and events; rather, we can connect with them through email, text, and social media. Today it is not necessary for us to be physically situated within our communities; instead, we can carry them with us in our pockets and backpacks. We do not have to interact with other community members face-to-face, in real time; rather, our communications can be and often are asynchronous. Our technologies now enable our communities to extend beyond the limitations of our physical beings and thus span the boundaries of time and place. Communities that are formed completely over the Internet have sprung up during the past decade. These associations, dubbed "virtual communities,"[3] develop over time. Jean Lave and Étienne Wenger illustrate a cycle of how users are incorporated into virtual communities.[4] They suggest five types of trajectories among a learning community:

1. *Peripheral* (i.e., Lurker). An outside, nonpublic, and unstructured participant.
2. *Inbound* (i.e., Novice). A newcomer is invested in the community and is heading toward full and public participation.
3. *Insider* (i.e., Regular). A fully committed community participant.
4. *Boundary* (i.e., Leader). An individual who sustains membership participation and brokers interactions.
5. *Outbound* (i.e., Elder). Someone in the process of leaving the community, due to new relationships, new positions, or new outlooks.

Virtual communities, by design, are also based on common interests. Such communities are characterized by "social aggregation and personal relationships,"[5] as well as by their members' ability to work across space and time.[6] While the benefits of being able to broaden the definition of community are clear, there are also costs, including the possibility of decreased human contact.[7] These technologies thus change the nature of community as well as our relationships and interaction with each other as human beings.

In higher education, the concept of community has begun to receive attention, and research has demonstrated that learning communities—which may include freshmen interest groups and linked courses, block scheduling and registration, and, at times, a living learning community, in which students are housed and take courses together—can enhance cognitive skills and intellectual growth, educational attainment and persistence, and moral development.[8] When we think about community within a particular course, however, it is a more difficult concept to define.[9]

There is something important about how students relate to each other within given courses, when they come together and coalesce, that seems to improve their satisfaction and thus their willingness to engage and learn, but there also is something indescribable about what it is. When we are teaching a course we know when have community, and we definitely know when we do not. The ways in which community might happen can differ from class to class. What we do know, however, is that when we teach onsite, there are things we share that help to bring us together as a group. We occupy the same physical space, and we spend time with each other. Our attention is focused on the same thing at the same time, whether it is the teacher talking, a student answering a question, a group working on a project, someone making a joke, and so forth. We engage in a course together, as a group, rather than as individual members of the class, and we identify with each other as part of this group. Just as with online communities, however, learning communities that form within a course are, by definition, transitory. They have a starting place, they develop, and they come to an end. Those phases can be accompanied by emotional intensity—the euphoria of having new friends, or a sense of loss at the community's dissolution. Technology can change this, allowing community to extend beyond the temporal and spatial confines of a classroom.

Changes to Faculty Experience with the Concept of Community When Teaching Online

When teaching happens online rather than onsite, some of that sense of sharing time, place, space, experience, and the like is lost. Thus community is different onsite than it is online. No longer can we or the students see community as something that happens within the space of the classroom; it is far less tangible than that. Without a shared physical space, community cannot be formed in the way that it typically unfolds in a traditional classroom. While online classes clearly do not produce the same kind of community created by onsite courses, they are not truly virtual communities, either. Thus the way in which community occurs in online courses is also different from the way in which it happens in virtual communities.[10]

Students in an online course may not have the same level of interest in the subject as a virtual community, in which membership is voluntary. They do, however, enter an established community in which there are experienced members who are already engaged. They do not have time to lurk and learn, but rather are expected to dive in as full members of the community. Online courses, then, reside at an uneasy juncture, sharing features with both onsite courses and virtual communities yet stubbornly refusing a characterization as either. They are their own entity, and new and different processes for establishing community apply, but we are not yet fully aware of what those are. For this reason, developing a sense of community can be challenging in an online course, and studies of student experiences suggest that students in online courses can feel isolated and alone.[11] It is important that we begin to take stock of the differences between communities in onsite and online courses, as well as how we might recognize and encourage community within online courses.

STRUCTURE OF COMMUNITY

The concept of a social network, in which individuals (represented as nodes) are connected to each other by relationships (represented by ties), is one that has utility for us in understanding the structure of community.[12] Networks create an overall group structure and have much to offer in our understanding of community. Terry Anderson discusses the concept of networks.

In examining complex networks, a given area within a network is thought to have a community structure when the nodes (i.e., individuals) are densely connected to each other. Thus networks are the overarching structure, and communities may form within them. Communities within a network may overlap or not. Cliques occur when all of the individuals in a community are directly connected to each other. Figure 12.1 (see p. 232) depicts a simple social-network structure. The nodes and ties collectively represent the network's structure. The grey circles represent relatively dense connections in the network and illustrate three separate

Networks and Sets

TERRY ANDERSON
Professor
Distance Education
Athabasca University, CA

When my colleagues Randy Garrison, Walter Archer, and I developed and tested the community-of-inquiry model, our view of online learning was constrained by the asynchronous text forums of the then-current computer conferencing tools. We documented the advantages and measured the type and quality of asynchronous communications, but we readily adopted more of the mixed-delivery methods—such as web conferencing and, later, immersive environments—as synchronous tools became available. Despite the change in our educational tools, we never had an opportunity to expand our teaching beyond the thirty-student virtual classroom and the security and comfort (for both students and teacher) of the closed online classroom.

Today, we are afforded new teaching and learning opportunities, based on networks and sets. As Jon Dron and I have been researching lately, networks allow learning to expand beyond the temporal bounds and role designations of this term's students and teachers and evolve into networks of current students, professionals, alumni, and guests. Networks leave traces of learning activity—visible strategies and artifacts—that enrich future students and informal learners from around the world who are not enrolled in the course.

Beyond networks, we see educational opportunities in the learner aggregations we refer to as sets: the collection of people interested in a topic, but not necessarily interested in tight group collaboration, or even a networked association. Web 2.0 tools such as Pinterest and learni.st, and

(continued)

even the cooperation of the collection of people who create any particular Wikipedia article, show early signs of the power of this emergent learning context.

In sum, the Internet first brought us the group-based classroom at a distance; now our pedagogical frontiers extend to developing networks and sets. Our challenge as teachers is to use all of these forms to create ever-more-powerful ways for learners and ourselves to acquire the knowledge and wisdom we need to more effectively manage our global home.

---

communities. In the third circle, all of the nodes are connected to each other and thus represent a clique.

When we teach onsite, community often is structured geographically. Students frequently choose to sit by individuals whom they already know and like, or they may elect to sit by those who display symbols with which the students identify (e.g., a sorority or fraternity emblem). Those students who sit next to each other probably have the most conversational exchanges. Many times, when we ask students to form groups, we often do so by asking students to work with their neighbors, particularly in large classroom settings, thus reinforcing the creation of community by geography. Therefore, it is relatively easy for the class as a whole to develop a community structure, and even for students to form cliques, which are more exclusive than communities and thus more difficult to join. In a given classroom, the community structure could resemble something very similar to the one depicted in figure 12.1.

In online courses, community still develops through patterns of communication, but the community structure typically is not determined by geography. Rather than individuals who are in close physical proximity creating communities and cliques, an online community can develop more evenly among the members of the class, because of the absence of spatial limitations. Thus an online community has a structure that potentially can be fairly inclusive, and barriers to entry into the course's community may be less rigid. That is not to say that individuals in online courses do not form separate communities and cliques, but rather that they are not predetermined by physical limitations. Moreover, the structure of an online community need not be limited to those enrolled in a course for credit; it has the potential to be more distributed and, even, out of bounds. Jim Groom, recently named a "tech innovator" by the *Chronicle of Higher Education*, describes how his institu-

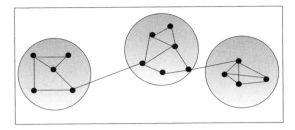

Figure 12.1. A simple social-network structure

tion is using technology to create learning spaces that extend beyond the walls of the traditional classroom, in a broader, and more distributed, view of learning online (see p. 234).

When we teach online, the community that forms is structured differently than the one created when we teach onsite. This has implications for our roles and responsibilities as teachers. When the class takes place onsite, in some cases it is easy to spot community. We know immediately when students sitting next to each other are engaged in mutual dialog. We can see students walk out of class together, talking of a future shared social event. Most of us could probably graph the nodes and ties of the students in our onsite classes in a manner similar to the diagram in figure 12.1. Online, we are not always as aware of the structure of the community. Many times community happens under the radar of the course, through private texting and emailing. We may not even be aware that a community has developed. Unless we are included in the communication loop, we can feel that an online course does not have the same level of community as an onsite one does.

COMMUNITY NORMS AND EXPECTATIONS

Norms are patterns of beliefs about behavior that is expected in certain situations or are circumstances that are shared by members of a given social group.[13] Norms are what regulate social behavior and thus what allow communities to function.[14] Norms thus serve as informal social controls. Moreover, they convey the collective conscience of a social group,[15] and the central and deep-seated values of the group.[16] Norms allow group survival and group identity.[17] Class norms are patterns of beliefs about behavioral expectations, or the rules of the class. Norms accepted by student groups influence the behavior of the group.[18] They are agreements among members of the community regarding how they will treat each other. Thus groups that accept strict academic norms will function at a high level of

Blogging as a Form of Learning at the University of Mary Washington

JIM GROOM
Director and Adjunct Professor
Division of Teaching and Learning
    Technologies
University of Mary Washington, US

The University of Mary Washington (UMW) in currently in the process of moving its whole public-facing website to an entirely open-source format. It will be using a mashup of WordPress and MediaWiki to deliver content on the web to visitors from around the world. The website will not simply be a space for "selling the school"—that is, a slick marketing campaign touting words like "excellence," "diversity," and "global"; rather, the umw .edu website will be transformed into an organic, community-authored representation of the life of the mind at UMW.

For over four years, UMW has seen an institution-wide adoption of blogging into the course curriculum—as well as the campus culture— employing the WordPress multiuser platform. As a result, we have had more than seven thousand users, with well over six thousand blogs that averaged 4.5 million page views over the 2011/12 academic year. UMW has developed a powerful web presence through its open approach to course blogging, which has begun to shape the overall tenor of the community at large. When it comes to web publishing at UMW, "open" (rather than "closed/private") is the default setting. The next stage is to make the process for publishing and sharing information about each academic department, faculty member, and student that much simpler and more transparent. UMW is pushing its publishing framework to accommodate everything from individual sites, to integrated course sites, to departmental sites, to college-wide sites. Through an innovative approach to creating a seamless series of networks across the various academic and administrative departments and colleges, UMW is truly on the verge of fostering a web presence for the university that encourages and enables a glimpse into the open, public domain of this academic community that goes beyond the siloed logic of a learning management system (LMS). The university website is no longer a colorful, hyperlinked brochure of what one imagines our ideal students and their parents want to see. Rather, the site has become a lively arena shooting forth and dancing with ideas, creativity, and the discourse that frames the intellectual activity on campus.

What is more, the website is a porous architecture aimed at integrating social-media services as a means of capturing and promoting the best of UMW around the web, rather than ignoring and diffusing this preexisting reality. Moving beyond an LMS means reintegrating the very heart of the open, dynamic web back into the university's publishing framework. It is no longer about divorcing the essence of the university's academic mission from its forward-facing web; it is about remarrying the public presence of UMW with open online spaces where teaching, learning, and engagement are everywhere present, permeable, and possible. It is about the university's website itself as an open, online learning space—what a novel concept!

---

achievement, and vice versa. Norms provide students with a basis from which to monitor and change their own behaviors.

When teaching onsite, the day-to-day interactions with each other by individuals in a given classroom govern norms. These contexts produce normative orientations that include participation, study behaviors, interactions with other students, faculty and student interactions, and so forth. It is the social interactions—the words, gestures, and behaviors—that set the norms. Norms are established by the students after they have had a chance to get to know each other. Some common norms in onsite classes are to attend class, to be on time, to be civil to the teacher and to each other, and to be honest. When we teach online, traditional norms are not necessarily in place, because there is no simultaneous group presence at a particular time in a specific locale. Students do not necessarily "attend" class at a given time; rather, they complete their work and interact in an asynchronous environment.

Civility in a text-based environment is less well established than civility in an onsite one.[19] But ideas about what constitutes "honesty" may be less clear where technology is involved.[20] Eric Rabkin describes his experience with academic honesty in an open online course.

Academic Honesty in an Online Course
What to Do about Plagiarism?

ERIC RABKIN
Arthur F. Thurnau Professor Emeritus,
    Professor Emeritus of English Language
    and Literature, and Professor Emeritus
    of Art and Design
College of Literature, Science, and the Arts
    (LSA) and Penny W. Stamps School of Art
    and Design
University of Michigan, US

Between July and October 2010, my massive open online course (MOOC), Fantasy and Science Fiction: The Human Mind, Our Modern World—created under the auspices of the University of Michigan and employing the technology and professional support of Coursera—was, according to journalistic reports, the world's first writing-intensive MOOC. By most measures, this course was enormously successful. It garnered about forty thousand participants from around the world, of whom approximately 15% finished the course, a completion rate typical of MOOCs. This MOOC involved a host of theoretical and practical questions regarding pedagogy, scholarship, and policy. Among these, although this was not a credit-bearing activity, two factors combined to foreground the question of plagiarism.

First, by calling it a "course," people—especially among those who completed all the timed tasks—wanted credit, and some of them wanted public assurance that this credit could be understood as a certification of an original contribution. Second, many institutions and organizations interested in MOOCs see them as alternatives or supplements to more traditional courses, offerings which historically issue credentials. If plagiarism goes undetected or is ignored, what happens to the value of the credentials (grades) that traditional educational institutions use to measure learners' efforts, which accumulate (as credits) into the ultimate credential (a degree) that many students feel they are purchasing not only with their effort, but also their money? Some "students" want to make sure that a MOOC is equivalent to a course, even though it has no admission requirements and costs them nothing, while some schools want to make sure that a MOOC doesn't count as the equivalent of a course unless its credentialing is trustworthy. Such enormous concerns must be addressed by a combination of policy decisions and technological solutions, ranging from rethinking what we mean by grades to retina scanners for distant students taking exams in order to achieve online authentication of who they are. These difficulties will need to be resolved if what are now MOOCs begin to become courses, not only in the sense of educating, but of credentialing.

I have many thoughts about these matters, but whatever shape a course takes—online or otherwise—a suspicion of plagiarism, no matter what else it prompts, should elicit education about this issue for all involved. When a minority concerned with plagiarism in my MOOC spoke out, I replied with a 1,200-word missive to all forty thousand participants. A few remained unsatisfied. Many wrote to thank me for this clarification, including two who self-identified as instructors themselves. Another offered to withdraw for having inadvertently plagiarized, but I declined the offer. In the context of a MOOC—it is open to all—what counts is the educational community. The overt consideration of how community is hurt by plagiarism—and by hasty accusations of plagiarism—matters, at least according to the many subsequent comments posted on the course forums and the subsidence of reports of plagiarism. For credentialing, the MOOC was imperfect, but then so are most lecture courses. For educating, it seems to have succeeded, even in ways that had not been anticipated at the outset. The suspicion of plagiarism provided one of those opportunities for education.

In my Fantasy and Science Fiction: The Human Mind, Our Modern World MOOC, those electing written work had the opportunity to submit a 270- to 320-word essay on each unit's reading, aiming to "enrich the reading of the intelligent, attentive fellow participant in the course." Each submitter then received four anonymous and randomized submissions by their fellows. Following instructions on video clips in the introductory unit that were synoptically reaffirmed in text on the web pages that presented those four essays, every submitter judged each of the writings of

(continued)

their four fellows on form and content (1 = unsuccessful; 2 = successful; 3 = outstanding) and had the opportunity to offer remarks under the headings "form," "content," and "comments in general." The grade was determined by the quality of one's writing, as judged by one's fellows (whose grades for the submissions were to fall within prescribed ranges, e.g., no more than 20% outstanding), and by one's participation, as judged by the quantity and timeliness of one's writing and evaluations. (Seven successful essay-and-response sets out of a possible ten could earn a B; nine an A). When plagiarism became an issue on the forums, I sent a message that, I am glad to say, seems to have mattered. Here is that message of August 14, 2012.

Dear Folks,

There has been some discussion about plagiarism on our forums. I would like to offer a few comments on that subject.

First, plagiarism, both legally and morally, is a variety of fraud. Claiming falsely to be the long-lost child of a recently deceased person in order to claim some of the estate is fraud; claiming falsely to be the originator of an idea in order to claim some credit for successful creation is fraud. In a course—or any intellectual community—misrepresentation of originality is unacceptable. It strikes at the heart of mutual trust, a condition one must have in order to support the deepest, freest discourse. For this reason Coursera has an honor code and I endorse it:

Coursera Honor Code

In order to ensure fairness, all students participating in any of our online classes must agree to abide by the following code of conduct:

> I will register for only one account. My answers to homework, quizzes, and exams will be my own work (except for assignments that explicitly permit collaboration).
> I will not make solutions to homework, quizzes, or exams available to anyone else. This includes both solutions written by me, as well as any official solutions provided by the course staff.
> I will not engage in any other activities that will dishonestly improve my results or dishonestly improve/hurt the results of others.

Second, precisely because plagiarism is so fundamental an attack on an intellectual community, an accusation of plagiarism is a deeply serious act and should be made only with concrete evidence behind it. An unjustified attack can be as damaging to the context of our conversation as can be the act of plagiarism itself. Both plagiarism and a careless accusation of plagiarism suggest a disrespect that we should all consider beneath us.

Third, plagiarism is hard to demonstrate for two reasons.

A. Most people don't cite sources for common knowledge. No one will think a writer is taking credit for coining the phrase "Honesty is the best policy" or the observation that Lewis Carroll enjoys creating linguistic paradoxes. The first is known to all educated native speakers of English (and we are reading and writing in English, so no one should expect a citation for that proverb) and the second should be obvious to the intelligent and attentive fellow participant in this course (and that person is our theoretical audience so, again, no citation is necessary). However, precisely because common knowledge is common and expectable in our readers, merely reporting common knowledge doesn't enrich our reading. There-fore, an essay full only of common knowledge doesn't fulfill our task. At least in content, it would earn a 1. An enriching essay needs to offer us more.

B. Good ideas often occur to more than one person at a time. Wallace and Darwin independently and nearly simultaneously articulated and promulgated the theory of evolution now known as Darwinism. Leibniz and Newton independently and nearly simultaneously articulated and promulgated what is now known as differential calculus. In reading *Dracula*, many people will notice that class structure or competitive sexuality are important. Merely noticing that does not constitute enrichment of others; however, noticing that, exploring that, and reaching conclusions about that does not inherently constitute plagiarism.

On the other hand, if you search the web for ideas about *Dracula* and find, say, a discussion of class in that novel and then present that as if it

(continued)

were your own, that is fraud; that is plagiarism; that is a violation of the Honor Code and, to my mind, more importantly, that is a violation of our mutual trust.

Why do it? Why lift someone else's idea and claim it as your own?

If you have no idea of your own and feel you need one, you might be tempted into this fraud. Don't do it. We all need to improve our ability to develop ideas; appropriating other people's ideas kills that opportunity for practice, growth, and pointed response. Ah, one might say, but I haven't time and I need the grade. Well, if you haven't time, just skip the essay. There's no requirement that each be submitted and in fact the course is structured so that you can miss one or two and still get an outstanding grade. But, one might say, I need even this essay to get that good grade. Do you really? This isn't a credit-bearing course. What will you do with a good grade other than know you've received it? Would anyone want to believe that they had received a grade by fraud rather than by accomplishment? Aren't we all here to enjoy the literature and grow together?

If you search the web and read an article that sticks with you and you inadvertently appropriate a brief phrase in your own essay, that is plagiarism. I know that one might feel wrongly accused in this case. After all, the error was accidental, not intentional. Well, folks, unfortunately, from the viewpoint of the community, that distinction is irrelevant. We have no way of knowing the motivations behind using a phrase encountered elsewhere. What we do know is that every disciplined scholar keeps track of their sources. If you are accused, with evidence, of plagiarism and feel your error was inadvertent, you should accept the unsatisfactory grade and apologize (at least in your own mind) not for plagiarism (there is no fraud by accident) but for intellectual carelessness. Learn to be more careful, maybe even in one's mind thank your accuser for catching your inadvertent mistake, and then go on in the course, looking forward to the next assignment, which you will address as a more careful scholar.

And if the plagiarism is demonstrable? If someone obviously lifts a whole paragraph, say, from another source and gives no credit, what then? Then that person should be confronted with the evidence and that person ought to consider publicly apologizing and even withdrawing from the course. If one is unwilling to support an intellectual community of mutual respect, one ought not to participate in it. If such a person cares to read the books and listen to the tapes, fine; but a plagiarist is not truly a part of our community and should not masquerade as such, asking us to read an essay as if it were truly original and asking us to respond to an essay as if the writer truly sought genuine dialog and coaching. We all deserve better than to be subjected to fraud. We owe each other honesty and, I am happy to say, that seems to be, in the enormous majority of our interactions, just what we give.

Anyway, why would one lift whole phrases, sentences, paragraphs without citation? Citation adds to your scholarly authority; it does not diminish it. True, if you say nothing more than what you have found in the work of others, you have not enriched our understanding. However, if you use the work of others to build an argument of your own, you have not only offered us the products of your thinking but of your scholarship. No one ever disparages a well-wrought argument that employs among its resources ideas and facts gathered from others.

Let me summarize. In our community, one should never commit the intellectual fraud of plagiarism, nor should one accuse someone of plagiarism simply on the basis of what might be accidental parallel efforts. However, when one does use sources other than one's own critical reading, one should cite anything that isn't common knowledge and build beyond what one has merely found. Together, with care and mutual respect, we can make our community an ever more nurturing place.

I look forward to all of us continuing to grow together.

Yours truly,

Eric Rabkin

Given the fuzziness of community norms in an online classroom, we may feel that few such standards exist. For this reason, we may work toward establishing firm expectations by way of the syllabus and ground rules for the course. We may feel that we need to be more explicit about doing so online than we would when we teach onsite.

Components of Community

While considering the structure of community is useful, so, too, are the ways in which individuals experience community. David McMillan and David Chavis's description of the key components of community is useful for highlighting the differences between the experiences of community when teaching online and onsite.[21] They identify four main areas of experience: community membership, influence, integration, and shared emotional connection.

COMMUNITY MEMBERSHIP

Membership means that individuals have invested themselves in a community and thus have earned the right to be a part of it.[22] Membership provides boundaries, which set the limits of who belongs to the community and who does not. The way participants in a group dress, the language they use, and their rituals can create a sense of boundaries. Membership gives individuals safety and security, which means that group intimacy can develop. Membership also provides individuals with a sense of belonging and identification. This characteristic is a feeling, belief, or expectation that one fits in with the group and has a place within it. It is a sense of acceptance by the group. Membership requires an individual to work for this feeling of belonging and acceptance, and membership will be more valuable because of that investment. Membership requires a system of common symbols. Understanding common symbols—which may involve a name, landmark, logo, or architectural style—is a prerequisite to understanding community.

In an onsite course, membership is established decisively and relatively quickly. It is bounded by the walls and doors of the classroom. Those on the inside are members; those on the outside are not. Members have an established sense of belonging; they have a right to be inside the walls of the classroom. Students often display common symbols, from similar styles of clothing to wearing school colors or logos, although some intentionally choose not to conform. They can also acknowledge membership and create intimacy through eye contact and nonverbal signals of agreement, such as nodding. In an online course, membership is not always as clear. The course may be taught in the open, with many people enrolling or with its content available for anyone to view. Even if courses do happen within a closed system, such as through an LMS, students do not necessarily possess the overt symbols that establish membership quickly. They often do not share course time and space, so their colors and logos are not as apparent. They do not have the same ability to acknowledge each other's membership and create intimacy within the group through nonverbal expressions; rather, they have to do so in text, such as by commenting on something a specific student has posted. Once they do establish community, however, it is based on knowing each other at an intellective level and sharing common interests. While community may not happen as quickly online, once it does happen, it has the potential to be deep and meaningful. But because of this lack of direct observations, instructors may not have a clear sense of the membership within a given community. As a result, we may feel that there is less of a community, or that we have to work harder to gauge it.

INFLUENCE IN COMMUNITIES

Influence in communities works in two ways.[23] Members of a community need to feel that they have some influence within the group. People who acknowledge others' values and options often are the most influential group members. Those who try to push themselves forward and dominate others are the least powerful members. Likewise, some influence by the group on its members is needed to create group cohesion. The influence of a member on a community and the influence of a community on a member operate concurrently. In an onsite course, individuals establish their influence quickly. The instructor may take up a position at the front of the room. Certain students may choose to sit at the front of the room, signaling their importance. Some students may raise their hands more frequently than others and thus have greater influence on the discussion than those who do not.

The group may also influence its members. If individuals in an onsite class sense a lack of participation, they may encourage others to join in, at times doing so overtly. If one student is dominating others, the group may send signals through body language or a lack of eye contact to discourage this behavior. Influence is not always established so quickly online. Rather than being the result of a front-to-back arrangement of students within a classroom, influence online comes from those individuals who are most central to the network, which is established through patterns of communication. Students in online classes often have to work harder for recognition of their place among their peers. Group members may have make greater efforts to encourage each other or discourage deviant behavior; they may handle an over-participator by ignoring his or her posts, which is not as immediate a signal as not making eye contact. Students who have operated primarily in an interpersonal world may lack the skills they need to establish and sway others and influence the group. Nonetheless, online courses can allow individuals to flourish, even if, for a variety of reasons, they might not have exerted their influence in the physical world yet. This shift can alter our experiences of community, as we see students changing places and making their mark in different ways.

INTEGRATION AND FULFILLMENT OF NEEDS

Integration and fulfillment of needs is a key element of community.[24] This characteristic involves reinforcement, where members feel rewarded in some way for their participation in the community. Reinforcement occurs through one's membership status, the success of the community, and the competence and capabilities of the other members. In an onsite course, members may receive recognition from their classmates through nonverbal behavior. For example, when a student makes a particularly good point, classmates can nod their approval. That student is recognized and thus is encouraged to participate in the future. The competence and capabilities of other students may also be assessed quickly, both through their comments and the acknowledgment given to them by their classmates. Online, however, students have to make an effort to write to another student to congratulate him or her on a point well made. Those opportunities are not often built into course design, so they are not natural and fluid, like nods. It may take a while to analyze text and gather a sense of the capabilities of others. Moreover, some students—and teachers—do not find text as rewarding as verbal and nonverbal recognition. Recognition and reinforcement online, however, are more tangible and more durable than onsite. A written response may ultimately provide more reinforcement than a nod of the head. As instructors, we may not have as much of a sense that our online students' need for community is being met, if indeed it is. If we are not aware of all the communication that is occurring, we may assume that there is less community. Thus we may try to over-structure opportunities for community in order to make up for this supposed deficit.

SHARED EMOTIONAL CONNECTION

Shared emotional connection is the "definitive element for true community."[25] It includes shared history (or at least an identification with that history) and mutual participation. If experienced to a higher degree, the following elements can even lead to shared emotional connection:

- *Contact.* The more people interact, the more likely they are to become close and establish intimacy.
- *Quality of interaction.* The more positive the experience and the relationships, the greater the bond.

- *Closure to events.* The more definite the tasks and the clearer the closure, the greater the connections groups will share. If interaction is ambiguous and tasks are left unresolved, cohesiveness will be inhibited.
- *Shared event.* The more important the shared event (e.g., a crisis) is to those involved, the greater the community bond.
- *Investment.* The more important the community's history and current status is to the members, the greater the connection (e.g., emotional or financial investment leads to more involvement).
- *Honor and humiliation.* Reward or humiliation in the presence of a community has a significant impact on the attractiveness (or adverseness) of that community to the person involved.
- *Spiritual bond / community spirit.* Positive feelings toward the group.

In an onsite course, students interact and have time to exchange ideas and information. There is a natural closure at the end of each class session. They share events, from funny ones, such as when a student has to leave class because his or her car is about to be towed, to serious ones, such as when someone has to leave class for a family crisis. They are investing time and energy with each other. In an online course, students may not have as much leisure to share ideas and information, even if they spend as much time on the interaction; it simply takes longer for most of us to type something than it does for us to say it. Often an online course is asynchronous and ongoing, without a specific end to each session. The important or pivotal events frequently are missing, are not shared, or are muted. When, however, they do occur, the emotional connections can be deep and can extend beyond the life of the course. As online instructors, we may feel as though we lack community and are missing out on the shared events; we may form poor opinions of community in an online course if we are not aware that community may still be present, but different.

Strategies for Promoting and Gauging Community in Online Courses

It can be difficult to achieve community in an online course and know whether it has developed, in part because we do not yet have a good sense of what community looks like in these courses. What we do know is that community is more than participation; it requires moving from participation to engagement, involvement, and action. Thinking through what appeals to us about other communities, whether

Developing Community in Online Courses

TODD CONAWAY
Instructional Designer
Teaching and eLearning Support
Yavapai College, US

Community has a personal investment. It is of great importance to those participating in the community, and that can be very hard to cultivate in online environments. Being personally engaged as an educator and serving as a role model—displaying commitment, drive, and care—are the first steps in developing a culture within a class that can foster a sense of community.

To me, this means that a teacher is an active learner in spaces where the students can witness that teacher behaving like a good learner. This can take place anywhere online or in physical spaces. The instructor is a cultivator of connections, and those connections to people and ideas are what need tending in order to create a community.

The use of various tools can help instructors create this type of environment, but it is not the tools themselves that will make it work. Teachers need to show that they are engaged in a community of practice in their profession and that they are contributing members, not just passive recipients of content. They publically need to share the good things they do. Likewise, they should be asking students to be contributors, not merely passive elements in the classroom.

Developing a sense of "ownership of stuff" for both instructors and students can help the class move toward a sense of mutual responsibility and community. When there is ownership, there can be the beginning of a sense of commitment and purpose that is the essence of community and the foundation for a lasting relationship with the class, the content, and the instructor.

spatial or online, can provide us with important clues about how to establish community online. Todd Conaway shares his ideas about developing community in online courses.

In addition to these suggestions, there are several steps we can take to promote community in an online course.

STRATEGY #1: PRESENT A SOCIAL PRESENCE AND HAVE STUDENTS DO SO AS WELL

Social presence is an important concept for developing community.[26] It is an individual's sense that he or she is connected to other real people, and that the reverse also applies.[27] Social presence requires being there and being seen as being there, and it is achieved through communication with others. Anecdotal information suggests that the medium of communication has an effect on social presence, which is influenced by a person's location in space and time. Face-to-face communication is thought to create the most social presence, real-time video conferencing has some social presence, and text-based communication is believed to allow the least amount of social presence. Some research, however, suggests that what the individuals do with a particular medium is more important than the media themselves.[28] There are several related factors that influence social presence: immediacy, or the psychological distance between communicators; interaction, when actions have an effect on each other; and intimacy, the notion that individuals will adjust their behaviors to maintain equilibrium.[29]

STRATEGY #2: CREATE OPPORTUNITIES FOR SHARING INFORMATION AND EXPERTISE

One factor that draws us to communities is the number of the rich resources that individuals provide. We like to be around others who are knowledgeable and from whom we can learn. Providing opportunities for students to share information is a useful tool in helping to develop community. A few options include:

- *Create study groups for the course.* Assign students to small groups. Suggest that they use the course-management system or, alternately, Google Hangout to work together. Doing so can help them learn to work in groups and make connections with their fellow students.
- *Include a "relevant resources" section for the course.* Ask students to post information happening in the outside world that is related to the course content. If students see the importance of that content, they will be more

engaged with it. Online articles, essays, YouTube clips, and so forth can add additional value. You can post in this section, as well.

- *Use a social-reading activity.* Social reading is a good way to build student collaboration and community. Social Book is an online social-reading platform that can support this activity.[30] Students annotate and comment on a book as they read it online, exchanging ideas and information along the way.
- *Use Pinterest as an information-exchange site.* Students can use Pinterest to post photos that express who they are, their responses to course material, and so forth. For example, some art instructors ask students to showcase their artwork through Pinterest.

STRATEGY #3: CREATE A SAFE CLASSROOM BY ESTABLISHING RULES AND NORMS

Students who feel they risk being shamed by other students will not engage in the classroom. Providing students with a set of rules for communication (e.g., no flaming, no put-downs, no hazing, no trolling, no dismissive responses, etc.) can help students know not only how to respond to each other, but can also give them with confidence that they may do so without fear of retribution. In addition, they might need information about netiquette.[31] Instructors can also establish guidelines to promote interaction, such as the following:

- *Participate.* Everyone is responsible for the course, and your participation is key to its success.
- *Follow the golden rule.* Treat others as you would like to be treated. This rule ensures that we are respectful of each other.
- *Don't flame / engage in personal attacks.* "Flaming" means to insult someone over the computer. In this course, no one should engage in personal attacks. All communication should be respectful and free of ridicule, condescending comments, or other disrespectful communication.
- *Don't type in ALL CAPS.* Typing in all capital letters is the equivalent of yelling online.
- *Respect other members' privacy.* Given the content of the course, some class members may share things, such as events from their lives, that may be germane to the class, but these should be considered private communications. Please note, however, that "private" does not mean confidential, as administrators have the right to review course documents.

- *Keep it PG-13.* This is a college-level course, and we are all adults. It can come back to haunt you, however, if you write something that's not appropriate. For this reason, keep communications at a level that would be appropriate for a younger audience.

Such rules can set the tone for the entire term.[32]

STRATEGY #4: CREATE COMMON SPACE

Rarely do online environments have aspects that can help students feel like they belong and create a sense of connection to the environment, as onsite ones do. Online courses rarely have common spaces equivalent to hallways, coffee shops, or quads. Thus students may not have the same opportunities to engage with those around them. Instructors can encourage a sense of communal space by designing a place for some informal interactions, such as a student lounge where discussions can take place.[33]

STRATEGY #5: USE TOOLS THAT ALLOW COMMUNITY TO FORM

Today we have a range of tools at our disposal that foster effective synchronous and asynchronous communications online. Many of the current tools listed in table 12.1 can be of use to give students opportunities to collaborate, and thus build community, in online courses.

Many learning platforms—such as Blackboard, Canvas, Desire2Learn, and Moodle—also have capabilities offering some of these tools, such as blogging, chat, web-conferencing, and wiki. Table 12.1 consists of tools that are not housed within such systems.

STRATEGY #6: USE COLLABORATIVE LEARNING

Reflecting the increase in interest about online learning and instructional approaches, several researchers have examined instructional approaches that can make a difference online. Some have studied the question of whether collaboration has a positive influence, especially in online courses. The answer is a resounding yes. In the US Department of Education's recent meta-analysis of more than two hundred studies, researchers found that the effect sizes of learning gains were larger for studies in which online instruction was collaborative or instructor-directed than in those studies where online learners worked independently.[34] Similarly, in their meta-analysis of seventy-four studies, Robert Bernard and his colleagues found that student-to-student and student-to-content interactions were

Table 12.1 Collaborative tools

Tool	Description and purpose	Sample current technologies
Bookmarks and annotation	Social-bookmarking tools are web-based means of sharing URLs, often labeling them with tags that permit organization and annotations. Social-bookmarking tools also allow students to share resources with each other	Diigo Delicious Bounce Google Bookmarks Markup/annotation tool Scribble SearchTeam (collaborative search engine)
Blog	At a fundamental level, blogs are web-sites maintained either by individuals or by groups of individuals that allow regular updating. Blogs permit users to write essay-style entries to which others may post comments. They allow students to try out new ideas and receive feedback from others	WordPress Edublogs Blogger Blackboard Collaborate
Microblogs	Microblogging is a form of blogging that is done on smaller scale. Microblogs allow users to reach others by publishing ideas in abbreviated form	Twitter Tumblr Edmodo
Discussion forums	A discussion forum is a message board intended as a discussion site in which individuals hold "conversations" in the form of posted messages. This tool allows participation through posting one's ideas in writing or by voice, connecting these ideas to others	Ning social network Yahoo groups Google groups VoiceThread Wimba Voice Facebook groups OpenStudy Blackboard Desire2Learn
Chat	Chat is the exchange of typed messages between individuals in real time	Google Chat
Instant messaging / text messaging (or texting)	Text-based synchronous communication that allows students to interact with each other immediately	Yahoo! Messenger AOL IM

Table 12.1   (continued)

Tool	Description and purpose	Sample current technologies
Email	A system for sending and receiving messages electronically over a computer network, such as between personal computers	Gmail Ymail
Voice over Internet Protocol (VoIP)	VoIP allows synchronous communication that involves video and audio. Users can see and hear each other as they talk together in real time	Skype Tinychat Gizmo5
Drawing	A drawing tool allows students to create freehand drawings in an online environment. Several tools exist in which students can collaborate remotely on drawings	CoSketch Draw it Live FlockDraw iBrainstrom Interactive Illimitably
Mind mapping	Mind-mapping tools allow users to create graphic representations that show relationships among ideas or concepts. Several tools exist in which students may collaborate on their maps in real time	MindMeister WiseMapping Mindmodo Diagram.ly Creately SpiderScribe Bubbl.us Cacoo TheBrain XTimeline Dipity Exploratree Lucidchart
Photo sharing	Photo sharing involves publishing photos online, which enables the user to share them with others	Flickr Instagram ZangZing Glogster
Presentation	Presentation tools allow users to create and host presentations online, which permits easier sharing with others. Some presentation tools, such as Prezi and Google Docs, also allow students to develop presentations together	Prezi Google Docs Zoho Show SlideRocket

(continued)

Table 12.1 (continued)

Tool	Description and purpose	Sample current technologies
Video	The term "video" means moving images and sound. While teachers have long used videos to illustrate content, many are now asking students to create and share their own videos	videos iMovie Windows live movie maker Masher Eyejot screencast videos Screencast-o-Matic Jing Camtasia animated videos Animoto Voki Blabberize distribution of videos YouTube Eyejot
Pin boards (also known as sticky-note boards, white boards, cork boards, bulletin boards)	Boards are a space for posting public messages intended to provide information. Many online boards allow real-time collaboration, drawing, and manipulation of the posted messages	Wallwisher Corkboard Popplet Pinterest Stixy.com RealtimeBoard Board 800 Conceptboard Scribblar Skrbl
Wiki documents	Wikis allow students to collaborate on a single document when they are separated by space and time. Each student can access the document, add to it, edit it, and so forth	Google Docs Tiki Wiki MediaWiki Wikispaces Sync Space Blackboard Collaborate
Social-network site	Social-network sites are websites where people can create a profile, make connections with other users, and communicate and share content	Google groups Yahoo groups Facebook groups Ning

Source: This table is adapted from Barkley, Cross, & Major (2014).

Note: Many learning platforms, such as Blackboard, Canvas, Desire2Learn, and Moodle, also have capabilities for some of these tools, such as blogging, chat, web conferencing, and wikis. The above list is composed of tools that are not housed within such systems.

more effective at producing positive learning outcomes than student-to-instructor ones.[35] In short, instructional methods are more important than technological aspects, and working and talking with other students through either discussions or collaborative projects improve student-learning outcomes in online courses.[36]

Collaborative learning requires students to work with each other, which can help reduce their feelings of isolation. In addition to simply being glad to know that others are in the same boat with them, online students appear to value interacting and forming relationships with their peers. Several research publications indicate that getting to know other learners in an online environment can improve an individual's overall experiences.[37] Moreover, students in some studies have suggested that their relationships with students in online courses were stronger than those in onsite courses.[38] These relationships form the basis of positive student experiences, and online collaborative learning provides a solid foundation on which to establish them. Collaborative learning techniques, such as Jigsaw, Collaborative Writing, and Paper Seminar, can be particularly effective in an online environment.[39]

Conclusion

The shifts in our views of what community is and what it does, occasioned by the development of communication technologies, have implications for teaching online. While community is ultimately a shared responsibility, instructors are responsible for creating opportunities that allow community to happen in an online environment. Accomplishing the elusive goal of planting the seeds from which a strong community can grow requires a combination of encouragement, patience, and the use of appropriate activities and tools. Developing a solid community in an online course is important not only for the students, but also for our own experiences with teaching online.

Conclusion

The future is already here—it's just not very evenly distributed.
—WILLIAM GIBSON

In higher education, we have a long history and culture,[1] an interlocking of the beliefs and values inherent in the system itself, of specific institutions, and of individuals who surround and populate the academy. The underlying ideals of academe are shared by its constituent members and often are represented by and communicated through a range of rites, rituals, symbols, artifacts, and so forth. Constituents use these ideals in a number of ways, such as establishing and conveying a sense of identity, communicating what we stand for, improving stability, and guiding sense-making.[2] Thus in higher education our ideals and values are important; they drive decisions and actions, and they are manifested in cultural products.

Likewise, there are many views about technology and culture.[3] Technology is designed within a cultural context and is a cultural artifact or expression; it is not separate from but rather is a representation of culture. Even so, there are some common values across technological tools. These may be instrumental (e.g., efficiency, reliability, ease of use), but they may also be social, ethical, or political (e.g., equality, openness, distribution). Such features may or may not express the values of a given culture and may work toward their own ends. That is, they are unique to technology itself, as a cultural form of its own; therefore the tools we select hold their own forms of values and intentions.

The values implicit in the technologies that we use for teaching online can come in conflict with those we hold dear in higher education, such as history and tradition. Technological tools imply innovation. In higher education, we prize the theoretical and the methodological. Technology comprises the logical and the practical. In higher education, we value individualism and autonomy. Technology supports system developments, constant connectivity, collective knowledge, and mass culture. It favors practicality and efficiency. Thus, as we attempt to integrate technology into higher education, our ideals from these two domains can be somewhat at odds with each other, creating a cultural dynamic that simultaneously favors and resists change.

The concept of disruptive innovation is useful in understanding the dynamic that occurs when a sector with values, such as higher education, is met with a technological innovation that can change the services the former provides. In introducing the term "disruptive innovations" in the late 1990s, Harvard business professor Clayton Christensen argues that a technologically driven innovation can create a new market and a different value network while disrupting existing ones.[4] This type of innovation is thought to improve a product or service in unexpected ways, first by expanding access to new consumers and then by lowering prices. Technologies are simultaneously creative and destructive, and the effects of their disruptions have possible repercussions. On the one hand, they can hurt successful and well-managed companies. On the other, if the disruptions are constructive, they can lead toward improved economic benefits, once their systemic benefits are understood and accepted.

Christensen has recently argued that online learning is a potentially disruptive innovation in higher education.[5] The technologies used for online courses certainly have the features of a disruptive innovation. They can help instruction that typically has been available only to a limited few reach a broader audience. Such technologies make instruction more convenient, and they have the potential to make it less expensive. Online learning seems to be gaining a market share. The growth of this instructional form, which was nearly 30% in 2009 and on the rise (see chapter 1), is evidence not only of its capacity for but also its increasing likelihood of creating disruption.

Some scholars agree with Christensen in believing the stage is set for a disruption of higher education. They see a convergence of forces—including budget cuts to higher education, rising tuition, record debt levels for student loans, and increased demand—that suggest a need for change, which can come about through online learning. They anticipate—and look forward to—a disruption, or revolution. Thomas Friedman, a journalist for the *New York Times*, makes this argument when describing several new providers of online learning:[6]

Welcome to the college education revolution. Big breakthroughs happen when what is suddenly possible meets what is desperately necessary. The costs of getting a college degree have been rising faster than those of health care, so the need to provide low-cost, quality higher education is more acute than ever. At the same time, in a knowledge economy, getting a higher-education degree is more vital than ever. And thanks to the spread of high-speed wireless technology, high-speed Internet, smartphones, Facebook, the cloud, and tablet computers, the world has gone from connected to hyperconnected in just seven years. Finally, a generation that has grown up on these technologies is increasingly comfortable learning and interacting with professors through online platforms. . . . When you consider how many problems around the world are attributable to the lack of education, that is very good news. Let the revolution begin.

Friedman later writes:[7]

LORD knows there's a lot of bad news in the world today to get you down, but there is one big thing happening that leaves me incredibly hopeful about the future, and that is the budding revolution in global online higher education. Nothing has more potential to lift more people out of poverty—by providing them an affordable education to get a job or improve in the job they have. Nothing has more potential to unlock a billion more brains to solve the world's biggest problems.

Other scholars are more cautious about welcoming the revolution. David Brooks, also a *New York Times* journalist, describes this potential change as a "campus tsunami" and considers possible problematic issues with online learning:[8]

Many of us view the coming change with trepidation. Will online learning diminish the face-to-face community that is the heart of the college experience? Will it elevate functional courses in business and marginalize subjects that are harder to digest in an online format, like philosophy? Will fast online browsing replace deep reading?

If a few star professors can lecture to millions, what happens to the rest of the faculty? Will academic standards be as rigorous? What happens to the students who don't have enough intrinsic motivation to stay glued to their laptop hour after hour? How much communication is lost—gesture, mood, eye contact—when you are not actually in a room with a passionate teacher and students?

In either case, a growing number of scholars see online learning as having the potential to create significant change.

As is evident in the quotations from these two journalists, the predictions of disruption are wide ranging, and it is easy to weigh them according to their possible advantages and disadvantages. Such predictions include discussions about the unbundling of higher education: breaking it into smaller parts, and perhaps allowing students to assemble credits from several different institutions to construct a degree. That means taking the diploma, which is a certification of completion, out of the hands of the higher education institutions that long have held a monopoly on it. Such a change may hold certain advantages for students, but questions about what a college degree really means challenge this assumption. Likewise, disruption may reduce the cost of a college degree for students and families, which, as Friedman notes, clearly could be an advantage. But what happens when students who can afford it receive onsite instruction, while those who cannot receive the online version? There also are predictions about what such a disruption could mean for faculty members' roles and responsibilities. The idea of sharing ideas and information with a wider student population may well hold some appeal, although the idea that the professoriate may change probably does not. Potential shifts could involve a growing reliance on contract-based rather than tenured or tenure-track faculty, or, as Brooks argues, an unbundling of faculty responsibilities, with the creation of course content is done by a select few, while others are relegated merely to grading papers.

As we decide whether and how to teach online, faculty should be mindful of the implications of online learning for students, for institutions, for the system, and for ourselves. Whether we acknowledge it or not, we are agents of change. Our practices have the potential to influence the system of higher education. When we teach online, we signal our buy-in to a new form of higher education and all of the issues that attend it. We challenge tradition, embrace a new learning environment, alter patterns of faculty work, and participate in what could be a disruption in the current system of higher education. For better or for worse, when we teach online, we endorse and participate in such change.

Notes

Introduction

1. A key characteristic of synthesis is the use of explicit search strategies, with the researcher providing a clear account of the hunt for and selection of relevant evidence so such strategies may be reproduced. I began my search for studies by framing one broad research question: how do faculty experience online teaching? This question allowed me to cast a wide initial net. I then explored online databases, such as the Educational Resources Information Center (ERIC), Academic Search Elite, and Google Scholar, and hand-searched the table of contents sections of several key journals as well as bibliographies of relevant articles. I adhered to a set of decision-making criteria to select articles based on their content and scope (faculty as participants in the study), timeframe (1998–present), report type (research and evaluation reports), and educational level (postsecondary, higher education, and two-year institutions).

2. For examples of my work investigating instructional change, see B. Palmer & Major (2007); Savin-Baden & Major (2007); Major (2006); Major & Palmer (2006).

3. For examples of my work giving faculty advice about instructional change, see Barkely, Cross, & Major (2014) and Savin-Baden & Major (2004).

4. For some of my publications about teaching online, see Blackmon & Major (2012); Major (2010); Bray, Harris, & Major (2007); E. Gibbs, Major, & Wright (2003).

5. For more information about Pedagogy First, the open online course concerning teaching online, see http://pedagogyfirst.org/wppf12/.

6. For my publications related to research synthesis, see Major & Savin-Baden (2010, 2011a, 2011b).

1. Teaching Online as Instructional Change

1. Heydenrych & Prinsloo (2010, pp. 8–9) describe the development of distance learning as an evolution. The following are models of distance-learning evolution that they review.

Moore & Kearsley (2005): *First generation*: correspondence—single medium (print)—mass production of technology—correspondence; *second generation*: radio and television broadcasting; *third generation*: combined approach—correspondence assisted by broadcasting (open universities); *fourth generation*: telelearning—interactive audio/video conferencing; *fifth generation*: online delivery—multimedia interactive content with online communication and support.

Lauzon & Moore (1989): *First generation*: correspondence—single medium (print)—mass production of content; *second generation*: teleconferencing—audio—communications network—synchronous; *third generation*: multimedia and computer-assisted learning—

interaction with content; *fourth generation*: Internet / World Wide Web (WWW)—students sharing collective intelligence.

Guglielmo (1998): *First generation*: correspondence—single medium (print)—mass production of content; *second generation*: multimedia and computer-assisted learning—interaction with content; *third generation*: group communication—Internet/WWW communication technologies.

J. Taylor (1995, 2001): *First generation*: correspondence—single medium (print)—mass production of content; *second generation*: teleconferencing—audio—communications network—synchronous; *third generation*: multimedia and computer-assisted learning—interaction with content; *fourth generation*: flexible learning via online delivery—communication enhanced online; *fifth generation*: intelligent flexible learning—automated content and responses and campus portals.

2. I. Allen & Seaman (2014) have one of the most extensive reports of the enrollment growth of online learning to date.

3. The Sloan Foundation findings about institutional offerings of online courses corresponds to those in a study by P. Taylor et al. (2011) conducted by the Pew Research Center. Researchers in this study found that 77% of the respondents (college presidents) indicated that their colleges offer online classes.

4. I. Allen & Seaman (2014) also detail administrator perceptions of the importance of online learning.

5. I. Allen & Seaman (2014) report administrator predictions about the future of online learning.

6. Findings from this study about faculty participation in online learning (I. Allen & Seaman, 2014) correspond to other studies, which also indicate that a growing number of faculty are beginning to teach online. Lederman & Jaschik (2013), for example, conducted a study with 2,251 faculty members. Their findings support those of J. Seaman's (2009) earlier study of more than 11,000 faculty, which indicated that by fall 2008, just over one-third (34.4%) had taught a course online and nearly one-quarter (23.6%) of all faculty were teaching one course online at that time.

7. Everett Rogers was a professor of rural sociology and an influential author. Rogers (1962/1983) is well known for his work outlining the adoption of innovations. Rogers's theory explains how, why, and at what rate new technologies spread through cultures. In his seminal work, *Diffusion of innovations,* he describes the process of innovation as communications that take place among members of a social system. The members join at different rates, beginning with innovators, moving to early adopters, then early majority, then late majority, and finally laggards. Four elements influence the rate and success of adoption: the innovation itself, communication channels, time, and the social system. According to Rogers, the innovation must have widespread adoption in order to become self-sustaining. Rogers suggests that it takes 25% of the adoptions by individuals to reach a "tipping point" of acceptance.

8. Verbeek (2000/2005), Mitcham (1994), and Ihde (1979, 1991) discuss the notion of technological mediation.

9. See Heidegger (1927).

10. See Ihde (1991).

11. The Paik (n.d.) quote offers a vision of how technology stands between us and reality.

12. Ihde (1991) frames his human/technology relations in philosophical terms: background relations, embodiment relations, hermeneutical relations, and alterity. I use more practical phrases to classify the relationships Ihde describes: technology as context, as an extension of selves, as a lens of interpretation, and as a human-like interface.

13. *Chronicle of Higher Education* reporter Jeffery Young (2009) describes a suggestion by José A. Bowen, dean of the Meadows School of the Arts, to teach without any machines, or naked.

14. In chapter 4, I describe three learning paths: centralized, decentralized, and distributed.

15. Veletsianos & Russell (2014) have conducted an impressive literature review on pedagogical agents.

16. Ihde (1979, 1991) provides extensive discussions about technological mediation.

17. Ihde (1990) describes the intentionality of technology.

18. McCaffrey (2012) offers an example of functional fixedness related to the *RMS Titanic* (people overlooked the fact that the iceberg could have served as a lifeboat). His post is available at the Harvard Business Review blog, http://blogs.hbr.org/cs/2012/05 /overcoming_functional_fixednes.html.

19. Gabriel (2008) argues that PowerPoint has fundamentally changed the lecture and that it can continue to do so by challenging the traditional model of the authority of the lecturer and drawing more on its multimedia capacities.

20. Verbeek (2006), Akrich (1992), and Latour (1992) provide extensive discussions about technological intentions.

21. Verbeek (2006), Akrich (1992), and Latour (1992) discuss the concepts of technological invitation and inhibition, or scripts. The quotation about scripts is from Verbeek (2006, p. 366).

22. Lane (2009) argues that learning management systems are drivers of pedagogical actions.

23. McLuan & Fiore (1967) and McLuhan (1964) declare that "the medium is the message" (sometimes spelled "message" and sometimes "massage" in McLuhan's publications), indicating that technology is a contributor to meaning.

24. Feenberg's (2002) factory and city models suggest two divergent views of technological learning initiatives.

25. Zuboff (1988) suggests that technology may change jobs in two ways: by automating or by "informating"; the former is positive and the latter, negative.

26. Panda & Mishra's (2007) and Parker's (2003) studies show that intellectual challenge is important to faculty when they decide to teach online.

27. Parker's (2003) study suggests that faculty can be incentivized to teach online.

28. Tomei (2006), Newton (2003), Pachnowski & Jurczyk (2003), and Wolcott (2003) have conducted studies suggesting that the perception of increased teaching time can be a deterrent to a faculty member's decision to teach online.

29. I. Allen & Seaman (2007) and Welker & Berardino (2005) have conducted studies that suggest that faculty may see course quality as a deterrent to teaching online.

30. DiRamio & Kops's (2004) study suggests that issues with intellectual property may be a deterrent to teaching online.

31. Kotze & Dreyer's (2002) study suggests that a lack of perceived value in promotion and tenure decisions could be a deterrent to teaching online.

32. Jamlan's (2004) and Grenzky & Maitland's (2001) studies show that providing educational access is important to faculty and is one reason why they choose to teach online.

33. L. Christianson, Tiene, & Luft's (2002) study indicates that some faculty choose to teach online for improved communications with faculty. Pachnowski & Jurcyzk's (2003), Parker's (2003), and Wolcott's (2003) studies suggest that some faculty teach online because they believe it will improve their teaching.

2. Faculty Knowledge

1. Professors who appear in films share several demographic characteristics, which have implications for our views of what a professor is and does. Such a discussion is generally beyond the scope of this book; however, I do address some issues related to technology and physical markers in chapter 8.

2. This question about the distinction between content and pedagogy is from Shulman (1986, p. 6).

3. This quotation about the distinction between content and pedagogical knowledge is from Shulman (1986, p. 8).

4. This quotation about pedagogical content knowledge is from Shulman (1987, pp. 9–10).

5. Zuboff (1988) calls skills such as abstraction "intellective skills."

6. See Van Manen (1991, p. 31) for a discussion of pedagogy and phenomenology.

7. Friesen (2011) describes how individuals learn online. He also makes a contribution in a sidebar to chapter 8.

8. This quotation about virtual artifacts is from Friesen (2011, p. 111).

9. Faculty can feel ill-equipped to take on the challenges of teaching online, in large part due to their lack of knowledge about it. In examining what factors might encourage or discourage faculty from teaching with Internet-enabled technology, several educational researchers have surveyed faculty about their perceptions. They found that faculty believe their knowledge of how to use available technologies and their knowledge of teaching with those technologies are among the primary factors influencing their willingness to adopt technology (e.g., Koehler, Mishra, & Yahya, 2007; Butler & Sellbom, 2002). In many of the studies, the results were weighted negatively; in short, faculty in these studies, most of whom are teaching online, generally do not feel that they have adequate preparation or knowledge for carrying out the work (e.g., Gahungu, Dereshiwsky, & Moan, 2006).

10. Herschback (1995) describes technology as knowledge and discusses the implications of this concept for instruction.

11. This quotation about knowledge and technology is from Landies (1980, p. 111).

12. Mesthene (1979) describes the concept of technical knowledge.

13. Herschback (1995) describes the notion of technology as knowledge and its implications for instruction.

14. Herschback (1995) also discusses technological knowledge.

15. Shulman (1986, 1987, 1991) describes his concepts of faculty knowledge across several different publications.

16. The authors describe TPACK more fully on their website, at www.tcpk.org, and in several publications, such as Koehler & Mishra (2009) and Mishra & Koehler (2006).

17. The diagram is available at www.tcpk.org.

18. Faculty may well appreciate the opportunity to participate in workshops, seminars, and other formal training, and faculty development and training improve attitudes toward online technology (e.g., Panda & Mishra, 2007; J. Lee & Busch, 2005; Kotze & Dreyer, 2002). Educational researchers have also suggested that improved knowledge in some areas boosted the likelihood of their adoption (see Dempsey et al., 2008). For example, an extensive prior use of computers and communications technology influences the likelihood of teachers attempting online distance technology (Walker & Johnson, 2008; Panda & Mishra, 2007). Self-efficacy in the use of technological tools is also a factor that influences their adoption (Parker, 2003).

19. Koehler & Mishra (2005a) surveyed master's degree students / in-service teachers to measure their technological knowledge, pedagogical knowledge, and content knowledge individually as well as in relation to each other. The researchers found that over time, the students/teachers began to demonstrate more interrelated knowledge (TPACK). Similarly, Koehler, Mishra, & Yahya (2007) used discourse analysis to study the conversations with master's students who were developing online courses. The researchers coded statements as content (CK), pedagogy (PK), technology (TK), or other (O). They found that early in the semester, knowledge areas were more discrete, while at the end of the semester, they were more interrelated. Thus technological pedagogical content knowledge develops over time.

20. Additional information about Pedagogy First is available at www.pedagogyfirst .org.

21. A. Seaman's (2013) blog post, at www.hybridpedagogy.com/Journal/files/Personal _Learning_Networks.html, provides a useful description of personal learning networks.

22. Shulman (1987) discusses his notion of the wisdom of practice.

23. Shulman (1987) describes the importance of documenting the wisdom of practice to overcome the amnesia that can otherwise accompany one's teaching practices.

24. Chickering & Gamson (1987) describe their principles of good practice.

25. Chickering & Ehrmann (1996) provide information about good practices as they relate to technology.

26. See Puzziferro & Shelton (2009).

27. There are at least two different categories of "good" practices. Evidence-based practices are those that have been proven effective by way of extensive empirical research and evaluation. Evidence-based practices traditionally rely on randomized controlled trials and, at times, on quasi-experimental designs, with the participants in controlled and experimental designs compared for changes in outcomes. Scholars have begun to see the importance of other forms of information as well, including data from survey-based research and qualitative case studies, to provide insights into people's experiences as well as information on why and how things might be working, such as in Meyer's sidebar.

28. Such portfolios focus on the course, rather than on teaching per se. They tend to address a specific question (e.g., the influence of the instructor's stance on student

perceptions of presence). A course portfolio requires the collection of data and an interpretation of these data. A course portfolio often contains a syllabus as well as a list of support materials and assignments, annotated with the instructor's reflections on what went well and what could be improved. It may also contain samples of students' performances and teacher reflections.

3. Views of Learning

1. The Mobile Learning Network defined M-learning as "the exploitation of ubiquitous handheld technologies, together with wireless and mobile phone networks, to facilitate, support, enhance, and extend the reach of teaching and learning. Learners involved may or may not be mobile. Learning can take place in any location, and at any time, including traditional learning environments, such as classrooms, as well as other locations including the workplace, at home, community locations, and in transit" (cited in Traxler, 2009, p. 2).

2. Bonk (2009) describes the concept of open learning.

3. Malcolm, Hodkinson, & Colley (2003) describe nonformal learning.

4. Schugurensky (2000) describes various types of informal learning.

5. I discuss MOOCs further in chapter 4.

6. Williams, Mackness, & Gumtau (2012) provide a useful description of the concept of emergent learning.

7. Sharples et al. (2012) provides an overview of Cormier's notion of rhizomatic learning.

8. Thomas & Brown (2011) outline their conception of the three kinds of learning.

9. Thomas & Brown (2011) argue that play is important for learning.

10. Freire (1972) was the first to outline the concept of a banking model of education.

11. Nowotny, Scott, & Gibbons (2001) describe socially accountable learning.

12. Only a few of the more recent studies have used experimental or controlled conditions (Zhao et al., 2005; Bernard et al., 2004; Anglin & Morrison, 2000), evidence that is well illustrated by two meta-analyses. Means et al. (2009) found only 176 studies that used random assignments or controlled quasi-experimental designs to compare learning outcomes between online and offline instruction. Because many of the 176 studies lacked sufficient methodological detail, researchers could only include 45 empirical research studies in their meta-analysis, and just 28 of these studies were purely of online courses (as opposed to blended or hybrid courses). Sitzmann et al. (2006), as part of a meta-analysis of 96 studies that compared web-based instruction with traditional classroom instruction, identified only 11 studies that used a true experimental design. These meta-analyses provide evidence of the low number of carefully designed and controlled research studies in the field of online learning. Some scholars suggest that merely a few studies are grounded in theory (Mishra & Koehler, 2006; Anglin & Morrison, 2000; Saba, 2000; Phipps & Merisotis, 1999; McIsaac & Gunawardena, 1996), although from my review of the research, it seems to me that scholars are beginning to address this deficit, as many new studies have a strong theoretical grounding.

13. Recent meta-analytic and research reviews suggest that the learning outcomes for online students are at least equivalent (Tallent-Runnels et al., 2006; Bernard et al., 2004;

M. Allen et al., 2002) and may be superior to (Means et al., 2009) those of classroom students.

14. The "no significant difference" bibliography is available at www.nosignificant difference.org/.

15. While there is a certain amount of compelling evidence to support the "no significant difference" finding, some educators argue that online learning is not as effective as onsite learning. Many of these have questioned the "no significant difference" research itself, raising issues from whether the studies were rigorous to whether they asked the right question. Criticisms of the "no significant difference" phenomenon can be found at www.educause.edu/EDUCAUSE+Review/EDUCAUSEReviewMagazineVolume41 /TheMythaboutNoSignificantDiffe/158103/.

16. Means et al. (2009) is the US Department of Education study referenced in this chapter, with this quotation from p. ix.

17. For most of us, the term "significant" means something akin to "important." To social science researchers within the context of statistics, it means "not likely to be due to chance."

18. This quotation is from Means et al. (2009, p. xv).

19. Several researchers have documented that online learning is an effective way to offer instruction. For example, see Bernard et al. (2009); Gunawardena & McIsaac (2004); Lockee, Moore, & Burton (2001); Clark (2000).

20. See New Media Consortium (2012). M. Brown (2012, p. 1) provides a useful description of learning analytics.

21. Several researchers have documented how learning analytics are providing answers to new questions. For example, see Liu, MacIntyre, & Ferguson (2012) for a study gauging the effectiveness of e-mentoring; V. Smith, Lange, & Huston (2012) for a study of analytics and identifying at-risk students; and Kop (2011) for a study of learner experiences in a MOOC.

22. Dringus (2012) has urged caution in relying on learning analytics.

23. For studies suggesting that some faculty believe course quality can be higher online, see Hartman, Dziuban, & Moskal (2000); National Education Association (2000).

24. Fredericksen et al. (2000) found that 45% of faculty felt their online students performed better than their classroom students did, and about 44% thought there was no difference.

25. J. Seaman (2009); I. Allen & Seaman (2007); Gahungu, Dereshiwsky, & Moan (2006); Welker & Berardino (2005); Hartman, Dziuban, & Moskal (2000); Hislop & Atwood (2000); and the National Education Association (2000) have documented faculty concerns about course quality.

26. The survey of faculty opinions is by J. Seaman (2009).

27. In an extensive review of the literature on learning styles, Pashler et al. (2008) found evidence that students do have learning styles or learning preferences, but they discovered no evidence to suggest that matching teaching approaches to learning styles improves learning outcomes.

28. Many of these learning-styles inventories are available online. See, for example, Grasha-Reichmann, at www.longleaf.net/teachingstyle.html; Solomon and Felder's index,

at www.engr.ncsu.edu/learningstyles/ilsweb.html; VARK, at www.vark-learn.com/english /index.asp.

29. For a sample philosophy-of-learning statement, see the blog entry at http:// teachpaperless.blogspot.com/2011/01/philosophy-of-learning.html.

4. Course Structure

1. Traditional online courses have been around since at least the mid-1980s. As of 1985, Nova Southeastern University was awarding degrees based on online courses (http://scis .nova.edu/admissions/faq.html). Online courses began to gain popularity in the mid- to late 1990s with the increased availability of personal computers and greater access to the Internet.

2. Watters (2012) identifies Cormier as the individual who coined the term "MOOC." Also, Cormier acknowledges having team taught one of the first courses dubbed a MOOC (www.xedbook.com).

3. More information about the connectivist MOOC 2012 is available at http://cck12 .mooc.ca/index.html.

4. Siemens (2012) names and identifies the differences in these two forms of MOOCs.

5. I provide additional information about the notion of connectivism in chapter 3.

6. Dave Cormier's take on MOOCs is available online in his "What is a MOOC?" presentation, at www.youtube.com/watch?v=eW3gMGqcZQc&feature=youtu.be/.

7. Thurn has recently announced a pivot, as Udacity is moving more toward vocational training. More information about this shift is available in Chalkin (2013).

8. Margaret Soltan's poetry MOOC (see chapter 1 for her description of the reasons for teaching them), Eric Rabkin's science fiction MOOC (see chapter 12 for his discussion of the issues of plagiarism and peer review), and Chuck Eesley's entrepreneurship MOOC (see chapter 1 for his description of using teamwork in a MOOC) all have high levels of student interaction and collaborative work.

9. Carey (2012) argues that online courses have the potential to provide access.

10. Carlson & Blumenstyk (2012) argue that MOOCs will contribute to the stratification of higher education.

11. Friedman (2012, 2013) argues that open online courses will revolutionize higher education.

12. Freedman (2013) argues that MOOCs will not challenge or change higher education greatly and, at best, will provide what amounts to educational outreach.

13. See I. Allen & Seaman (2007).

14. More information about Blackboard is available at www.blackboard.com.

15. More information about Desire2Learn is available at www.desire2learn.com.

16. More information about Moodle is available at https://moodle.org.

17. More information about Canvas is available at www.instructure.com.

18. "Web Course in the Box," which was developed in the mid-1990s, was among the first learning management systems.

19. More information about Coursera is available at https://www.coursera.org.

20. More information about EdX is available at https://www.edx.org.

21. More information about Udacity is available at www.udacity.com.

22. More information about Venture Lab is available at https://novoed.com.

23. More information about WordPress is available at http://wordpress.org.

24. More information about EduBlogs is available at http://edublogs.org.

25. More information about Blogger is available at www.blogger.com.

26. More information about Twitter is available at https://twitter.com.

27. More information about Tumblr is available at https://www.tumblr.com.

28. Rheingold's *Net smart*, published in 2012, is an excellent introduction to the skills individuals need to successfully navigate the Internet.

29. While multiuser dungeons (MUDs) were developed in the 1970s and fully graphical MUDs were developed in the 1990s, as were massively multiplayer online games (MMOGs), the 3D technologies that enabled multiuser virtual environments (MUVEs) have taken hold as an important platform for immersive online courses.

30. More information about Second Life is available at www.secondlife.com.

31. More information about Activeworlds is available at www.activeworlds.com.

32. More information about OpenSimulator is available at http://opensimulator.org /wiki/Main_Page.

33. Duncan, Miller, & Jiang (2012) provide a taxonomy of virtual-world usage in education.

34. I describe community more fully in chapter 12.

35. If course conversations can happen in Facebook, on Twitter, on Google Hangout, and other potential places, a student who misses a Google Hangout opportunity may feel that he or she has lost out on an important part of the conversation. Likewise, a student who does not regularly follow his or her Twitter feed may feel like he or she has missed important discussions.

36. C.-Y. Lee et al. (2012) describe different institutional approaches that dictate the level of autonomy faculty have when making decisions about online courses.

5. Course Planning

1. Additional examples of commonly adopted instructional design models include the 4C-ID model (Jeroen van Merriënboer), algo-heuristic theory (Lev Landa), the ASSURE model (Robert Heinich, Michael Molenda, James Russell, & Sharon Smaldino), conditions of learning theory (Robert Gagné), component display theory (M. David Merrill), criterion referenced instruction (Robert Mager), the Dick and Carey model (Walter Dick & Lou Carey), elaboration theory (Charlie Reigeluth), the Gerlach-Ely model (Vernon Gerlach & Donald Ely), the Hannafin-Peck model (Michael Hannafin & Kyle Peck), the Knirk and Gustafson model (Frederick Knirk & Kent Gustafson), instructional systems design (ISD), the integrative learning design framework for online learning (Nada Dabbagh, the spiral model (Barry Boehm), rapid prototyping (Steven Tripp & Barbara Bichelmeyer), the Kemp design model (Gary Morrison, Steven Ross, & Jerrold Kemp), and the organizational elements model (OEM) (Roger Kaufman).

2. I provide further information about cognitivism as a learning theory in chapter 2.

3. As faculty, we typically make decisions about goals and objectives, but many institutions, colleges, departments, and programs have some structures already in place.

4. Paulson (2002) states that there are several distinct areas of responsibility within a faculty member's instructional role: design, development, delivery, mediation, assessment, and management. These, Paulson asserts, may be covered in new ways, particularly

in virtual settings, as is done in for-profit institutions like Western Governors University and the University of Phoenix. She makes recommendations for reducing instructional costs, such as using teaching professionals in the same manner as undergraduate teaching assistants, to replace "expensive labor" with "cheap labor" (p. 133). She also suggests that with online learning, faculty could focus on content, while instructional-development officers could translate subject matter into instructional materials.

5. See chapter 6 for a further discussion about ownership issues.

6. A *goal* is a broad statement about what students will accomplish (e.g., students will learn problem solving). An *objective* is a narrower statement than a goal and specifies what students will do that can be measured (e.g., students will perform the following steps when presented with a problem: identify the central question or issue, identify what they know about it, identify what they require to solve the problem).

7. Many institutions use student-readiness assessments, such as the University System of Georgia's Student Online Readiness Tool (SORT), at www.occc.edu/OnlineResources /sort/html/tool.html; the Penn State Learning Design Community Hub's Online Readiness Self-Assessment, at http://ets.tlt.psu.edu/learningdesign/assessment/onlinecontent /online_readiness/; and the San Diego Community College District's Online Learning Pathways, at www.sdccdonline.net/assess.htm.

8. Angelo & Cross's (1993) classic text, *Classroom assessment techniques*, is a useful resource for those who wish to use classroom assessment.

9. The limited amount research that has been done has produced mixed findings about faculty experiences with assessment. Some faculty interviewed for qualitative studies have indicated that assessment is an ongoing and natural part of the process of online teaching. Others, however, have noted that the opposite is true, indicating that assessment becomes more rote and less intuitive. Faculty members interviewed in qualitative studies frequently have noted differences in online and face-to-face ways to gauge learning; at times they seemed to value the former. See, for example, Pallof & Pratt (2008); Conceição (2006): Comeaux (2004).

10. Many of the models also include identifying materials as a factor in instructional design. I discuss materials in chapter 6.

11. Dave Cormier describes the concept of the rhizomes in chapter 3.

12. Singham (2007) argues that we should eliminate the syllabus.

13. Some institutions, however, make the decisions about the technology that faculty will use to teach online.

14. Vai & Sosulski (2011) provide a full description of design.

15. The Grasha-Reichmann teaching-style survey, at www.longleaf.net/teachingstyle .html, is a useful tool for helping faculty understand the different preferences faculty may have as teachers.

16. A teaching-philosophy statement is a narrative that typically contains a description of the professor's view of teaching, a description of the way the professor teaches, and a justification of why one teaches in a given way. The University of Iowa's Center for Teaching Excellence contains a useful description of teaching-philosophy statements, at www .celt.iastate.edu/teaching/philosophy.html.

17. The design process involving inspiration, ideation, and implementation is a well-known form of design thinking, as described in T. Brown & Wyatt (2010).

18. Figure 5.1 is reprinted with permission of the developer of the model, Ruben R. Puentedura.

6. Intellectual Property

1. Copyright protects forms of expression (e.g., prose, poetry, art, music, photographs); it does not protect ideas, logos, slogans, or works in the public domain. To date, the terms of copyright extend to the life of the author plus seventy years (see the US copyright law and related laws contained in title 17 of the United States Code, at www.copyright.gov /title17/92chap3.html).

2. This definition of copyright is from 17 USC, section 106.

3. This quotation about the moment that copyright is fixed is from 17 USC, section 102.

4. I am not a lawyer; thus this chapter should be viewed as a discussion of an educational issue, rather than as a document providing legal advice.

5. This quotation is from the Policy and Global Affairs National Research Council (2002) report.

6. For additional information about course readers, see Evans & Willinsky (2013).

7. The doctrine of fair use indicates that "the fair use of a copyrighted work, including such use by reproduction in copies or phonorecords or by any other means specified by that section [of the USC], for purposes such as criticism, comment, news reporting, teaching (including multiple copies for classroom use), scholarship, or research, is not an infringement of copyright" (17 USC, section 107).

8. Additional information about the statutory factors of fair use may be found in 17 USC, section 107.

9. With online learning, litigation of copyright infringement in online courses has become more common. In 2008, for example, several publishers (Cambridge University Press, Oxford University Press, and Sage Publications) sued four faculty members at Georgia State University for the "systematic, widespread, and unauthorized copying and distribution of a vast amount of copyrighted works . . . through a variety of online systems and outlets utilized and hosted by the University for the digital distribution of course reading material" (*Cambridge University Press et al. v. Patton et al.*, 2008). While the court rejected most of the allegations, it did find that the plaintiffs' copyrights were violated.

10. The fair-use guidelines for educational multimedia are:

- Students may incorporate others' works into their multimedia creations and perform and display them for academic assignments.
- Faculty may incorporate others' works into their multimedia creations to produce curriculum materials for educational use. (Note: Faculty may retain these multimedia products incorporating the copyrighted works of others for a period of two years. After that, permission must be sought.)
- Faculty may provide for multimedia products using copyrighted works to be accessible at a distance (i.e., distance learning), provided that only those students may access the material.
- Faculty may demonstrate their multimedia creations at professional symposia and retain the same in their own portfolios.

- For motion media (e.g., video clips), use is limited to 10% or three minutes, whichever is less.
- For text, use is limited to 10% or 1,000 words, whichever is less.
- For poems, use is limited to 250 words, three poems per poet, and five poems by different poets from an anthology.
- For music, use is limited to 10% or thirty seconds, whichever is less.
- For photos and images, use is limited to five works from one creator and 10% or fifteen works, whichever is less, from a collection.
- For database information, use is limited to 10% or 2,500 fields or cell entries, whichever is less.

This information is also cited in Ko & Rossen (2010); the University of South Carolina's library page, at www.sc.edu/beaufort/library/pages/liblink/fairuse.shtml; Ithaca College's website, at www.ithaca.edu/policies/vol2/volume_2-232/; and elsewhere.

11. Section 101 of the Copyright Act (title 17 of the US Code) defines a "work made for hire" in two parts (see www.copyright.gov/circs/circ09.pdf):

a. a work prepared by an employee within the scope of his or her employment
or
b. a work specially ordered or commissioned for use
   1. as a contribution to a collective work,
   2. as a part of a motion picture or other audiovisual work,
   3. as a translation,
   4. as a supplementary work,
   5. as a compilation,
   6. as an instructional text,
   7. as a test,
   8. as answer material for a test, or
   9. as an atlas,
if the parties expressly agree in a written instrument signed by them that the work shall be considered a work made for hire.

12. See the *Works made for hire* web document (p. 2), at www.copyright.gov/circs/circ09.pdf.

13. The information about part-time employees comes from Levy (2003).

14. The copyright protection for work made for hire is 95 years from date of publication or 120 years from date of creation, whichever comes first (www.copyright.gov/circs/circ09.pdf).

15. Lectures that are not captured by video are not copyrightable (Eisler, 2001).

16. The list of instructional materials that may be copyrighted is from Rowe, Webb, & Hartwell-Hunnicutt (1998).

17. While there is some relationship between plagiarism and copyright, they are different issues. Plagiarism is using another person's work without attribution and indicating that it is original work by the author using it. Plagiarism is an ethical offense that involves intellectual dishonesty and is governed by intellectual peers. Copyright infringement, as indicated earlier in this chapter, involves using another person's work without

permission, whether citing the source or not. Copyright infringement is a legal offense, governed by the courts. Thus it is possible to both plagiarize and infringe on copyright simultaneously.

18. Ko & Rossen (2010, p. 231) discuss these guidelines.

19. This suggestion is more appropriate for those faculty teaching traditional online courses, and it is probably one reason why so many of the faculty teaching MOOCs choose open-access materials.

20. Evans & Willinsky (2013) reviewed 110 course readers and found that 45% of the materials were free and accessible online. The authors argue that in addition to offering economic benefits, having students access these materials helps them develop important Internet skills. They also posit that these online documents have other advantages, such as linked references.

21. CC has explicit agreements for the different licensing types, available at http://creativecommons.org.

22. For open and available texts, see Project Gutenberg, at www.gutenberg.org; Open Textbook, at http://oerconsortium.org/discipline-specific/.

23. Images of CC's licensing symbols are available at http://blog.misterhamada.com/resources/creative-commons/.

7. Instructional Time

1. Cooper (2002, p. 121) describes time as a category of existence.

2. Cooper (2002) describes how time affects our relationships with each other.

3. In his novel *The time machine*, H. G. Wells (1895, p. 18) summed up the time/space relationship: "There is no difference between Time and any of the three dimensions of Space except that our consciousness moves along it. . . . Scientific people . . . know very well that Time is only a kind of Space."

4. This quotation is from Levine & Sun (2002, pp. 5–6).

5. The quotation regarding faculty concerns about their workloads is from Palloff & Pratt (2001, p. 40).

6. The quotation suggesting that the workload is two to three times higher is from Palloff & Pratt (1999, p. 49).

7. The quotation concluding that online instructors spend more time on teaching is from Young (2002, p. A31).

8. Research has documented faculty concerns about the amount of time that goes into teaching an online course. A Sloan Foundation study of more than 11,000 faculty members found that a majority of them believe that online courses take more time to develop and teach than a comparable onsite course (J. Seaman, 2009). More than 85% of all faculty with experience in online course development said that it takes "somewhat more" or "a lot more" effort to develop online courses than it does to develop onsite ones. Less than 2% of these faculty members believed that online course development required less effort than onsite course development. Nearly 64% said that it takes "somewhat more" to "a lot more" effort to teach an online course than an onsite one; only 12% thought that teaching online took less effort than teaching onsite. Seaman also found that faculty members' perception of a need for increased time and effort was the most important barrier to their

participation in online teaching. Moreover, his research indicated that increased participation in online learning leads to more positive attitudes about online instruction. For
smaller studies that concur with Seaman's evidence that faculty believe teaching online
takes more time, see Pachnowski & Jurczyk (2003); Pajo & Wallace (2001); Hartman,
Dziuban, & Moskal (2000); McKenzie et al. (2000); National Education Association
(2000); Berge (1998); Daugherty & Funke (1998); C. Wilson (1998).

9. Several studies suggest that time may be a barrier to faculty participation in online
learning, such as Naidu (2004); Frey & Donehue (2003); Newton (2003); Pajo & Wallace
(2001).

10. Several qualitative studies document the issue of faculty time, such as Samarawickrema & Stacey (2007); Bongalos et al. (2006); Conceição (2006); Lao & Gonzales (2005);
McShane (2004); Coppola, Hiltz, & Rotter (2002); Jones, Asensio, & Goodyear (2000). As
an instructor who participated in interviews for one of these studies said, "There is just
not enough time to do it all: answer all of my emails, design a course or courses, teach them,
manage them, grade, research advise, and so on" (Oomen-Early & Murphy, 2009, p. 229).

11. Some faculty who participated in interview studies have described time as a percentage. For example, one faculty member suggested that it took 50% more time to deliver
an online course than a classroom-based course (Conceição, 2006, p. 38). Other faculty
who were interviewed said that teaching online added several additional hours to their day.
See, for example, the study by Coppola, Hiltz, & Rotter (2002, p. 181).

12. Several researchers have attempted to document faculty time in online versus onsite courses, such as Tomei (2006); Cavanaugh (2005); Reinheimer (2005); D. Bender,
Wood, & Vredevoogd (2004); Hislop & Ellis (2004); DiBiase (2000); Visser (2000).

13. D. Bender, Wood, & Vredevoogd (2004) conducted a study of teaching time in two
"comparable" computer-aided design courses by analyzing the time and task records of the
teaching assistants. The two courses were taught at two different institutions, however,
and the study populations were different (students in the online course were older than
those in the onsite course), factors that certainly could have contributed to differences in
the amount of time spent by the instructor and the teaching assistants.

Cavanaugh's (2005) study of preparation and teaching time, based on teaching assistants' time-logs, investigated two different versions of the same economics course; the author, however, did not provide sufficient information about student characteristics to
determine whether there were noteworthy differences in the populations studied. Reinheimer's (2005) study of teaching time, assessing the instructor's contact time with
students in a section of an online English course versus an onsite one, also indicated more
time was spend in the former. The sections were taught by different instructors, however,
which could have accounted for the differences in the amount of time spent.

Tomei's (2006) study of eleven online and onsite versions of a technology and education course provided a point of comparison. The same instructor taught both sections, the
instructor had online and onsite experience in teaching the courses, both sections were
mature courses, the courses had eleven students per section, the duration of the sections
was similar, and the assignments were similar. Emails, chats, end-of-session posts, and an
electronic portfolio were used. Important details about the study, however, were omitted
in the descriptions, such as the average age of the students and the amount of technical

support available. Moreover, while calculations—such as the word-counts per response divided by typing time—were interesting, it was not entirely clear how the researcher arrived at the amount of time spent composing responses.

Visser's (2000) study compared the time that he spent designing and teaching his first online graduate course in his area of specialization (public administration) to three other comparable graduate-level courses he had taught previously. He offered the online course over a twelve-week period through a course management system and used several modalities, including web-based lectures, asynchronous discussions, synchronous chats, interactive video, and a web-based case study. He used an "experiential case approach" to study the courses, in which he analyzed time-logs, the data for which came from his planning calendar and his estimates, to compare the online course with the traditional courses. Visser, who was both the researcher and the course instructor, found that the online course took substantially more time (415 hours) than the onsite course (223 hours) to develop and teach. He estimated that the design and development time for the online course was about 85% greater than that for the onsite course, but the delivery time was approximately 13% less for the former. Visser's study, however, has a limitation, in that he did not include the efforts of a graduate assistant, who focused on the "technical work in posting, redesigning, and formatting materials for the course website, and checking and maintaining external links, into his estimate of delivery time. The assistant also provided technical troubleshooting assistance for students during course delivery" (p. 24). Visser asserted that including the assistant's time would have increased the amount of development and delivery time for the course by 220 hours.

14. Hislop & Ellis (2004) investigated the time spent teaching onsite courses that their online counterparts offered as a part of a Master of Science in Information Systems program, but the authors did not include the time spent designing the courses in their analysis. The seven pairs of onsite/online courses included in this study were software project management (two pairs, or four sections), database management, applied information-database technology, evaluation of information systems, human/computer interactions, and information systems analysis design. The asynchronous sections were all mature courses that relied on text and graphics focused on interaction, rather than static materials or independent study. The instructors were experienced in both onsite and online teaching, and the course pairs were taught by the same instructors without the benefit of teaching assistants, although technical-support staff were available to both faculty and students. The average class size for the online courses was 19.3 for the online section and 26 for the traditional section. The research approach involved instructors logging the time they spent in each of the courses. Hislop & Ellis found that the amount of time spent was approximately equivalent in the online and onsite courses (6.26 hours per student for the online section, and 6.17 hours per student for the onsite section). Like Visser (2000), however, Hislop & Ellis (2004) omitted accounting for the time spent by the technical-support staff, who assisted both students and faculty with general technical issues and technology problems. Omitting this information from their time estimates is a limitation in their findings.

Lazarus (2003) used a stopwatch to record the number of minutes spent in reading and responding to emails; reading, participating in, and grading online discussions; and grading assignments in three asynchronous online courses. She concluded that the course fell within "reasonable expectations" for teaching either a live or an online course (p. 53).

McLain (2005) also sought to investigate faculty workloads for interactions through online discussions and email. The author used email and discussion-board transcripts and analyzed them, based on average typing speeds, to estimate faculty time in seven online graduate courses. She concluded that the amount of time fell within "normal expectations" for faculty office hours for six of the seven courses (p. 54).

These latter two studies appear to support Hislop & Ellis's (2004) finding that teaching online falls within an expected level of time for teaching an onsite course, but none of them directly answered the question of whether teaching online takes more or less time than teaching onsite.

15. DiBiase (2004) compared the time it took him to deliver two versions of the same geography course. His study used time-logs to compare an asynchronous online course (four sections) with its synchronous classroom course (two sections), both delivered over a year. All were mature courses that had been offered at least twice previously, and the instructor/researcher already had online teaching experience. The courses were similar in their learning objectives, activities, and favorable ratings by students. The online courses had 18 students enrolled, while the onsite ones had 112 registered each term. The author found that the online course took less overall time (190 hours compared with 260 hours); adjusting for class size, the online version also took slightly less time per student (an average of 2.7 hours per student for the online course versus 3.2 hours per student for the onsite course). He found that the percentage of days per term spent on the course, however, was greater for the online course (70% of total days) than the onsite course (57% of total days). DiBiase, however, had vastly different student populations in the two versions of the course (an average age of twenty-one in the face-to-face courses, and average age of thirty-nine in the online course), the class sizes differed dramatically (112 in the face-to-face courses versus 18 in the online sections), and the versions differed in duration, all significant limitations of this study.

DiBiase also conducted a notable follow-up study (DiBiase & Rademacher, 2005). Examining the same asynchronous course for four additional iterations, he found a strong relationship between course enrollment and instructor effort. The relationship was curved, however, rather than linear, and DiBiase asserted that he was able to achieve increased efficiency when considering the amount of time spent per student. The authors noted that this increased efficiency was achieved without a discernible decrease in student satisfaction. They also indicated that the ability to achieve efficiency varies by pedagogy, the level of support, the experience of the instructor, and the suitability of the content.

16. The studies that include a direct assessment of time in their analyses include Tomei (2006); Reinheimer (2005); D. Bender, Wood, & Vredevoogd (2004); Hislop & Ellis (2004); DiBiase (2000).

17. A few studies included development time in their analyses, such as Cavanaugh (2005); Visser (2000).

18. Some of the studies documenting faculty time examined faculty work in mature courses, such as Tomei (2006); Cavanaugh (2005); Hislop & Ellis (2004); DiBiase (2000).

19. Some of the studies documenting faculty time examined faculty work in new courses, such as Reinheimer (2005); D. Bender, Wood, & Vredevoogd (2004); Visser (2000).

20. Several studies have a finding of increased faculty contact time with students, such as Tomei (2006); Cavanaugh (2005); McLain (2005); Thompson (2004).

21. Several studies suggest that the online course-development process increases the amount of faculty time spent, such as Pachnowski & Jurczyk (2003); Visser (2000).

22. Studies suggesting that design time decreases with additional course offerings include Pachnowski & Jurczyk (2003); DiBiase (2000).

23. Some studies indicate that increased faculty time is related to the technological aspect of teaching online, such as Reinheimer (2005); D. Bender, Wood, & Vredevoogd (2004).

24. Visser (2000) found that varying the tools and pedagogies used increases the amount of time spent teaching online.

25. Kern (1983) has suggested that the advent of communications technologies, particularly newspapers, telegraphs, and telephones, created the first sense of simultaneity. He posits that a sense of the present was *deepened* when large numbers of people felt they were experiencing the same events (p. 171).

26. Suler (2004b) discusses the difference between asynchronous and synchronous communication.

27. Suler (2004b) describes the zone of reflection that accompanies asynchronous teaching.

28. Thompson (2004, p. 86) notes that uninterrupted time spans, which many faculty members view as necessary, no longer exist; rather they are "chopped up" into shorter and, in effect, less-productive spans of time. Critical theorist Virilio (1991, p. 82) suggests that "time is lived—physiologically, sociologically, politically—to the extent that it is interrupted."

29. Some faculty have reported feeling that online students need additional attention. See, for example, DiBiase (2004).

30. As McLain (2005, p. 54) notes: "Perceptions of excessive workload may be better explained by the dynamics of online interaction indicated in this study. Online students attempted to contact their instructors twenty-four hours per day, seven days per week. . . . This is a radical shift from the traditional office hours [in] offline interaction normally experienced by university faculty. . . . Faculty find that there is no 'down' time for online teaching."

31. Some researchers have found that the work of teaching seems more fragmented, such as Lao & Gonzales (2005); Coppola, Hiltz, & Rotter (2002).

32. Some studies suggest that teaching online requires greater effort, such as Hislop & Ellis (2004, p. 29).

33. Samarawickrema & Stacey (2007) report findings from a case study that relied heavily on interviews with twenty-two faculty who use web-based learning to teach at Monash University's six Australian campuses. They suggest that many faculty discover that teaching expands to fill whatever time it is allowed. One faculty member in their study stated: "Teaching, I have to say, takes a lot of my time. . . . It's a bit like gas where it exp[and]s,

whatever room you put it in, it will exp[and], whatever time I give it, it'll just take . . . so I have to put very strict limits" (pp. 321–322).

34. Some studies have indicated that faculty believe teaching online takes time away from their other activities. See, for example, McShane (2004); Coppola, Hiltz, & Rotter (2002); Jones, Asensio, & Goodyear (2000).

35. Some studies suggest that faculty believe teaching online takes away from personal time, including Samarawickrema & Stacey (2007); Conceição (2006); McShane (2004).

36. Surveys of faculty have also suggested that an important reason that faculty choose to teach online is for the flexibility it offers. See, for example, J. Lee & Busch (2005); Hartman, Dziuban, & Moskal (2000).

37. Crews et al. (2008) and Shi, Bonk, & Magjuka (2006) suggest that writing specifically for the web is an important time-management strategy for online courses.

38. Sheridan (2006) and Collis & Nijhuis (2000) recommend keeping a "what's new" section.

39. Collis & Nijhuis (2000) recommend developing standardized responses.

40. Sheridan (2006) recommends holding virtual office hours for time management.

41. See Raines (2011).

42. Raines (2011) recommends social bookmarking as a time-management strategy.

8. Teacher Persona

1. Much like J. Alfred Prufrock, the narrator in T.S. Elliot's poem, suggests, "There will be time, there will be time / To prepare a face to meet the faces that you meet."

2. Several scholars, such as Lasky (2005) and Zembylas (2003), have written about the concept of teacher identity. A few have written about teacher identity in online courses, such as Irwin & Hramiak (2010) and Wheeler, Kelly, & Gale (2005). There are many different definitions of identity, but one constant across them is that identity appears to be at least partially fixed and partially validated by a set of credentials. Validation could be through fingerprints, dental records, and DNA scans. Proof of identity may include a social security number, a passport, and so forth. Thus at least part of one's identity rests with one's genetic constitution, country of origin, and the like. According to P. Palmer (1998, p. 12), identity can be summed up as "an evolving nexus where all the forces that constitute my life converge in the mystery of self: my genetic makeup, the nature of the man and woman who gave me life, the culture in which I was raised, people who have sustained me and people who have done me harm, the good and ill I have done to others and to myself, the experience of love and suffering—and much, much more. In the midst of that complex field, identity is a moving intersection of the inner and outer forces that make me who I am, converging in the irreducible mystery of being human." What some of the authors listed here really seem to be describing, however, is teacher persona, rather than a more fully encompassing notion of identity.

3. Lang's (2007) article in the *Chronicle of Higher Education* describes persona in onsite classes.

4. Lang (2007) successfully argues that there should be consistency between a teacher's persona and his or her educational objectives and classroom practices.

5. Blackmon (2013) describes online instructors' descriptions of their online personas as doppelgangers.

6. Many faculty interviewed in qualitative studies have described developing a "completely different personality" (Coppola, Hiltz, & Rotter, 2002, p. 182). Faculty also have reported being conscious of a need to change: "I found that my persona did not work well online. . . . I found myself in a position where I needed to change my teaching style, and I didn't know how to do that" (Coppola, Hiltz, & Rotter, 2002, p. 181).

7. See Suler (2002).

8. Faculty interviewed in several qualitative studies noted that they had shifting beliefs about teacher centrality in the learning process. As one faculty member said: "It has gotten me to think about the fact that class does not revolve around me, which is what every new teacher thinks. They are more concerned about themselves and what they are doing" (Coppola, Hiltz, & Rotter, 2002, p. 180). One faculty member offered an explanation of the difference between face-to-face and online courses: "In a face-to-face class the instructor initiates the action: meeting the class, handing out the syllabus, etc. In on-line instruction the student initiates the action by going to the website, posting a message, or doing something" (G. Smith, Ferguson, & Caris, 2002, p. 353).

9. Faculty in interview studies described a number of ways in which they deconstructed and then reconstructed their personas with students. Faculty found that they had to renegotiate their professional status with students. They also mentioned a need to establish that status online. As one individual stated, "Sometimes I think they forget I'm there!!!" (G. Smith, Ferguson, & Caris, 2002, p. 354). In addition, they felt a need to assert their presence at each point of communication with students, noting that "on-line you establish yourself again and again with each response" (G. Smith, Ferguson, & Caris, 2002, p. 353).

10. See Goodyear et al. (2001). Faculty in interview studies also often noted an increase in their roles and responsibilities. As one faculty member put it, "You become an administrator and a teacher and a multimedia developer and you are a researcher and whatever else that I've left out" (Samarawickrema & Stacey, 2007, p. 323).

11. McLuhan & Fiore (1967) argued that the medium is part of the message.

12. Parini's (2005) *Art of teaching* describes the author's evolution into a teacher while also meeting the creative demands of publish-or-perish university life. His book provides insights and advice, and he argues that it is important to find a teaching identity.

13. Showalter's (2003) *Teaching literature* is part manual and part memoir, a blend of narrative and scholarship related to the subject of teaching English.

14. In his article about identity management in cyberspace, Suler (2002) describes how the selection of a username or an avatar may reveal an individual's hidden beliefs or values.

15. Suler (2002) describes how we grapple with unconscious elements of our personalities in an online environment.

16. Several authors recommend virtual office hours, including Li & Pitts (2009) and Lavooy & Newlin (2008).

17. I provide additional information about the topic of student engagement in chapter 11.

9. Communication

1. Littlejohn & Foss (2005) argue that finding a single definition of communication has been impossible.

2. The model created by Tubbs & Moss (2006, pp. 12–14) defines verbal and nonverbal messages. Verbal messages are any type of spoken communication that uses one or

more words. Intentional verbal messages are conscious attempts to communicate with others through speech. Unintentional verbal messages involve saying things without necessarily meaning to do so. Nonverbal messages are all of the messages transmitted without words, or over and above the actual words used. Intentional nonverbal messages are those that are deliberately transmitted. Unintentional nonverbal messages are unarticulated aspects of behavior transmitted without conscious control.

3. Both Clanchy (1993) and Goody (1987) provide fuller discussions of these advances.

4. The fundamental difference between online courses and correspondence courses is that an online course requires regular and substantive communication between the instructor and the students, while a correspondence course does not. The drafters of the Higher Education Opportunity Act (2009), which reauthorized the Higher Education Act of 1965, determined that faculty and student interactions are an essential part of online learning, clearly differentiating it from correspondence study. The updated act states that "distance education" involves "the use of one or more technologies to deliver instruction to students who are separated from the instructor and to support regular and substantive interaction between the students and the instructor, either synchronously or asynchronously." This marks a clear distinction between online learning and correspondence courses, in which "interaction between the instructor and the student is limited, is not regular and substantive, and is primarily initiated by the student. Correspondence courses are typically self-paced" (Electronic Code of Federal Regulations). A lack of definition in the terms "regular and substantive" in the act, however, leads to the question of what "regular and substantive interaction" means.

Online learning has fast asynchronous or, at times, synchronous communication, while a correspondence course traditionally has slow asynchronous communication that requires an exchange of letters and print materials between the student and the instructor. Today, however, correspondence courses often are delivered through an electronic medium. For a history of correspondence courses, see Watkins & Wright (1991).

5. The electronic text used in online learning may not seem as personal, or at least as official, as the formal letters for correspondence study, given the former's standardized fonts, spellcheck, and use of media. Written letters require a careful crafting of handwritten text or the use of a formal letterhead. Electronic text does not have the physicality of a letter. It is, however, much faster and, in a sense, more immediate. In this way, electronic text also encourages more frequent communication.

6. Several studies document that social presence influences learner attitudes and learning outcomes. See, for example, Hostetter & Busch (2006); Russo & Benson (2005); Swan & Shea (2005); Richardson & Swan (2003); Picciano (2002); Shin (2002); Gunawardena et al. (2001).

7. A *New York Times* article, at www.nytimes.com/2012/05/03/education/harvard-and -mit-team-up-to-offer-free-online-courses.html, documents the rise of massively open online courses.

8. More information about the origins of the Internet is available in "Brief history of the Internet," at www.internetsociety.org/internet/internet-51/history-internet/brief -history-internet/.

9. Suler (2004b) describes the ways in which text, and differences in text, communicate meaning.

10. See Garrison & Archer (2003) and Rourke et al. (2001).

11. Suler (2004b) describes the ways in which the temporal aspects of online environments influence communication patterns.

12. Vonderwell (2003) suggests that shy students tend to participate more in online discussions.

13. Coppola, Hiltz, & Rotter (2002, p. 179) explain that faculty in their qualitative study "noted the absence of nonverbal cues, such as facial expressions, eye contact, voice qualities, and body movement, which are used in the classroom to support and encourage students on both conscious and unconscious levels."

14. Faculty in some qualitative studies indicated concern about decreased interactions among and with students and inadequate visual clues to help them "read" students. See, for example, Coppola, Hiltz, & Rotter (2002, p. 183).

15. While redefining and reasserting status could become challenging, some faculty interviewed in qualitative studies saw a benefit in being freed from the preconceptions students might hold. See, for example, McShane (2004) and G. Smith, Ferguson, & Caris (2002). Many of the faculty members interviewed in such studies explained similar changes in how they perceived students in the absence of physical markers.

16. Faculty in many of the qualitative studies described an increase in their closeness with students. Some learned more about their students on an intellectual level online than they did in face-to-face courses, providing a point of connection with these students. For such faculty, the online environment created a "kind of a purified atmosphere" (G. Smith, Ferguson, & Caris, 2001). For some faculty, this enhanced knowledge about their students at an intellectual level replaced visual cues and physical markers.

17. Suler (2004b) argues that relationships *are* the documents themselves.

18. Many faculty interviewed in qualitative studies have described the responsibility associated with responding to student emails and postings. Faculty often found that they had more time to think when teaching online, which many believed allowed them to become more "thoughtful," "articulate," and "intellectual." See Conceição (2006); McShane (2004); Coppola, Hiltz, & Rotter (2002). The permanence of the written word gives faculty an added feeling of scrutiny and accountability for their responses.

19. Suler (2004b) describes the process of distortions of meaning in written text.

20. Suler (2004a) describes the ways in which individuals change in cyberspace, either through inhibition or a lack of inhibition.

21. Several researchers have noted the importance of the instructor's responsibility (sometimes called "instructor presence") in establishing a social presence throughout the course. See, for example, T. Anderson et al. (2001); Rourke et al. (2001); Garrison, Anderson, & Archer (2000); Gunawardena (1995).

22. Aragon (2003) provides a list of specific strategies, some of which overlap, including course-design strategies (e.g., limiting class size), instructor strategies (e.g., providing frequent feedback), and participant strategies (e.g., sharing personal stories).

23. Rovai (2001, 2002a, 2002b) argues for the importance of collaborative learning in establishing social presence.

24. I discuss netiquette further in chapter 12.

25. T. Bender (2012) argues for the importance of communication when teaching online.

26. Several authors have argued that the social nature of the Internet influences relationships. See, for example, Baym, Zhang, & Lin (2004); Morahan-Martin & Schumacher (2003); Walther & Parks (2002).

27. Laffey, Lin, & Lin (2006) and Shea et al. (2001) also document that effective communication is critical when teaching online.

10. Student Rights

1. I am not a lawyer; thus this chapter should be viewed as a discussion of an educational issue, rather than as a document providing legal advice.

2. Bill of Rights and Principles for Learning in the Digital Age.

3. The authors of the Bill of Rights and Principles of Learning in the Digital Age have come under some criticism, as expressed in a *Chronicle of Higher Education* article by Kolowich (2013).

4. The full report on disability from the World Health Organization is available at www .who.int/disabilities/world_report/2011/en/.

5. For additional information about disabilities, see 3PlayMedia (2013).

6. The full version of the Rehabilitation Act is available at www2.ed.gov/policy/speced /reg/narrative.html.

7. A summary of the Rehabilitation Act, as well as sections 504 and 508, is available at http://webaim.org/articles/laws/usa/rehab#s504.

8. The text of the Americans with Disabilities Act is available at www.ada.gov/pubs /ada.htm.

9. In their white paper, 3PlayMedia (2013) lists the disabilities students may have.

10. See the Bill of Rights and Principles for Learning in the Digital Age (line 28).

11. See the Bill of Rights and Principles for Learning in the Digital Age (line 31).

12. Additional information about what constitutes acceptable and unacceptable sharing of information in online classes is available from the Virginia Commonwealth University Center for Teaching and Learning, at www.vcu.edu/cte/resources/OTLRG/04_10 _FERPA.html.

13. This information about FERPA and social media is from Lavagnino (2010).

14. Orlando (2011) describes the issue of FERPA and social media.

15. Bathon (2008) describes FERPA rules.

16. I have a fuller discussion of copyright in chapter 6.

17. A *Chronicle of Higher Education* article (Hendry, 2009) provides additional information about the student lawsuit against Turnitin, which reached a settlement.

18. Mitriano (2011) provides further details about the students who created the iPhone app and argues that these students should retain the intellectual-property rights to it.

19. Bill of Rights and Principles for Learning in the Digital Age (line 37).

20. Indiana University–Bloomington supplies additional information about third-party technology providers in their Teaching Handbook, available at http://teaching.iub.edu /wrapper_big.php?section_id=tech.

21. Lavagnino (2010) provides additional information about issues involved in using what she call "third-party tools," which include social media.

22. I culled this list of suggestions from several institutional websites and articles focused on ADA compliance.

23. I adapted the list of suggestions for using social media from Orlando (2011).

24. Creative Common provides information about how to license your work at http://creativecommons.org/choose/.

11. Student Engagement

1. This chapter is about student intellectual engagement in a specific course, not about the broader notion of student engagement during the college experience, as measured by instruments such as the National Study of Student Engagement (NSSE).

2. This quotation about engagement is from Bowen (2005, p. 3).

3. Brophy (2004) describes the concept of motivation.

4. The definition of attention is derived from J. Anderson (2004).

5. This quotation is from Astin (1984, p. 301).

6. See Marton & Säljö (1976).

7. Marton & Säljö's (1976) seminal work on surface learning has launched much additional research on these two concepts.

8. Säljö (1979) describes the different levels of learning as "interrelated" and "building."

9. Ramsden (1992) elaborates on the concepts of deep- and surface-learning.

10. Biggs, Kember, & Leung (2001) developed the Study Process Questionnaire.

11. The eighteen-item Approaches and Study Skills Inventory is available in Entwistle (2010).

12. See Marton & Säljö (1976).

13. The quotation about engagement is from Shulman (2002 , p. 37).

14. This quotation about engagement comes from Pascarella & Terenzini (1991, p. 616).

15. The quotation about agency comes from Martin (2004, p. 135).

16. Andersen (1979) and Mehrabian (1969, 1971) offer their perspectives on the concept of immediacy.

17. Most of the research on the concept of immediacy in higher education focuses on the immediacy of teachers. A smaller number of studies have examined student immediacy, although it is directly related to the student experience.

18. Some studies have documented the relationship between student immediacy and teacher affinity. See, for example, Barringer & McCroskey (2000).

19. Edgerton (2001).

20. Knowles (1950) is well known for his work in adult learning and his attendant theory of andragogy.

21. Reeves, Herrington, & Oliver (2002, p. 564) offer this description of the elements composing authentic activities in online courses.

22. In addition, Alan Levine's description of ds 106 in chapter 4 provides information about an open online course on digital storytelling.

23. Several scholars have identified evidence of the effectiveness of different types of punctuated lectures, including Benedict & Apple (2005); Boyce & Hineline (2002); Crouch & Mazur (2001).

24. Reuell (2013) documents the usefulness of tests in an online learning environment.

25. Curation is the act of discovering, gathering, and presenting the digital content that surrounds specific subject matter. It requires evaluation and synthesis skills, which places it squarely as a higher-order thinking skill.

26. Figure 11.1, along with an essay about student engagement, is available at Wheeler's (2013) blog.

12. Community

1. The quotation defining community comes from Schwier (2011, pp. 18–19).

2. Wenger's (1998, pp. 72–73) community-of-practice model has several characteristics:

- *Mutual Engagement.* Through participation in the community, members establish norms and build collaborative relationships. These relationships are the ties that bind the members of the community together as a social entity.
- *Joint Enterprise.* Through their interactions, community members create a shared understanding of what binds them together. The joint enterprise is (re) negotiated by its members and is sometimes referred to as the "domain" of the community.
- *Shared Repertoire.* As part of its practice, the community produces a set of communal resources. This is used in the pursuit of their joint enterprise and can include both literal and symbolic meanings.

The community-of-inquiry model has a long history, dating back to nineteenth-century pragmatists such as Dewey (1938) and Peirce (1877).

3. Rheingold (2000, p. 5) defines virtual communities as "social aggregations that emerge from the [Internet] when enough people carry on those public discussions long enough, with sufficient human feeling, to form webs of personal relationships in cyberspace." The concept has been applied to online learning by Garrison & Anderson (2003) and Garrison, Anderson, & Archer (2000). In their community-of-inquiry model, these authors suggest that a virtual community has three main components: instructor presence, social presence, and cognitive presence.

4. See Lave & Wenger (1991).

5. The quotation about communities is from Rheingold (2000, p. 3).

6. Mowshowitz (1997) describes the ways in which communities can cross time and space.

7. Scholars have suggested that virtual communities can lead to less-frequent interactions with humans in traditional settings (C. H. Lee et al., 2004), as well as attitude polarization and increased prejudices (Parsell, 2008).

8. Pascarella & Terenzini's (2005) extensive review synthesizes research on the ways in which college influences student learning, including the relationship between regular student-faculty and student-student interactions and learning outcomes.

9. Some scholars have suggested that community may not even be the best descriptive term for what goes on when groups learn together. Schwier (2011), for example, argues that community is not a completely convincing metaphor to explain all the complexities of learning groups, such as resiliency, authenticity, and so forth. It may simply be the best term we have to date.

10. Siemens (2002) notes that learner-learner interactions in an online course can be viewed as a four-stage continuum:

1. *Communication.* People "talking," discussing.
2. *Collaboration.* People sharing ideas and working together (and occasionally sharing resources) in a loose environment.
3. *Cooperation.* People doing things together, but each with his or her own purpose.
4. *Community.* People striving for a common purpose.

This continuum of involvement provides a useful framework for thinking about scaffolding with learners through progressively more complex interaction skills, thus leading to the creation of an effective working group.

11. Blackmon & Major (2012) synthesize studies of student experiences in online courses.

12. The notion of a network is one that is frequently applied in descriptions of online courses. It has been used to characterize communication (in which individuals are connected to the course and each other; see chapter 2), learning (in which individuals are connected to knowledge across distributed sources; see chapter 3), and social networks (in which individuals are connected to each other; discussed in this chapter).

13. Caboni et al. (2005); Rossi & Berk (1985); and J. Gibbs (1981) describe the concept of norms.

14. Caboni et al. (2005); Hechter & Opp (2001); and Horne (2001) describe the functions of norms.

15. Caboni et al. (2005, p. 520) describe the concept of a collective conscience.

16. Durkheim (1982) argues that norms represent cultural values.

17. Feldman (1984) argues that norms are essential to survival.

18. Braxton & Caboni (2005) document ways in which norms influence academic behavior.

19. I provide additional information about communication patterns in chapter 9.

20. Several scholars have expressed concern about problems with Internet-based assessments and academic honesty, such as G. Smith, Ferguson, & Caris (2001) and Kennedy et al. (2000). King, Guyette, & Piotrowski (2009) found that 73.8% of the students they surveyed felt it was easier to cheat in an online class. Research by Lanier (2006) revealed that out of 1,262 college students, student cheating in online courses was significantly higher than in onsite classes. Some studies, however, point in a different direction. Based on survey data, Grijalva, Nowell, & Kerkvliet (2006) concluded that there was no significant difference between the amount of cheating on regular paper assessments and web-based assessments. Moreover, Stuber-McEwen, Wiseley, & Hoggatt (2009) found that students were less likely to cheat in online classes, as did Watson & Sottile (2010).

21. See McMillan & Chavis (1986).

22. McMillan & Chavis (1986) describe the concept of membership.

23. McMillan & Chavis (1986) argue that influence is an important aspect of community.

24. McMillan & Chavis (1986) argue that integration and the fulfillment of needs are critical to community.

25. McMillan & Chavis (1986) argue that emotional connection is a critical component of community, and they identify shared emotional connection as the definitive element of community (p. 14).

26. The notion of social presence is tied to communication, particularly in the work of Short, Williams, & Christie (1976). In literature on education, it often is linked with the community-of-inquiry model developed by Garrison, Anderson, & Archer (2000).

27. Social presence is a slippery concept, since scholars define it in several different ways. Garrison (2009, p. 352) characterizes social presence as "the ability of participants to identify with the community (e.g., course of study), communicate purposefully in a trusting environment, and develop inter-personal relationships by way of projecting their individual personalities." Garrison & Archer (2003, p. 29) define it as "the ability of participants in a community of inquiry to project themselves socially and emotionally as 'real people' through the medium of communication being used." Tu & McIsaac (2002, p. 140) call social presence "the degree of feeling, perception, and reaction of being connected" to another person. Tu (2002, p. 38) defines it as "the degree of salience of another person in an interaction and the consequent salience of an interpersonal relationship." Picciano (2002, p. 22) classifies social presence as students' perceptions of being in and belonging in an online course. Finally, Leh (2001, p. 110) suggests that it is the learners' ability to project themselves socially and affectively into the learning environment.

28. Wise et al. (2004) conclude that the medium is not as important as the interactions among individuals.

29. In their study of social presence, Tu & McIsaac (2002) found that several variables can influence social presence, including the social context (e.g., the degree of familiarity between teacher and students, trust relationships, attitudes toward technology, etc.), online communication (e.g., communication accuracy, the use of emoticons and paralanguage, language skills, and characteristics of the environment, such as a chat or a discussion board), and interactivity (e.g., the timeliness of responses, communication styles, the length of messages, etc.). All of these factors then influence a student's sense of being there and realizing that others are also present.

30. More information about Social Book is available at http://theopenutopia.org/social-book/.

31. Virginia Shea has an online book that provides some useful advice about netiquette, at www.albion.com/bookNetiquette/.

32. The *People for Education* blog provides a solid overview of netiquette, available at http://discuss.peopleforeducation.ca/forum/topics/online-discussion-netiquette/.

33. Ko & Rossen (2010) recommend a common space, such as a virtual student lounge, to help build community in an online course.

34. The US Department of Education's meta-analysis (Means et al., 2009), has been widely cited, but it also has been the subject of some criticism, due to questions about its methodology.

35. Bernard et al. (2009) is a widely cited meta-analysis, and Bernard's discussion about the future of research on online learning is available in a sidebar in chapter 3.

36. Çavuş, Uzunboylu, & Ibrahim (2007) and Bernard et al. (2004) have documented within-course effects for specific instructional approaches.

37. Some authors indicate that it is important for students in online courses to get to know each other. See, for example, Blackmon & Major (2012) and Motteram & Forrester (2005).

38. Some authors argue that students in online courses can form deeper relationships than they do in onsite ones. See, for example, Zembylas, Theodorou, & Pavlakis (2008).

39. Barkely, Cross, & Major (2014) outline thirty-five different collaborative learning techniques and indicate how these may be implemented online.

Conclusion

1. There is no single, agreed-upon definition of culture to be found in the literature. In general, however, culture is the product of the systems of knowledge shared by a group, and it may be represented by observable cultural artifacts, such as norms and practices, symbols, ideology, rituals, myths, and ceremonies (Kuh & Whitt, 1988; Tierney, 1988). Culture, however, also represents the work of selecting, challenging, and arranging cultural artifacts; thus culture is the process through which tradition is reconfigured (Slack & Wise, 2005).

2. Toma, Dubrow, & Hartley (2005) discuss how we use ideals in higher education.

3. Much of the discussion about technology and culture centers on the notion of technological determinism (the idea that technology drives change) and the social construction of technology (the idea that human actions shape technology, rather than the other way around). Each perspective has its champions, but some scholars are finding both views to be too narrow.

4. Christensen (1997) and Bower & Christensen (1995) discuss the notion of disruptive technologies.

5. Christensen & Eyring (2011) apply the notion of disruptive innovations to higher education, as do Christensen et al. (2011).

6. This quotation about the potential benefits of online learning to higher education is from Friedman (2012).

7. This additional quotation about the potential benefits of online learning to higher education is from Friedman (2013).

8. This quotation about the potential challenges of online learning for higher education is from Brooks (2012).

References

Abt, C. (1970). *Serious games*. New York: Viking Press.

Ainsworth, S., Prain, V., & Tytler, R. (2011). Drawing to learn in science. *Science, 333*(6046), 1096–1097.

Akrich, M. (1992). The description of technological objects. In W. E. Bijker & J. Law (Eds.), *Shaping technology-building society: Studies in Sociotechnical Change*. Cambridge, MA: MIT Press, 205–224.

Alexander, B. (2011). *The new digital storytelling: Creating narratives with new meaning*. Westport, CT: Praeger.

Allen, I. E., & Seaman, J. (2007). *Online nation: Five years of growth in online learning*. Needham, MA: Sloan Consortium. Retrieved on June 25, 2014, from http://sloanconsortium .org/publications/survey/index.asp.

Allen, I. E., & Seaman, J. (2014). *Grade change: Tracking online education in the United States*. Babsom Park, MA: Babson Survey Research Group and Quahog Research Group.

Allen, M., Bourhis, J., Burrell, N., & Mabry, E. (2002). Comparing student satisfaction with distance education to traditional classrooms in higher education: A meta-analysis. *American Journal of Distance Education, 16*(2), 83–97.

Andersen, J. F. (1979). Teacher immediacy as a predictor of teaching effectiveness. In D. Nimmo (Ed.), *Communication yearbook*, volume 3. New Brunswick, NJ: Transaction Books, 543–559.

Anderson, J. R. (2004). *Cognitive psychology and its implications* (6th edition). New York: Worth.

Anderson, R. C. (1984). Role of the reader's schema in comprehension, learning, and memory. In R. C., Anderson, J. Osborn, & R. Tierney (Eds.), *Learning to read in American schools*. Hillsdale, NJ: Erlbaum, 243–257.

Anderson, T., Rourke, L., Garrison, D. R., & Archer, W. (2001). Assessing teaching presence in a computer conferencing context. *Journal of Asynchronous Learning Networks, 5*(2), 1–17.

Andrade, J. (2010). What does doodling do? *Applied Cognitive Psychology, 24*(1), 100–106.

Angelo, T. A., & Cross, P. K. (1993). *Classroom assessment techniques: A handbook for college teachers* (2nd edition). San Francisco: Jossey-Bass.

Anglin, G. J., & Morrison, G. R. (2000). An analysis of distance education research: Implications for the instructional technologist. *Quarterly Review of Distance Education, 1*(3), 189–194.

Annetta, L., Murray, M., Laird, S., Bohr, S., & Park, J. (2006). Serious games: Incorporating video games in the classroom. *EDUCAUSE Quarterly, 29*(3), 16–22.

Aragon, S. R. (2003). Creating social presence in online environments. *New Directions for Adult and Continuing Education, 2003*(100), 57–68.

Astin, A. W. (1984). Student involvement: A developmental theory for higher education. *Journal of College Student Personnel, 25*, 297–308.

Bandura, A. (1977). *Social learning theory*. New York: General Learning Press.

Baran, P. (1962). *On distributed communication networks*. Santa Monica, CA: Rand Corporation.

Barkham, M., & Mellor-Clark, J. (2000). Rigour and relevance: Practice-based evidence in the psychological therapies. In N. Rowland & S. Goss (Eds.), *Evidence-based counselling and psychological therapies: Research and applications*. London: Routledge, 127–144.

Barkley, E., Cross, K. P., & Major, C. H. (2014). *Collaborative learning techniques: A handbook for college faculty* (2nd edition). San Francisco: Jossey-Bass.

Barringer, D. K., & McCroskey, J. C. (2000). Immediacy in the classroom: Student immediacy. *Communication Education, 49*(2), 178–186.

Bateson, G. (1991). *A sacred unity: Further steps to an ecology of mind*. New York: Cornelia & Michael Bessie.

Bathon, J. (2008). Controversial new FERPA rules take effect next week. *EdJurist*. Retrieved on June 25, 2014, from edjurist.com/blog/controversial-new-ferpa-rules-take-effect-next-week.html.

Baym, N. K., Zhang, Y. B., & Lin, M.-C. (2004). Social interaction across media: Interpersonal communication on the Internet, telephone, and face-to-face. *New Media & Society, 6*(3), 299–318.

Bender, D. M., Wood, B. J., & Vredevoogd, J. D. (2004). Teaching time: Distance education versus classroom instruction. *American Journal of Distance Education, 18*(2), 103–114.

Bender, T. (2012). *Discussion-based online teaching to enhance student learning: Theory, practice and assessment* (2nd edition). Sterling, VA: Stylus.

Benedict, J. O., & Apple, K. J. (2005). Just-in-time teaching: A web-based teaching approach. In B. K. Saville, T. E. Zinn, & V. W. Hevern (Eds.), *Essays from excellence in teaching*. Retrieved on June 25, 2014, from http://teachpsych.org/Resources/Documents/ebooks/eit2009.pdf.

Berge, Z. L. (1998). Barriers to online teaching in post-secondary institutions: Can policy changes fix it? *Online Journal of Distance Learning Administration, 1*(2). Retrieved on June 25, 2014, from www.westga.edu/~distance/Berge12.html.

Bernard, R. M., Abrami, P. C., Borokhovski, E., Wade, A., Tamim, R., Surkes, M., & Bethel, E. C. (2009). A meta-analysis of three interaction treatments in distance education. *Review of Educational Research, 79*(3), 1243–1289.

Bernard, R. M., Abrami, P. C., Lou, Y., Borokhovski, E., Wade, A., Wozney, L., Wallet, P. A., Fiset, M., & Huang, B. (2004). How does distance education compare with classroom instruction? A meta-analysis of the empirical literature. *Review of Educational Research, 74*(3), 379–439.

Biggs, J., Kember, D., & Leung, D. Y. P. (2001). The revised two-factor Study Process Questionnaire: R-SPQ-2F. *British Journal of Educational Psychology, 71*(1), 133–147.

Biktimirov, E. N., & Nilson, L. B. (2003). Mapping your course: Designing a graphic syllabus for introductory finance. *Journal of Education for Business*, 78(6), 308–312.

Bill of Rights and Principles for Learning in the Digital Age. Retrieved on June 25, 2014, from https://github.com/audreywatters/learnersrights/blob/master/billofrights.txt.

Blackmon, S. J. (2013). Faculty perspectives of persona in a virtual world. Unpublished dissertation. University of Alabama, Tuscaloosa.

Blackmon, S. J., & Major, C. H. (2012). Student experiences in online courses: A qualitative research synthesis. *Quarterly Review of Distance Education*, 13(2), 77–85.

Blanchard, J. (2010). The teacher exception under the work-for-hire doctrine: Safeguard of academic freedom or vehicle for academic free enterprise? *Innovative Higher Education*, 35(1), 61–69.

Bloom, B. S. (1984). The 2-sigma problem: The search for methods of group instruction as effective as one-to-one tutoring. *Educational Researcher*, 13, 4–16.

Bongalos, Y. Q., Bulaon, D. D. R., Celedonio, L. P., de Guzman, A. B., & Ogarte, C. J. F. (2006). University teachers' experiences in courseware development. *British Journal of Educational Technology*, 37(5), 695–704.

Bonk, C. J. (2009). *The world is open: How web technology is revolutionizing education.* San Francisco: Jossey-Bass.

Bowen, S. (2005). Engaged learning: Are we all on the same page? *Peer Review*, 7(2), 4–7.

Bower, J. L., & Christensen, C. M. (1995). Disruptive technologies: Catching the wave. *Harvard Business Review*, 73(1), 43–53.

Boyce, T. E., & Hineline, P. N. (2002). Interteaching: A strategy for enhancing the user-friendliness of behavioral arrangements in the college classroom. *Behavior Analyst*, 25, 215–226.

Braxton, J. M., & Caboni, T. C. (2005). Using student norms to create positive learning environments. *About Campus*, 9(6), 2–7.

Bray, N., Harris, M., & Major, C. H. (2007). New verse or the same old chorus? Looking holistically at distance education research. *Research in Higher Education*, 48(7), 889–908.

Brooks, D. (2012). The campus tsunami. *New York Times*, May 3. Retrieved on June 25, 2014, from www.nytimes.com/2012/05/04/opinion/brooks-the-campus-tsunami.html.

Brophy, J. (2004). *Motivating students to learn* (2nd edition). Mahwah, NJ: Lawrence Erlbaum Associates.

Brown, J. S., Collins, A., & Duguid, S. (1989). Situated cognition and the culture of learning. *Educational Researcher*, 18(1), 32–42.

Brown, M. (2012). Learning analytics: Moving from concept to practice. *EDUCAUSE Learning Initiative*. Retrieved on June 25, 2014, from http://net.educause.edu/ir/library/pdf/ELIB1203.pdf.

Brown, T., & Wyatt, J. (2010). Design thinking for social innovation. *Stanford Social Innovation Review*, 8(1), 31–35.

Butler, D. L., & Sellbom, M. (2002). Barriers to adopting technology for teaching and learning. *EDUCAUSE Quarterly*, 2, 22–28. Retrieved on June 25, 2014, from http://net.educause.edu/ir/library/pdf/EQM0223.pdf.

Caboni, T. C., Braxton, J. M., Deusterhous, M. B., Mundy, M. E., McClendon, S. A., & Lee, S. D. (2005). Toward an empirical delineation of a normative structure for college students. *Journal of Higher Education, 70*, 519–544.

Cambridge University Press et al. v. Patton et al., No. 1:2008cv01425 (N.D. Ga. 2008).

Carey, K. (2012). Into the future with MOOC's. *Chronicle of Higher Education*, September 3. Retrieved on June 25, 2014, from http://chronicle.com/article/Into-the-Future-With-MOOCs/134080/.

Carlson, S., & Blumenstyk, G. (2012). For whom is college being reinvented? *Chronicle of Higher Education*, December 17. Retrieved on June 25, 2014, from http://chronicle.com /article/The-False-Promise-of-the/136305/.

Cavanaugh, J. (2005). Teaching online: A time comparison. *Online Journal of Distance Learning Administration, 8*(1). Retrieved on June 25, 2014, from www.westga.edu/~distance /ojdla/spring81/cavanaugh81.htm.

Çavuş, N., Uzunboylu, H., & Ibrahim, D. (2007). Assessing the success of students using a learning management system together with a collaborative tool in web-based teaching of programming languages. *Journal of Educational Computing Research, 36*(3), 301–321.

Chalkin, M. (2013). Udacity's Sebastian Thurn, godfather of free online education, changes course. Retrieved on June 25, 2014, from www.fastcompany.com/3021473/udacity -sebastian-thrun-uphill-climb/.

Cheney, A., & Sanders, R. L. (2011). *Teaching and learning in 3D immersive worlds: Pedagogical models and constructivist approaches.* Hershey, PA: Information Science Reference.

Chickering, A., & Ehrmann, S. C. (1996). Implementing the seven principles: Technology as lever. *AAHE [American Association of Higher Education] Bulletin, 49*(2), 3–6.

Chickering, A., & Gamson, Z. (1987). Seven principles for good practice in undergraduate education. *AAHE [American Association of Higher Education] Bulletin, 39*, 3–7.

Christensen, C. M. (1997). *The innovator's dilemma: When new technologies cause great firms to fail.* Boston: Harvard Business School Press.

Christensen, C. M., & Eyring, H. J. (2011). *The innovative university: Changing the DNA of higher education from the inside out.* San Francisco: Jossey-Bass.

Christensen, C. M., Horn, M. B., Soares, L., & Caldera, L. (2011, February 8). *Disrupting college: How disruptive innovation can deliver quality and affordability to postsecondary education.* Center for American Progress. Retrieved on June 25, 2014, from http:// americanprogress.org/issues/labor/report/2011/02/08/9034/disrupting-college/.

Christianson, L., Tiene, D., & Luft, P. (2002). Examining online instruction in undergraduate nursing education. *Distance Education, 23*(2), 213–229.

Clanchy, M. T. (1993). *From memory to written record: England, 1066–1307.* Oxford: Blackwell.

Clark, R. E. (2000). Evaluating distance education: Strategies and cautions. *Quarterly Review of Distance Education, 1*(1), 3–16.

Collis, B., & Nijhuis, G. G. (2000). The instructor as manager: Time and task. *Internet and Higher Education, 3*(1–2), 75–97.

Comeaux, P. (2004). *Assessing online learning.* San Francisco: Jossey-Bass.

Conceição, S. C. O. (2006). Faculty lived experiences in the online environment. *Adult Education Quarterly, 57*(1), 26–45.

Cook, D. A. (2009). The failure of e-learning research to inform educational practice, and what we can do about it. *Medical Teacher, 31*(2), 158–162.

Cooper, S. (2002). *Technoculture and critical theory: In the service of the machine?* London: Routledge.

Coppola, N. W., Hiltz, S. R., & Rotter, N. (2002). Becoming a virtual professor: Pedagogical roles and asynchronous learning networks. *Journal of Management Information Systems, 18*(4), 169–190.

Crews, T. B., Wilkinson, K., Hemby, K. V., McCannon, M., & Wiedmaier, C. (2008). Workload management strategies for online educators. *Delta Pi Epsilon Journal, 50*(3), 132–149.

Crouch, C. H., & Mazur, E. (2001). Peer instruction: Ten years of experience and results. *American Journal of Physics, 69*, 970–977.

Daugherty, M., & Funke, B. L. (1998). University faculty and student perceptions of web-based instruction. *Journal of Distance Education, 13*(1), 21–39. Retrieved on June 25, 2014, from www.jofde.ca/index.php/jde/article/view/134/.

Dempsey, J. V., Fisher, S. F., Wright, D. E., & Anderton, E. K. (2008). Training and support, obstacles, and library impacts on e-learning activities. *College Student Journal, 42*(2), 630–636.

Dewey, J. (1938). *Logic: The theory of inquiry.* New York: Henry Holt.

DiBiase, D. (2000). Is distance teaching more work or less? *American Journal of Distance Education, 14*(3), 6–20.

DiBiase, D. (2004). The impact of increasing enrollment on faculty workload and student satisfaction over time. *Journal of Asynchronous Leaning Networks, 8*(2). Retrieved on June 25, 2014, from https://www.e-education.psu.edu/files/sites/file/Scaling_Up_II.pdf.

DiBiase, D., & Rademacher, H. (2005). Scaling up: Faculty workload, class size, and student satisfaction in a distance learning course on geographic information science. *Journal of Geography in Higher Education, 29*(1), 139–158.

DiRamio, D., & Kops, G. (2004). Distance education and digital intellectual property issues. *Planning for Higher Education, 32*(3), 37–46.

Doering, A., Miller, C., & Veletsianos, G. (2008). Adventure learning: Educational, social, and technological affordances for collaborative hybrid distance education. *Quarterly Review of Distance Education, 9*(3), 249–265.

Doering, A., Veletsianos, G., Scharber, C., & Miller, C. (2009). Using the technological, pedagogical, and content knowledge framework to design online learning environments and professional development. *Journal of Educational Computing Research, 41*(3), 319–346.

Downes, S. (2005, December 22). An introduction to connective knowledge. *Stephen's Web.* Retrieved on June 25, 2014, from www.downes.ca/post/33034/.

Downes, S. (2006, October 16). Learning networks and connective knowledge. *Instructional Technology Forum: Paper 92.* Retrieved on April 26, 2007, from http://it.coe.uga.edu/itforum/paper92/paper92.html [no longer available].

Downes, S. (2007, February 6). Msg. 2 Re: *What connectivism is.* Online Connectivism Conference, University of Manitoba.

Dringus, L. P. (2012). Learning analytics considered harmful. *Journal of Asynchronous Learning Networks, 16*(3), 87–100.

Driscoll, M. P. (2000). *Psychology of learning for instruction* (2nd edition). Boston: Allyn and Bacon.

Duncan, I., Miller, A. H. D., & Jiang, S. (2012). A taxonomy of virtual worlds usage in education. *British Journal of Educational Technology, 43*(6), 949–964.

Durkheim, E. (1982). *Rules of sociological method.* New York: Free Press.

Edgerton, R. (2001). *Education white paper.* Washington, DC: Pew Forum on Undergraduate Learning [update of his 1997 *Higher education white paper* prepared for the Pew Charitable Trusts].

Eisler, D. L. (2001). Higher education communication and information systems policy. *New Directions for Higher Education, 2001*(115), 71–82.

Electronic Code of Federal Regulations. Title 34: Education, part 600. Retrieved on June 25, 2014, from http://ecfr.gpoaccess.gov/cgi/t/text/text-idx?c=ecfr&sid=702c7e87ace3 5f7eefc7466b2beb3c3f&rgn=div8&view=text&node=34:3.1.3.1.1.1.23.2&idno=34)/.

Entwistle, N. (2010). Taking stock: An overview of key research findings. In J. C. Hughes & J. Mighty (Eds.), *Taking stock: Research on teaching and learning in higher education.* Kingston, ON: School of Policy Studies, Queens University, 45–81.

Evans, B. J., & Willinsky, J. (2013). Setting aside the course reader: The legal, economic, and pedagogical reasons. *Innovative Higher Education, 38*(5), 341–354.

Feenberg, A. (2002). *Transforming technology: A critical theory revisited.* Oxford: Oxford University Press.

Feldman, D. C. (1984, January). The development and enforcement of group norms. *Academy of Management Review, 9*(1), 47–53.

Fredericksen, E., Pickett, A., Pelz, W., Swan, K., & Shea, P. (2000). Student satisfaction and perceived learning with on-line courses: Principles and examples from the SUNY learning network. In J. Bourne (Ed.), *Learning effectiveness and faculty satisfaction,* volume 1 of *Online education.* Nashville, TN: Center for Asynchronous Learning Networks, 7–36.

Freedman, J. (2013). MOOCs: Usefully middlebrow. *Chronicle Review.* Retrieved on June 25, 2014, from http://chronicle.com/article/MOOCs-Are-Usefully-Middlebrow /143183/.

Freire, P. (1970). *Pedagogy of the oppressed.* Harmondsworth, UK: Penguin.

Freire, P. (1972). *Cultural action for freedom.* Harmondsworth, UK: Penguin.

Freire, P. (1973). *Education for critical consciousness.* London: Sheed and Ward.

Frey, B. A., & Donehue, R. (2003). Making the transition from traditional to cyberspace classrooms. *PAACE [Pennsylvania Association for Adult Continuing Education] Journal of Lifelong Learning, 12,* 69–84.

Friedman, T. L. (2012). Come the revolution. *New York Times,* May 16. Retrieved on June 25, 2014, from www.nytimes.com/2012/05/16/opinion/friedman-come-the-revolution .html?_r=0/.

Friedman, T. L. (2013). Revolution hits the universities. *New York Times,* January 27. Retrieved on June 25, 2014, from www.nytimes.com/2013/01/27/opinion/sunday/friedman -revolution-hits-the-universities.html?src=me&ref=general/.

Friesen, N. (2011). *The place of the classroom and the space of the screen.* New York: Peter Lang.

Gabriel, Y. (2008). Against the tyranny of PowerPoint: Technology-in-use and technology abuse. *Organization Studies, 29*(2), 255–276.

Gagné, R. M., & Dick, W. (1983). Instructional psychology. *Annual Review of Psychology, 34*, 261–295.

Gahungu, A., Dereshiwsky, M., & Moan, E. (2006). Finally I can be with my students 24/7, individually and in groups: A survey of faculty teaching online. *Journal of Interactive Online Learning, 5*(2), 118–142.

Garrison, D. (2009). Implications of online learning for the conceptual development and practice of distance education. *Journal of Distance Education, 23*(2), 93–104.

Garrison, D., & Anderson, T. (2003). *E-learning in the 21st century: A framework for research and practice.* London: Routledge/Falmer.

Garrison, D., Anderson, T., & Archer, W. (2000). Critical inquiry in a text-based environment: Computer conferencing in higher education. *Internet and Higher Education, 2*(2–3), 87–105.

Garrison, D., & Archer, W. (2003). Community of inquiry framework for online learning. In M. G. Moore & W. G. Anderson (Eds.), *Handbook of distance education.* New York: Lawrence Erlbaum Associates, 113–127.

Garrison, D., & Kanuka, H. (2004). Blended learning: Uncovering its transformative potential in higher education. *Internet and Higher Education, 7*(2), 95–105.

Gibbs, E., Major, C. H., & Wright, V. (2003). Faculty perceptions of the costs and benefits of instructional technology: Implications for faculty work. *Journal of Faculty Development, 19*(2), 77–88.

Gibbs, J. P. (1981). *Norms, deviance, and social control: Conceptual matters.* New York: Elsevier.

Goody, J. (1987). *The interface between the written and the oral.* Cambridge: Cambridge University Press.

Goodyear, P., Salmon, G., Spector, J., Steeples, C., & Tickner, S. (2001). Competencies for online teaching: A special report. *Educational Technology Research and Development, 49*(1), 65–72.

Gose, B. (2012). 4 massive open online courses and how they work. *Chronicle of Higher Education*, October 1. Retrieved on June 25, 2014, from http://chronicle.com/article/4 -MOOCsHow-They-Work/134664/.

Grandin, T. (1996). *Thinking in pictures: And other reports from my life with autism.* New York: Vintage Books.

Grandin, T. (2010). The world needs all kinds of minds. Retrieved on June 25, 2014, from www.ted.com/talks/temple_grandin_the_world_needs_all_kinds_of_minds/.

Grenzky, J., & Maitland, C. (2001). Focus on distance education. *Update, 7*(2), 1–6.

Grijalva, T., Nowell, C., & Kerkvliet, J. (2006). Academic honesty and online courses. *College Student Journal, 40*(1), 180–185.

Guglielmo, T. (1998). Computer conferencing systems as seen by a designer of online courses. *Educational Technology, 38*(3), 36–43.

Gunawardena, C. N. (1995). Social presence theory and implications for interaction and collaborative learning in computer conferences. *International Journal of Educational Telecommunications, 1*(2), 147–166.

Gunawardena, C. N., & McIsaac, M. S. (2004). Distance education. In D. H. Jonassen (Ed.), *Handbook of research for educational communications and technology* (2nd edition). Mahwah, NJ: Lawrence Erlbaum Associates, 355–396.

Gunawardena, C. N., Nolla, A. C., Wilson, P. L., López-Islas, J. R., Ramírez-Angel, N., & Megchun-Alpízar, R. M. (2001). A cross-cultural study of group process and development in online conferences. *Distance Education, 22*(1), 85–121.

Haraway, D. (1991). A cyborg manifesto: Science, technology, and socialist-feminism in the late twentieth century. In *Simians, cyborgs and women: The reinvention of nature.* New York: Routledge, 149–181. Retrieved on June 25, 2014, from www9.georgetown.edu /faculty/irvinem/theory/Haraway-CyborgManifesto.html.

Hartman, J., Dziuban, C., & Moskal, P. (2000). Faculty satisfaction in ALNs: A dependent or independent variable? *Journal of Asynchronous Learning Networks, 4*(3), 155–179.

Hays v. Sony Corporation of America, 847 F.2d 412 (7th Cir. 1988). Retrieved on June 25, 2014, from http://openjurist.org/847/f2d/412/hays-v-sony-corporation-of-america/.

Hechter, M., & Opp, K. D. (Eds.). (2001). *Social norms.* New York: Russell Sage Foundation.

Heidegger, M. (1927). *Sein und Zeit.* Tübingen, Germany: Max Niemeyer. [(1962). *Being and Time,* trans. J. Macquarrie and E. Robinson. New York: Harper and Row].

Hendry, E. (2009). Students reach settlement in Turnitin lawsuit. *Chronicle of Higher Education,* August 3. Retrieved on June 25, 2014, from http://chronicle.com/blogs/wired campus/students-reach-settlement-in-turnitin-suit/7569/.

Herschback, D. R. (1995). Technology as knowledge: Implications for instruction. *Journal of Technology Education, 7*(1), 31–42. Retrieved on June 25, 2014, from http://scholar .lib.vt.edu/ejournals/JTE/v7n1/herschbach.jte-v7n1.html.

Heydenrych, J. F., & Prinsloo, P. (2010). Revisiting the five generations of distance education: Quo vadis? *Progressio, 32*(1), 5–26.

Higher Education Opportunity Act. (2009). Retrieved on June 25, 2014, from www2.ed .gov/policy/highered/leg/hea08/index.html.

Hill, J. R., Song, L., & West, R. E. (2009). Social learning theory and web-based learning environments: A review of research and discussion of implications. *American Journal of Distance Education, 23*(2), 88–103.

Hislop, G. [W.], & Atwood, M. (2000). ALN teaching as routine faculty workload. *Journal of Asynchronous Learning Networks, 4*(3), 216–230. Retrieved on June 25, 2014, from http://sloanconsortium.org/jaln/v4n3/aln-teaching-routine-faculty-workload/.

Hislop, G. W., & Ellis, H. J. C. (2004). A study of faculty effort in online teaching. *Internet and Higher Education, 7*(1), 15–31.

Horne, C. (2001). Sociological perspectives on the emergence of social norms. In M. Hechter & K. Opp (Eds.), *Social Norms.* New York: Russell Sage Foundation, 3–34.

Hostetter, C., & Busch, M. (2006). Measuring up online: The relationship between social presence and student learning satisfaction. *Journal of Scholarship of Teaching and Learning, 6*(2), 1–12.

Ihde, D. (1979). *Technics and praxis.* Dordrecht, The Netherlands: D. Reidel.

Ihde, D. (1990). *Technology and the lifeworld: From garden to earth.* Bloomington: Indiana University Press.

Ihde, D. (1991). *Instrumental realism: The interface between philosophy of science and philosophy of technology.* Bloomington: Indiana University Press.

Irvine, V. (2009). The emergence of choice in "multi-access" learning environments: Transferring locus of control of course access to the learner. In G. Siemens & C. Fulford (Eds.), *ED-MEDIA 2009: Proceedings of World Conference on Educational Multimedia, Hypermedia and Telecommunications.* Chesapeake, VA: AACE [Association for the Advancement of Computing in Education], 746–752.

Irvine, V., Code, J., & Richards, L. (2013). Realigning higher education for the 21st-century learner through multi-access learning. *MERLOT: Journal of Online Teaching and Learning, 9*(2). Retrieved on June 25, 2014, from http://jolt.merlot.org/vol9no2/irvine_0613 .htm.

Irwin, B., & Hramiak, A. (2010). A discourse analysis of trainee teacher identity in online discussion forums. *Technology, Pedagogy and Education, 19*(3), 361–377.

Jamlan, M. (2004). Faculty opinions towards introducing e-learning at the University of Bahrain. *International Review of Research in Open and Distance Learning, 5*(2), 1–14. Retrieved on June 25, 2014, from www.irrodl.org/index.php/irrodl/article/view/185/802/.

Jonassen, D. H. (2006). *Modeling with technology: Mindtools for conceptual change* (3rd edition). Upper Saddle River, NJ: Pearson Education.

Jones, C., Asensio, M., & Goodyear, P. (2000). Networked learning in higher education: Practitioners' perspectives. *ALT-J: Association for Learning Technology Journal, 8*(2), 18–28.

Kapp, K. M., & O'Driscoll, T. (2010). *Learning in 3D: Adding a new dimension to enterprise learning and collaboration.* San Francisco: John Wiley and Sons.

Kennedy, K., Nowak, S., Raghuraman, R., Thomas, J., & Davis, S. (2000). Academic dishonesty and distance learning: Student and faculty views. *College Student Journal, 34*(2), 309–314.

Kern, S. (1983). *The culture of time and space, 1880–1918.* Cambridge, MA: Harvard University Press.

King, C., Guyette, R., & Piotrowski, C. (2009). Online exams and cheating: An empirical analysis of business students' views. *Journal of Educators Online, 6*(1), 1–11.

Knowles, M. S. (1950). *Informal adult education.* Chicago: Association Press.

Ko, S., & Rossen, S. (2010). *Teaching online: A practical guide* (3rd edition). New York: Routledge.

Koehler, M. J., & Mishra, P. (2005a). What happens when teachers design educational technology? The development of technological pedagogical content knowledge. *Journal of Educational Computing Research, 32*(2), 131–152.

Koehler, M. J., & Mishra, P. (2005b). Teachers learning technology by design. *Journal of Computing in Teacher Education, 21*(3), 94–102.

Koehler, M. J., & Mishra, P. (2009). What is technological pedagogical content knowledge? *Contemporary Issues in Technology and Teacher Education, 9*(1), 60–70. Retrieved on June 25, 2014, from www.citejournal.org/vol9/iss1/general/article1.cfm.

Koehler, M. J., Mishra, P., Hershey, K., & Peruski, L. (2004). With a little help from your students: A new model for faculty development and online course design. *Journal of Technology and Teacher Education, 12*(1), 25–55.

Koehler, M. J., Mishra, P., & Yahya, K. (2007). Tracing the development of teacher knowledge in a design seminar: Integrating content, pedagogy, & technology. *Computers and Education, 49*(3), 740–762.

Kolowich, S. (2013, January 25). Authors of "Bill of Rights" for online learners face criticism. *Wired Campus*. Retrieved on June 25, 2014, from http://chronicle.com/blogs/wiredcampus/authors-of-bill-of-rights-for-online-learners-face-criticism/41971/.

Kop, R. (2011). *The challenges to connectivist learning on open online networks: Learning experiences during a massive open online course*. NRC Publications Archive. Retrieved on June 25, 2014, from http://nparc.cisti-icist.nrc-cnrc.gc.ca/npsi/ctrl?action=rtdoc&an=18150443&lang=en/.

Kop, R., & Hill, A. (2008). Connectivism: Learning theory of the future or vestige of the past? *International Review of Research in Open and Distance Learning, 9*(3), 1–13.

Kotze, Y., & Dreyer, C. (2002). Concerns of lecturers delivering distance education. *South African Journal of Higher Education, 16*(2), 130–138.

Kress, G., & Pachler, N. (2007). Thinking about the "M" in M-learning. In N. Pachler (Ed.), *Mobile learning: Towards a research agenda*. London: WLE Centre, 7–32. Retrieved on June 25, 2014, from http://eprints.ioe.ac.uk/5402/1/mobilelearning_pachler_2007.pdf.

Kuh, G., & Whitt, E. (1988). *The invisible tapestry: Culture in American colleges and universities*. Washington, DC: Association for the Study of Higher Education.

Laffey, L., Lin, G. Y., & Lin, Y. (2006). Assessing social ability in online learning environments. *Journal of Interactive Learning Research, 17*(2), 163–177.

Landies, D. (1980). The creation of knowledge and technique: Today's task and yesterday's experience. *Daedalus, 109*(1), 111–1120.

Lane, L. M. (2009). Insidious pedagogy: How course management systems impact teaching. *First Monday, 14*(10). Retrieved on June 25, 2014, from http://firstmonday.org/htbin/cgiwrap/bin/ojs/index.php/fm/article/view/2530/2303/.

Lang, J. M. (2007). Crafting a teaching persona. *Chronicle of Higher Education, 53*(23), C2–C3.

Lanier, M. (2006). Academic integrity and distance learning. *Journal of Criminal Justice Education, 17*(2), 244–261.

Lao, T., & Gonzales, C. (2005). Understanding online learning through a qualitative description of professors' and students' experiences. *Journal of Technology and Teacher Education, 13*(3), 459–474.

Lasky, S. (2005). A sociocultural approach to understanding teacher identity, agency and professional vulnerability in a context of secondary school reform. *Teaching and Teacher Education, 21*(8), 899–916.

Latour, B. (1992). Where are the missing masses? The sociology of a few mundane artifacts. In W. E. Bijker & J. Law (Eds.), *Shaping technology–building society: Studies in sociotechnical change*. Cambridge, MA: MIT Press, 225–259.

Lauzon, A. C., & Moore, G. A. B. (1989). A fourth-generation distance education system: Integrating computer assisted learning and computer conferencing. *American Journal of Distance Education, 3*(1), 38–49.

Lavagnino, M. B. (2010). Policy as an enabler of student engagement. *EDUCAUSE Review, 45*(5), 104–105. Retrieved on June 22, 2014, from www.educause.edu/ero/article/policy-enabler-student-engagement/.

Lave, J., & Wenger, E. (1991). *Situated learning: Legitimate peripheral participation*. Cambridge: Cambridge University Press.

Lavooy, M., & Newlin, M. (2008). Online chats and cyber-office hours: Everything but the office. *International Journal on e-Learning, 7*(1), 107–116.

Lazarus, B. D. (2003). Teaching courses online: How much time does it take? *Journal of Asynchronous Learning Networks, 7*(3), 47–54.

Lederman, D., & Jaschik, S. (2013, August 27). Survey of faculty attitudes on technology. *Inside Higher Education.* Retrieved on June 25, 2014, from www.insidehighered.com /news/survey/survey-faculty-attitudes-technology#.UhzeVkQNAbM.twitter/.

Lee, C. H. M., Cheng, Y. W., Rai, S., & Depickere, A. (2004). What affect student cognitive style in the development of hypermedia learning system? *Computers and Education, 45*(1), 1–19.

Lee, C.-Y., Dickerson, J., & Winslow, J. (2012). An analysis of organizational approaches to online course structures. *Online Journal of Distance Learning Administration, 15*(1). Retrieved on June 25, 2014, from www.westga.edu/~distance/ojdla/spring151/lee _dickerson_winslow.html.

Lee, J., & Busch, P. E. (2005). Factors related to instructors' willingness to participate in distance education. *Journal of Educational Research, 99*(2), 109–115.

Leh, A. C. (2001). Computer-mediated communication and social presence in a distance learning environment. *International Journal of Educational Telecommunications, 7*(2), 109–128.

Levine, A., & Sun, J. C. (2002). *Barriers to distance education* (6th in a series). Distributed Education: Challenges, Choices, and a New Environment. Washington, DC: American Council on Education Center for Policy Analysis and EDUCAUSE.

Levy, S. (2003). Six factors to consider when planning online distance learning programs in higher education. *Online Journal of Distance Learning Administration, 6*(1).

Li, L., & Pitts, J. P. (2009). Does it really matter? Using virtual office hours to enhance student-faculty interaction. *Journal of Information Systems Education, 20*(2), 175–185. Retrieved on June 25, 2014, from http://jise.org/Volume20/20-2/Pdf/V20N2P175-abs .pdf.

Littlejohn, S. W., & Foss, K. A. (2005). *Theories of human communication* (8th edition). Belmont, CA: Thompson Wadsworth.

Liu, H., MacIntyre, R., & Ferguson, R. (2012). Exploring qualitative analytics for e-mentoring relationships building in an online social environment. *Proceedings of the 2nd international conference on learning analytics and knowledge, New York.* New York: ACM [Association for Computing Machinery], 179–183.

Lockee, B., Moore, M., & Burton, J. (2001). Old concerns with new distance education research. *EDUCAUSE Quarterly, 24*(2), 60–62.

Major, C. H. (2006). Graduate program experiences that can influence confidence for faculty roles and responsibilities. *Journal of Graduate Teaching Assistant Development, 10,* 87–105.

Major, C. H. (2010). Do virtual professors dream of electric students? University faculty experiences with online distance education. *Teachers College Record, 112*(8), 2154–2208.

Major, C. H., & Palmer, B. (2006). Reshaping teaching and learning: Changing faculty pedagogical content knowledge. *Higher Education, 51*(4), 619–647.

Major, C. H., & Savin-Baden, M. (2010). Qualitative research synthesis: The scholarship of integration in practice. In C. H. Major & M. Savin-Baden (Eds.), *New approaches to qualitative research: Wisdom and uncertainty.* London: Routledge, 108–118.

Major, C. H., & Savin-Baden, M. (2011a). *An introduction to qualitative research synthesis: Managing the information explosion in social science research.* London: Routledge.

Major, C. H., & Savin-Baden, M. (2011b). Integration of qualitative evidence: Towards construction of academic knowledge in social science and professional fields. *Qualitative Research, 11*(6), 645–663.

Malcolm, J., Hodkinson, P., & Colley, H. (2003). The interrelationships between informal and formal learning. *Journal of Workplace Learning, 15*(7), 313–318.

Mangan, K. (2012). A first for Udacity: A US university will accept transfer credit for one of its courses. *Chronicle of Higher Education,* September 6. Retrieved on June 25, 2014, from http://chronicle.com/article/A-First-for-Udacity-Transfer/134162/.

Martin, A. (2004). Addressing the gap between theory and practice: IT project design. *JITTA: Journal of Information Technology Theory and Application, 6*(2), 23–42.

Marton, F., & Säljö, R. (1976). On qualitative differences in learning: Outcome as a function of the learner's conception of the task. *British Journal of Educational Psychology, 46*(2), 115–127.

McCaffrey, T. (2012, May 10). *Functional fixedness.* Retrieved on June 25, 2014, from http://blogs.hbr.org/cs/2012/05/overcoming_functional_fixednes.html.

McIsaac, M. S., & Gunawardena, C. N. (1996). Distance education. In D. H. Jonassen (Ed.), *Handbook of research for educational communications and technology: A project of the Association for Educational Communications and Technology.* New York: Macmillan, 403–437. Retrieved on June 25, 2014, from http://umsl.edu/~wilmarthp/modla-links-2011/Distance%20education%20McIsaac%20and%20Gunawardena.pdf.

McKenzie, B. K., Mims, N., Bennett, E., & Waugh, M. (2000). Needs, concerns and practices of online instructors. *Online Journal of Distance Learning Administration, 3*(3). Retrieved on June 24, 2014, from www.westga.edu/~distance/ojdla/fall33/mckenzie33.html.

McLain, B. (2005). Estimating faculty and student workload for interaction in online graduate music courses. *Journal of Asynchronous Learning Networks, 9*(3), 47–56. Retrieved on June 25, 2014, from http://sloanconsortium.org/jaln/v9n3/estimating-faculty-and-student-workload-interaction-online-graduate-music-courses/.

McLuhan, M. (1964). *Understanding media: The extensions of man.* New York: McGraw-Hill.

McLuhan, M., & Fiore, Q. (with Agel, J.). (1967). *The medium is the massage: An inventory of effects.* New York: Random House.

McMillan, D. W., & Chavis, D. M. (1986). Sense of community: A definition and theory. *Journal of Community Psychology, 14*(1), 6–23.

McShane, K. (2004). Integrating face-to-face and online teaching: Academics' role concept and teaching choices. *Teaching in Higher Education, 9*(1), 3–16.

Means, B., Toyama, Y., Murphy, R., Bakia, M., & Jones, K. (2009). *Evaluation of evidence based practices in online learning: A meta-analysis and review of online learning studies.* Washington, DC: US Department of Education. Retrieved on June 25, 2014, from www2.ed.gov/rschstat/eval/tech/evidence-based-practices/finalreport.pdf.

Mehrabian, A. (1969). Some referents and measures of nonverbal behavior. *Behavior Research Methods and Instrumentation, 1*, 203–207.

Mehrabian, A. (1971). *Silent messages.* Belmont, CA: Wadsworth.

Mesthene, E. G. (1979). The role of technology in society. In A. H. Teich (Ed.), *Technology and the future.* New York: St. Martin's Press, 77–99.

Miller, G. A. (1956). The magical number seven, plus or minus two: Some limits on our capacity for processing information. *Psychological Review, 63*(2), 81–97.

Mishra, P., & Koehler, M. J. (2006). Technological pedagogical content knowledge: A framework for teacher knowledge. *Teachers College Record, 108*(6), 1017–1054.

Mishra, P., Koehler, M. J., & Zhao, Y. (Eds.). (2007). *Faculty development by design: Integrating technology in higher education.* Greenwich, CT: Information Age.

Mitcham, C. (1994). Thinking through technology: *The path between engineering and philosophy.* Chicago: University of Chicago Press.

Mitriano, T. (2011, February 1). Who owns student work product? *Inside Higher Education.* Retrieved on June 25, 2014, from www.insidehighered.com/blogs/law_policy_and_it /who_owns_student_work_product/.

Moore, M. G., & Kearsley, G. (2005). *Distance education: A systems view* (2nd edition). Washington, DC: Wadsworth.

Morahan-Martin, J., & Schumacher, P. (2003). Loneliness and social uses of the Internet. *Computers in Human Behavior, 19*(6), 659–671.

Motteram, G., & Forrester, G. (2005). Becoming an online distance learner: What can be learned from students' experiences of induction to distance programmes? *Distance Education, 26*(3), 281–298.

Mowshowitz, A. (1997). Virtual organization. *Communications of the ACM, 40*(9), 30–37.

Naidu, S. (2004). Trends in faculty use and perceptions of e-learning. *Asian Journal of Distance Education, 2*(2). Retrieved on June 25, 2014, from http://asianjde.org.hosting .domaindirect.com/2004v2.2.Naidu.pdf.

National Education Association. (2000, June). *A survey of traditional and distance learning higher education members.* Washington, DC: National Education Association. Retrieved on June 25, 2014, from www.nea.org/assets/docs/HE/DistanceLearningFacultyPoll .pdf.

Newell, A., Shaw, J. C., & Simon, H. A. (1958). Elements of a theory of human problem solving. *Psychological Review, 65*(3), 151–166.

New Media Consortium. (2012). *Horizon report.* Austin, TX: New Media Consortium.

Newton, R. (2003). Staff attitude to the development and delivery of e-learning. *New Library World, 104*(10), 412–425.

Nowotny, H., Scott, P., & Gibbons, M. (2001). *Re-thinking science: Knowledge and the public in an age of uncertainty.* Cambridge: Polity Press.

Oomen-Early, J., & Murphy, L. (2009). Self-actualization and e-learning: A qualitative investigation of university faculty's perceived needs for effective online instruction. *International Journal on e-Learning, 8*(2), 223–240.

Orlando, J. (2011, February 2). FERPA and social media. *Faculty Focus.* Retrieved on June 25, 2014, from www.facultyfocus.com/articles/teaching-with-technology-articles/ferpa -and-social-media/.

Pachler, N., Bachmair, B., & Cook, J. (2010). *Mobile learning: Structures, agency, practices.* New York: Springer.

Pachnowski, L. M., & Jurczyk, J. (2003). Perceptions of faculty on the effect of distance learning technology on faculty preparation time. *Online Journal of Distance Learning Administration, 6*(3). Retrieved on June 25, 2014, from www.westga.edu/~distance/ojdla/fall63/pachnowski64.html.

Paik, N. J. (n.d.). Quotation in Nam June Paik biography and artwork. *MetroArtWork.* Retrieved on June 25, 2014, from http://metroartwork.com/Nam-June-Paik-biography-artwork-m-148.html.

Pajo, K., & Wallace, C. (2001). Barriers to the uptake of web based technology by university teachers. *Journal of Distance Education, 16*(1), 70–84.

Palloff, R. M., & Pratt, K. (1999). *Building learning communities in cyberspace.* San Francisco: Jossey-Bass.

Palloff, R. M., & Pratt, K. (2001). *Lessons from the cyberspace classroom: The realities of online teaching.* San Francisco: Jossey-Bass.

Palmer, B., & Major, C. (2007). Engendering the scholarship of teaching: A case study. *International Journal for the Scholarship of Teaching, 1*(2), 1–15.

Palmer, P. J. (1998). *The courage to teach: Exploring the inner landscape of a teacher's life.* San Francisco: Jossey-Bass.

Panda, S., & Mishra, S. (2007). Faculty attitude towards, and barriers and motivators of e-learning in a mega open university. *Educational Media International, 44*(4), 323–338.

Papert, S., & Harel, I. (1991). Situating constructionism. In S. Papert & I. Harel (Eds.), *Constructionism.* Norwood, NJ: Ablex. Retrieved on June 25, 2014, from www.papert.org/articles/SituatingConstructionism.html.

Parini, J. (2005). *The art of teaching.* Oxford: Oxford University Press.

Parker, A. (2003). Motivation and incentives for distance faculty. *Online Journal of Distance Learning Administration, 6*(3). Retrieved on June 25, 2014, from www.westga.edu/~distance/ojdla/fall63/parker63.htm.

Parrish, P. (2008). Plotting a learning experience. In L. Botturi & T. Stubbs (Eds.), *Handbook of visual languages for instructional design: Theories and practices.* Hershey, PA: Information Science Reference, 91–111.

Parsell, M. (2008). Pernicious virtual communities: Identity, polarisation and the Web 2.0. *Ethics and Information Technology, 10*(1), 41–56.

Pascarella, E. T., & Terenzini, P. T. (1991). *How college affects students: Findings and insights from twenty years of research.* San Francisco: Jossey-Bass.

Pascarella, E. T., & Terenzini, P. T. (2005). *How college affects students: A third decade of research.* San Francisco: Jossey-Bass.

Pashler, H., McDaniel, M., Rohrer, D., & Bjork, R. (2008). Learning styles: Concepts and evidence. *Psychological Science in the Public Interest, 9*(3), 105–119.

Paulson, K. (2002). Reconfiguring faculty roles for virtual settings. *Journal of Higher Education, 73*(1) 123–140.

Pear, J. J. (2004). Enhanced feedback using computer-aided personalized system of instruction. In W. Buskist, V. W. Hevern, B. K. Saville, & T. Zinn (Eds.), *Essays from e-xcellence in teaching, 2003.* [Kennesaw, GA]: Society for the Teaching of Psychology, chapter 11.

Retrieved on June 25, 2014, from http://teachpsych.org/resources/e-books/eit2003/eit03
-11.pdf.

Peirce, C. S. (1877). The fixation of belief. *Popular Science Monthly, 12*(November), 1–15.

Phipps, R., & Merisotis, J. (1999). *What's the difference? A review of contemporary research on the effectiveness of distance learning in higher education.* Washington, DC: Institute for Higher Education Policy.

Piaget, J. (1985). *Equilibration of cognitive structures.* Chicago: University of Chicago Press.

Picciano, A. (2002). Beyond student perceptions: Issues of interaction, presence, and performance in an online course. *Journal of Asynchronous Learning Networks, 6*(1), 21–40.

Policy and Global Affairs National Research Council. (2002). *Preparing for the revolution: Information technology and the future of the research university.* Washington, DC: National Academies Press.

Puzziferro, M., & Shelton, K. (2009). Supporting online faculty: Revisiting the seven principles (a few years later). *Online Journal of Distance Learning Administration, 7*(3). Retrieved on June 25, 2014, from www.westga.edu/~distance/ojdla/fall123/puzziferro123.html.

Raines, D. A. (2011, January 24). Be efficient, not busy: Time management strategies for online educators. *Faculty Focus.* Retrieved on June 25, 2014, from www.facultyfocus.com/articles/online-education/be-efficient-not-busy-time-management-strategies-for-online-teaching/.

Ramsden, P. (1992). *Learning to teach in higher education.* London: Routledge.

Reeves, T. C., Herrington, J., & Oliver, R. (2002). Authentic activities and online learning. In A. Goody, J. Herrington, & M. Northcote (Eds.), *Quality conversations: Research and development in higher education*, volume 25. Jamison Centre, ACT, Australia: HERDSA [Higher Education Research and Development Society of Australasia], 562–567.

Reinheimer, D. A. (2005). Teaching composition online: Whose side is time on? *Computers and Composition, 22*(4), 459–470.

Reuell, P. (2013). Online learning: Varying lectures with tests improves attention, note-taking, and retention. *Harvard Gazette*, April 3. Retrieved on June 25, 2014, from http://news.harvard.edu/gazette/story/2013/04/online-learning-its-different/.

Rheingold, H. (2000). *The virtual community: Homesteading on the electronic frontier.* London: MIT Press.

Rheingold, H. (2012). *Net smart: How to thrive online.* Cambridge, MA: MIT Press.

Richardson, J. C., & Swan, K. (2003). Examining social presence in online courses in relation to students' perceived learning and satisfaction. *Journal of Asynchronous Learning Networks, 7*(1), 68–88.

Rogers, E. M. (1962/1983). *Diffusion of innovations.* New York: Free Press of Glencoe.

Rossi, P. H., & Berk, R. A. (1985). Varieties of normative consensus. *American Sociological Review, 50*, 333–347.

Rothkopf, E. Z. (1970). The concept of mathemagenic activities. *Review of Educational Research, 40*(3), 325–336.

Rourke, L., Anderson, T., Garrison, D. R., & Archer, W. (2001). Assessing social presence in asynchronous text-based computer conferencing. *Journal of Distance Education, 14*, 1–18. Retrieved on June 25, 2014, from http://auspace.athabascau.ca/bitstream/2149/732

/1/Assessing%20Social%20Presence%20In%20Asynchronous%20Text-based %20Computer%20Conferencing.pdf.

Rovai, A. P. (2001). Building classroom community at a distance: A case study. *Educational Technology Research and Development, 49*(4), 33–48.

Rovai, A. P. (2002a). A preliminary look at the structural difference of higher education classroom communities in traditional and ALN courses. *Journal of Asynchronous Learning Networks, 6*(1), 41–56.

Rovai, A. P. (2002b). Development of instrument to measure classroom community. *Internet and Higher Education, 5*(3), 197–211.

Rowe, J., Webb, L. D., & Hartwell-Hunnicutt, K. (1998). Who owns multimedia courseware—faculty or the institution? A critical issue in development and delivery of technology-based education. In T. Ottmann & I. Tomak (Eds.), *ED-MEDIA 1998: Proceedings of World Conference on Educational Multimedia, Hypermedia and Telecommunications.* Charlottesville, VA: AACE [Association for the Advancement of Computing in Education], 1197–1202.

Russo, T., & Benson, S. (2005). Learning with invisible others: Perceptions of online presence and their relationship to cognitive and affective learning. *Educational Technology & Society, 8*(1), 54–62.

Saba, F. (2000). Research in distance education: A status report. *International Review of Research in Open and Distance Learning, 1*(1). Retrieved on June 25, 2014, from www .irrodl.org/index.php/irrodl/article/view/4/337/.

Sachse, P., Hacker, W., & Leinert, S. (2004). External thought: Does sketching assist problem analysis? *Applied Cognitive Psychology, 18*(4), 415–425.

Säljö, R. (1979). Learning about learning. *Higher Education, 8*(4), 443–451.

Salomon, G. (1997). *Distributed cognitions.* New York: Cambridge University Press.

Samarawickrema, G., & Stacey, E. (2007). Adopting web-based learning and teaching: A case study in higher education. *Distance Education, 28*(3), 313–333.

Savin-Baden, M., & Major, C. H. (2004). *Foundations of problem-based learning.* Maidenhead, UK: Society for Research in Higher Education and Open University Press.

Savin-Baden, M., & Major, C. H. (2007). Using interpretive meta-ethnography to explore the relationship between innovative approaches to learning and innovative methods of pedagogical research. *Higher Education, 54*(6), 833–852.

Schugurensky, D. (2000). *The forms of informal learning: Towards a conceptualization of the field.* NALL [New Approaches to Lifelong Learning] Working Paper No. 19-2000. Retrieved on June 25, 2014, from https://tspace.library.utoronto.ca/bitstream/1807/2733 /2/19formsofinformal.pdf.

Schwier, R. A. (2011). *Connections: Virtual learning communities.* Retrieved on June 25, 2014, from http://rickscafe.wordpress.com/2011/06/01/connections-virtual-learning -communities-ebook-launch/.

Scott, S. S., McGuire, J., & Foley, T. E. (2001). *Principles of universal design for instruction.* Storrs: University of Connecticut, Center on Postsecondary Education and Disability.

Seaman, A. (2013). *Personal learning networks: Knowledge sharing as democracy.* Retrieved on June 22, 2014, from www.hybridpedagogy.com/Journal/files/Personal_Learning _Networks.html.

Seaman, J. (2009). *The paradox of faculty voices: Views and experiences with online learning*, volume 2 in *Online learning as a strategic asset*. Washington, DC: Association of Public and Land-Grant Universities & Babson Survey Research Group. Retrieved on June 25, 2014, from www.aplu.org/document.doc?id=1879/.

Sharples, M., McAndrew, P., Weller, M., Ferguson, R., FitzGerald, E., Hirst, T., Mor, Y., Gaved, M., & Whitelock, D. (2012). *Innovating pedagogy 2012: Open University innovation report 1*. Milton Keynes, UK: Open University.

Shea, P. J., Fredericksen, E., Pickett, A., Pelz, W., & Swan, K. (2001). Measures of learning effectiveness in the SUNY learning network. In J. Bourne & J. C. Moore (Eds.), *Learning effectiveness, faculty satisfaction, and cost effectiveness*, volume 2 in *Online education*. Needham, MA: SCOLE [Sloan Center for Online Education], 31–54.

Sheridan, R. (2006). Reducing the online instructor's workload: Tips on designing and administering online courses. *EDUCAUSE Quarterly, 29*(3), 65–67. Retrieved on June 25, 2014, from www.educause.edu/EDUCAUSE+Quarterly/EDUCAUSEQuarterlyMaga zineVolum/ReducingtheOnlineInstructorsWo/157409/.

Shi, M., Bonk, C. J., & Magjuka, R. J. (2006). Time management strategies for online teaching. *International Journal of Instructional Technology and Distance Learning, 3*(2), 3–10.

Shin, N. (2002). Beyond interaction: The relational construct of "transactional presence." *Open Learning: Journal of Open, Distance, and e-Learning, 17*(2), 121–137.

Short, J., Williams, E., & Christie, B. (1976). *The social psychology of telecommunications*. London: John Wiley.

Showalter, E. (2003). *Teaching literature*. Malden, MA: Blackwell.

Shulman, L. (1986). Those who understand: Knowledge growth in teaching. *Educational Researcher, 15*(2), 4–14.

Shulman, L. (1987). Knowledge and teaching: Foundations of the new reform. *Harvard Educational Review, 57*(1), 1–23.

Shulman, L. (1991). Ways of seeing, ways of knowing: Ways of teaching, ways of learning about teaching. *Journal of Curriculum Studies, 23*(5), 393–395.

Shulman, L. (2002). Making differences: A table of learning. *Change, 34*(6), 36–45.

Siemens, G. (2002, September 30). Instructional design in elearning. *Elearnspace: Everything elearning*. Retrieved on June 25, 2014, from www.elearnspace.org/Articles /InstructionalDesign.htm.

Siemens, G. (2005a, August 10). Connectivism: Learning as network creation. *Elearnspace: Everything elearning*. Retrieved on June 25, 2014, from www.elearnspace.org/Articles /networks.htm.

Siemens, G. (2005b, updated April 5). *Connectivism: A learning theory for the digital age*. Retrieved on June 25, 2014, from www.elearnspace.org/Articles/connectivism.htm.

Siemens. G. (2006a). *Knowing knowledge*. Retrieved on June 25, 2014, from www.elearn space.org/KnowingKnowledge_LowRes.pdf.

Siemens G. (2006b, November 12). Connectivism: Learning theory or pastime of the self-amused? *Elearnspace: Everything elearning*. Retrieved on June 25, 2014, from www .elearnspace.org/Articles/connectivism_self-amused.htm.

Siemens, G. (2008). *Learning and knowing in networks: Changing roles for educators and designers*. University of Georgia IT Forum, Paper No. 105. Retrieved on June 22, 2014, from http://itforum.coe.uga.edu/Paper105/Siemens.pdf.

Siemens, G. (2012, July 25). MOOCs are really a platform. *Elearnspace: Learning, Networks, Knowledge, Technology, Community*. Retrieved on June 25, 2014, from www.elearnspace .org/blog/2012/07/25/moocs-are-really-a-platform/.

Singham, M. (2007). Death to the syllabus! *Liberal Education*, 93(4), 52–56. Retrieved on June 25, 2014, from www.aacu.org/liberaleducation/le-fa07/le_fa07_myview .cfm.

Sitzmann, T., Kraiger, K., Stewart, D., & Wisher, R. (2006). The comparative effectiveness of web-based and classroom instruction: A meta-analysis. *Personnel Psychology*, 59(3), 623–664.

Slack, J. D., & Wise, J. M. (2005). *Culture + technology: A primer*. New York: Peter Lang.

Smith, G. G., Ferguson, D., & Caris, M. (2001, April 1). Teaching college courses online vs. face-to-face. *T.H.E. Journal*. Retrieved on June 25, 2014, from http://thejournal.com /Articles/2001/04/01/Teaching-College-Courses-Online-vs-FacetoFace.aspx/.

Smith, G. G., Ferguson, D., & Caris, M. (2002). Teaching online versus face-to-face. *Journal of Educational Technology Systems*, 30(4), 337–364.

Smith, V. C., Lange, A., & Huston, D. R. (2012). Predictive modeling to forecast student outcomes and drive effective interventions in online community college courses. *Journal of Asynchronous Learning Networks*, 16(3), 51–61.

Stuber-McEwen, D., Wiseley, P., & Hoggatt, S. (2009). Point, click, and cheat: Frequency and type of academic dishonesty in the virtual classroom. *Online Journal of Distance Learning Administration*, 12(3), 1–10. Retrieved on June 25, 2014, from www.westga.edu /~distance/ojdla/fall123/stuber123.html.

Suler, J. R. (2002). Identity management in cyberspace. *Journal of Applied Psychoanalytic Studies*, 4(4), 455–460. Retrieved on June 25, 2014, from http://users.rider.edu/~suler /psycyber/identitymanage.html.

Suler, J. R. (2004a). Extending the classroom into cyberspace: The discussion board. *CyberPsychology and Behavior*, 7, 397–403. Retrieved on June 25, 2014, from http://users .rider.edu/~suler/psycyber/extendclass.html.

Suler, J. R. (2004b). The psychology of text relationships. In R. Kraus, J. Zack, & G. Striker (Eds.), *Online counseling: A manual for mental health professionals*. London: Elsevier Academic Press, 20–50. Retrieved on June 25, 2014, from http://users.rider.edu/~suler /psycyber/emailrel.html.

Swan, K., & Shea, P. (2005). The development of virtual learning communities. In S. R. Hiltz & R. Goldman (Eds.), *Asynchronous learning networks: The research frontier*. New York: Hampton Press, 239–260. Retrieved on June 25, 2014, from www.rcet.org /research/publications/chapter_11.pdf.

Tallent-Runnels, M. K., Thomas, J. A., Lan, W. Y., Cooper, S., Ahern, T. C., Shaw, S. M., & Liu, X. (2006). Teaching courses online: A review of the research. *Review of Educational Research*, 76(1), 93–135.

Tan, E. (2012). Bitten by the online teaching bug. *Chronicle of Higher Education*, October 24. Retrieved on June 25, 2014, from http://chronicle.com/article/Bitten-by-the-Online -Bug/135260/.

Taylor, J. C. (1995). Distance education technologies: The fourth generation. *Australian Journal of Educational Technology*, 11(2), 1–7.

Taylor, J. C. (2001). *Fifth-generation distance education.* Higher Education Series Report No. 40. Australia: Department of Education, Training and Youth Affairs. Retrieved on June 25, 2014, from www.c3l.uni-oldenburg.de/cde/media/readings/tayloro1.pdf.

Taylor, P., Parker, K., Lenhart, A., & Patten, E. (2011). *The digital revolution and higher education: College presidents, public differ on value of online learning.* Washington, DC: Pew Research Center, Social & Demographic Trends. Retrieved on June 25, 2014, from http://eric.ed.gov/PDFS/ED524306.pdf.

Thomas, D., & Brown, J. S. (2011). *A new culture of learning: Cultivating the imagination for a world of constant change.* Lexington, KY: CreateSpace2.

Thompson, M. M. (2004). Faculty self-study research project: Examining the online workload. *Journal of Asynchronous Learning Networks, 8*(3), 84–88. Retrieved on June 25, 2014, from http://sloanconsortium.org/jaln/v8n3/faculty-self-study-research-project -examining-online-workload/.

3PlayMedia. (2013). *2014 roadmap to web accessibility in higher education.* Retrieved on June 25, 2014, from http://info.3playmedia.com/wp-web-accessibility.html.

Tierney, W. S. (1988). Organizational culture in higher education. *Journal of Higher Education, 59*(1), 2–21.

Toma, J. D., Dubrow, G., & Hartley, M. (2005). *The uses of institutional culture: Strengthening identification and building brand equity in higher education.* San Francisco: Jossey-Bass.

Tomei, L. (2006). The impact of online teaching on faculty load: Computing the ideal class size for online courses. *Journal of Technology and Teacher Education, 14*(3), 531–541.

Traxler, J. (2009). Learning in a mobile age. *International Journal of Mobile and Blended Learning, 1*(1), 1–12.

Tu, C. H. (2002). The measurement of social presence in an online learning environment. *International Journal on e-Learning, 1*(2), 34–45.

Tu, C. H., & McIsaac, M. (2002). The relationship of social presence and interaction in on-line classes. *American Journal of Distance Education, 16*(3), 131–150.

Tubbs, S., & Moss, S. (2006). *Human communication: Principles and contexts.* New York: McGraw-Hill.

University of Louisiana System. (2012). Intellectual property and shared royalties. *Policy and Procedures Memorandum.* University of Louisiana System, Policy Number FS.III. VI-la. Retrieved on June 25, 2014, from www.ulsystem.net/assets/docs/searchable /boards/FS-III.VI.-1a%20Intellectual%20Property%2010_23_2012.pdf.

University of Minnesota. (2007). Copyright policy: Background and resource page. *Academic Affairs & Provost.* Retrieved on June 25, 2014, from www.academic.umn.edu /provost/reports/copyright.html.

University of Minnesota. (2008). Copyright ownership. *UWIDE Policy Library.* Retrieved on June 24, 2014, from http://policy.umn.edu/Policies/Research/COPYRIGHT.html.

Vai, M., & Sosulski, K. (2011). *Essentials of online course design: A standards-based guide.* New York: Routledge.

Van Manen, M. (1991). *The tact of teaching: The meaning of pedagogical thoughtfulness.* Albany: State University of New York Press.

Veletsianos, G., & Russell, G. (2014). Pedagogical agents. In M. Spector, D. Merrill, J. Elen, & M. J. Bishop (Eds.), *Handbook of Research on Educational Communications and Technology* (4th edition). New York: Springer Academic, 759–769.

Verbeek, P.-P. (2000/2005). *What things do: Philosophical reflections on technology, agency, and design*, trans. R. P. Crease. University Park: Pennsylvania State University Press.

Verbeek, P.-P. (2006). Materializing morality: Design ethics and technological mediation. *Science, Technology, & Human Values, 31*(3), 361–380.

Verhagen P. (2006). Connectivism: A new learning theory? *Surf e-learning themasite*. Retrieved on February 21, 2008, from http://elearning.surf.nl/e-learning/english/3793/ [no longer available].

Virilio, P. (1991). *Last dimension*. New York: Semiotext(e).

Visser, J. A. (2000). Faculty work in developing and teaching web-based distance courses: A case study of time and effort. *American Journal of Distance Education, 14*(3), 21–32.

Vonderwell, S. (2003). An examination of asynchronous communication experiences and perspectives of students in an online course: A case study. *Internet and Higher Education, 6*(1), 77–90.

Vygotsky, L. (1978). *Mind in society*. London: Harvard University Press.

Walker, G., & Johnson, N. (2008). Faculty intentions to use components for web-enhanced instruction. *International Journal on e-Learning, 7*(1), 133–152.

Walther, J. B., & Parks, M. R. (2002). Cues filtered out, cues filtered in. In M. L. Knapp & J. A. Daly (Eds.), *Handbook of interpersonal communication*. Thousand Oaks, CA: Sage Publications, 529–563.

Watkins, B. L., & Wright, S. J. (1991). *The foundations of American distance learning: A century of collegiate correspondence study*. Dubuque, IA: Kendall/Hunt.

Watson, G., & Sottile, J. (2010). Cheating in the digital age: Do students cheat more in online courses? *Online Journal of Distance Learning Administration, 13*(1).

Watters, B. (2012, December 18). Top ed-tech trends of 2012: MOOCs. *Inside Higher Education*. Retrieved on June 25, 2014, from www.insidehighered.com/blogs/hack-higher -education/top-ed-tech-trends-2012-moocs/.

Welker, J., & Berardino, L. (2005). Blended learning: Understanding the middle ground between traditional classroom and fully online instruction. *Journal of Educational Technology Systems, 34*(1), 33–55.

Wells, H. G. (1895). *The time machine*. Project Gutenberg. Retrieved on June 25, 2014, from www.gutenberg.org/cache/epub/35/pg35.html.

Wenger, E. (1998). *Communities of practice: Learning, meaning, and identity*. Cambridge: Cambridge University Press.

Wheeler, S. (2013, May 10). Just how far can they go? *Learning with "e"s*. Retrieved on June 25, 2014, from http://steve-wheeler.blogspot.co.uk/2013/05/just-how-far-can-they-go .html.

Wheeler, S., Kelly, P., & Gale, K. (2005). The influence of online problem-based learning on teachers' professional practice and identity. *Research in Learning Technology, 13*(2), 125–137.

Williams, R. T., Mackness, J., & Gumtau, S. (2012). Footprints of emergence. *International Review of Research in Open and Distance Learning, 13*(4), 49–90. Retrieved on June 22, 2014, from www.irrodl.org/index.php/irrodl/article/view/1267/.

Wilson, C. (1998). Concerns of instructors delivering distance learning via the WWW. *Online Journal of Distance Learning Administration, 1*(3). Retrieved on June 25, 2014, from www.westga.edu/~distance/wilson13.html.

Wilson, K., & Korn, J. (2007). Attention during lectures: Beyond ten minutes. *Teaching of Psychology, 34*(2), 85–89.

Wise, A., Chang, J., Duffy, T., & Del Valle, R. (2004). The effects of teacher social presence on student satisfaction, engagement, and learning. *Journal of Educational Computing Research, 31*(3), 247–271. Retrieved on June 25, 2014, from https://www.gse.harvard.edu /usableknowledge/otpd/participants/papers/duffy_sp_paper.pdf.

Wolcott, L. (2003). Dynamics of faculty participation in distance education: Motivations, incentives, and rewards. In M. G. Moore & W. G. Anderson (Eds.), *Handbook of Distance Education*. Mahwah, NJ: Lawrence Erlbaum Associates, 549–565.

Young, J. R. (2002). The 24-hour professor. *Chronicle of Higher Education, 48*(38), A31–A33.

Young, J. R. (2009). When computers leave classrooms, so does boredom. *Chronicle of Higher Education*, July 20. Retrieved on June 25, 2014, from http://chronicle.com/article/Teach -Naked-Effort-Strips/47398/.

Young, J. R. (2012). 4 professors discuss teaching free online courses for thousands of students. *Chronicle of Higher Education*, June 11. Retrieved on June 25, 2014, from http:// chronicle.com/article/4-Professors-Discuss-Teaching/132125/.

Zembylas, M. (2003). Interrogating "teacher identity": Emotion, resistance, and self-formation. *Educational Theory, 53*(1), 107–127.

Zembylas, M., Theodorou, M., & Pavlakis, A. (2008). The role of emotions in the experience of online learning: Challenges and opportunities. *Educational Media International, 45*(2), 107–117.

Zhao, Y., Lei, J., Yan, B., Lai, C., & Tan, H. (2005). What makes the difference? A practical analysis of research on the effectiveness of distance education. *Teachers College Record, 107*(8), 1836–1884.

Zuboff, S. (1988). *In the age of the smart machine: The future of work and power*. New York: Basic Books.

Contributors

Bryan Alexander, Consultant, Educational Technology, Bryan Alexander
   Consulting, US
Terry Anderson, Professor, Distance Education, Athabasca University, CA
Fil J. Arenas, Associate Professor, Organizational Leadership Studies, Maxwell Air
   Force Base (Alabama), US
Tisha Bender, online teacher trainer and writer, Rutgers University, US
Robert M. Bernard, Professor, Educational Technology, Centre for the Study of
   Learning and Performance, Concordia University, CA
J. Patrick Biddix, Associate Professor, Higher Education, University of Tennessee, US
Stephanie Blackmon, Assistant Professor, Adult and Higher Education, University of
   Oklahoma, US
Curtis J. Bonk, Professor, Instructional Systems Technology, School of Education,
   Indiana University, US
Amanda E. Brunson, Research Assistant and ESL Instructor, Higher Education
   Administration Program and English Language Institute, University of
   Alabama, US
Gardner Campbell, Vice Provost for Learning Innovation and Student Success,
   Virginia Commonwealth University, US
Todd Conaway, Instructional Designer, Teaching and eLearning Support, Yavapai
   College, US
Dave Cormier, Manager, Web Communications and Innovations, University of
   Prince Edward Island, CA
Alec Couros, Associate Professor, Education, University of Regina, CA
Cris Crissman, Adjunct Assistant Professor, College of Education, North Carolina
   State University, US
William M. Cross, Director, Copyright and Digital Scholarship Center, North
   Carolina State University Libraries, US
André R. Denham, Assistant Professor, Department of Educational Leadership,
   Policy, and Technology Studies, University of Alabama, US

Aaron Doering, Associate Professor and Codirector of the LT Media Lab, College of
Education and Human Development, University of Minnesota, US

Wendy Drexler, Chief Innovation Officer, ISTE Leadership Team, International
Society for Technology in Education (ISTE), US

Chuck Eesley, Assistant Professor and Morgenthaler Faculty Fellow, Department
of Management Science and Engineering (MS&E), Stanford University, US

David Evans, Professor, Computer Science, University of Virginia, US

Giulia Forsythe, Special Projects Facilitator, Centre for Teaching, Learning &
Educational Technologies, Brock University, CA

Norm Friesen, Associate Professor, Education, Boise State University, US

Jim Groom, Director and Adjunct Professor, Division of Teaching and Learning
Technologies, University of Mary Washington, US

Neal H. Hutchens, Associate Professor in the Higher Education Program and Senior
Research Associate in the Center for the Study of Higher Education, Pennsylvania State University, US

Valerie Irvine, Assistant Professor, Education, University of Victoria, CA

Matthew J. Koehler, Professor, College of Education, Michigan State University, US

Lisa Lane, Instructor, History, MiraCosta Community College, US

Alan Levine, Consultant, Educational Technology, CogDog IT, US

Susan Lucas, Academic Chair, Higher Education and Adult Learning, Kaplan
University, US

Ted Major, Instructor, Business, Shelton State University, US

Rose Marra, Professor, Learning Technologies, College of Education, University of
Missouri–Columbia, US

Katrina Meyer, Professor, College of Education, Health, and Human Sciences,
University of Memphis, US

Charles Miller, Associate Professor and Codirector of the LT Media Lab, College of
Education and Human Development, University of Minnesota, US

Kenley Obas, Assistant Professor and Associate Vice President of Information
Technology, Alabama State University, US

Norbert Pachler, Professor and Director of International Teacher Education,
Institute of Education, University of London, UK

Laura Paciorek, Instructor, Child Development, MiraCosta College and San Diego
Miramar College, US

Eric Rabkin, Arthur F. Thurnau Professor Emeritus, Professor Emeritus of English
Language and Literature, and Professor Emeritus of Art and Design, College of

Literature, Science, and the Arts (LSA) and Penny W. Stamps School of Art and Design, University of Michigan, US

Howard Rheingold, critic, writer, teacher, and founder, Rheingold University, US

Maggi Savin-Baden, Professor, Higher Education Research, Coventry University, UK

Margaret Soltan, Associate Professor, English, George Washington University, US

Marilyn J. Staffo, Director of the Faculty Resource Center, Center for Instructional Technology, University of Alabama, US

Bonnie Stewart, educator and writer, University of Prince Edward Island, CA

Jesse Stommel, Assistant Professor, Department of Liberal Studies and the Arts, University of Wisconsin–Madison, US

Wanda Sullivan, Associate Professor, Art, Spring Hill College, US

Alex Tabarrok, Associate Professor, Economics, George Mason University and Marginal Revolution University (MRUniversity.com), US

Eloise Tan, Lecturer and Teaching and Learning Developer, Learning Innovation Unit, Dublin City University, IE

Chad Tindol, Director of Risk Management and Deputy General Counsel, University of Alabama System, US

Index

Abt, Clark, 220
Academic Earth, 161
access. *See* educational access
Activeworlds, 85
aesthetics, 127–28
Akrich, Madeleine, 13
Alexander, Bryan, "Digital Storytelling," 224–25
Allen, I. Elaine, 82
Americans with Disabilities Act (ADA), 195
analysis, design, development, implementation, evaluation (ADDIE), 109
Anderson, Terry, "Networks and Sets," 231–32
andragogy, 217
anywhere, anytime learning, 52
Approaches and Study Skills Inventory for Students (ASSIST), 211
Archer, Walter, 231, 284n27
Arenas, Fil J., "Multiplayer Educational Role-Playing Games," 220–23
The Art of Teaching (Parini), 169, 277n12
assignments, 38, 83, 94, 218–19; due dates for, 93, 160; and student engagement, 208, 218, 223, 226
Astin, Alexander, 209
asynchronous courses, 83, 106–7, 154, 214
attention, relevance, confidence, satisfaction (ARCS), 109
attention and concentration, 124, 153, 155, 158, 223; as factor in student engagement, 209
authentic activities, 219, 223

backward design, 109
basic-guidelines approach, 105
Bateson, Gregory, 71
Bathon, Justin, 199
behaviorism, 46, 47, 61
Bender, D. M., 272n13
Bender, Tisha, "Suggestions for Effective Online Communication," 189–91

Bernard, Robert M., 249, 253; "Future Research in Online Learning," 69–70
Biddix, J. Patrick, "A New Online Course Using Social Media," 92–95
Bill of Rights and Principles for Learning in the Digital Age, 194, 196, 197, 200
Blackboard, 13, 14, 83, 90, 191, 249; about, 116, 117–18, 119
Blackmon, Stephanie, "Ten Technologies to Help Establish Teacher Persona in Online Courses," 175–77
blended courses, 51, 81–82
Blogger, 85, 93, 174
blogs and blogging, 38, 40, 85, 191, 204, 217, 224; as collaborative tool, 249, 250; as form of learning, 234–35; as method to communicate with students, 174
Bloom, B. S., 21n1
Bonk, Curtis, "Informal and Extreme Learning," 62–63
Bookhenge in Second Life, 97
Brooks, David, 256, 257
Brown, John S., 50n3, 64
Brunson, Amanda E., "Access for All," 201–2

Caine, Michael, 24
Campbell, Gardner, "Caution in Learning Analytics," 71–72
Canvas, 83, 249
Carnegie, Dale, 157
Cavanaugh, J., 272n13
centralized pathways, 85–86
Chapman, Peter, 103
chat, 39, 67, 153, 176, 184, 187; as collaborative tool, 249, 250
Chavis, David, 241–42
cheating, student, 283n20. *See also* plagiarism
Chickering, Arthur, 41

Christensen, Clayton, 255
civility, 190, 235
classical conditioning, 47, 48n4
cliques, 230, 232
cMOOCs, 80–81
Code, Jillianne, 59
cognitivism, 46, 47, 109–10
collaborative learning, 186, 253; and
    community, 249, 253
Collaborative Writing, 253
Collins, A., 50n3
communication, 178–92, 277–80; about,
    178–79, 277–78n2; changes to faculty
    experience with, 180–86; and course
    design, 186; differences between online
    and onsite, 180, 278n4; durability of,
    184–86; effectiveness in, 189–91; expecta-
    tions for, 182–83; and feedback, 188–89;
    forms of, 181–82; instructor-led, 186, 191;
    management of, 159; and media, 168–69;
    patterns of, 180; and presence, 187–88;
    reflection and, 182; skills required for,
    183–84; strategies for managing, 186–92;
    teaching as, 178, 188; technology and,
    14–15, 179; verbal and nonverbal, 178,
    277–78n2
community, 227–53, 282–85; about, 227–29;
    changes to faculty experience with, 229–41;
    and collaborative learning, 249, 253; and
    common space, 249; components of,
    241–45; concept of, 229, 282n9; developing
    culture of, 246; emotional connection and,
    245, 247; honesty in, 235, 236–41, 283n20;
    influence in, 243; integration and fulfill-
    ment of needs in, 244; membership in,
    242–43; norms and expectations in, 233,
    235, 241, 248–49; online classes and, 230,
    283n10; and sharing information, 247–48;
    and social presence, 247; strategies for
    promoting and gauging, 245–53; structure
    of, 230, 232–33; tools to help create, 246,
    249, 250–52
computer-assisted instruction (CAI), 47n1
Conaway, Todd, "Developing Community in
    Online Courses," 246
CONFU (Conference on Fair Use), 134
connectivism, 49–50, 80
Connexions, 161
constructivism, 46, 47, 48, 49, 220
content knowledge (CK), 26, 27, 31
ConvinceMe, 118

Copyleft, 148
copyright: Cross on, 135–39; and fair use, 135,
    269n7; ownership patterns in, 139–41; use
    of copyrighted materials, 132–34; what it is,
    131, 269n1. See also intellectual property
copyright infringement, 131–32, 144,
    270–71n17; litigation over, 269n9
core values, 15, 17
Cormier, Dave, 64, 78, 266n2
correspondence courses, 180, 278n4
cost, higher education, 255
Couros, Alec, "Open Courses," 79–80
course planning, 109–30, 267–69; about,
    109–10; case studies in, 113–14, 117–18,
    122–23; changes to, when teaching online,
    110–20, 268n4; and course conception,
    120–21; creating learning environment,
    119–20; design process, 121, 127–28, 186,
    268n17; faculty members working together
    in, 110–11; personal philosophies and ideals
    in, 121; setting goals in, 111, 113, 268n6;
    strategies for, 120–30; and student needs,
    121, 122–23
course portfolios, 42, 263–64n28
Coursera, 80, 83, 236; honor code of, 238–39
course structure, 76–108, 266–67; about,
    76; assessing potential learners, 111–12;
    blending of online and onsite, 81–82; case
    studies of, 87, 88–91, 92–95, 96–101, 102–5;
    changes to faculty experience with, 77–87;
    choosing assessments, 112, 113–14, 268n9;
    choosing online tools, 115–16, 118–19;
    developing learning materials, 114;
    institutional approaches to, 87, 105;
    selecting instructional activities, 115;
    strategies for approaching, 87–108;
    structural elements of, 106–8
Cowbird, 224
Creative Commons (CC), 147–48
Crissman, Cris, "An Open Online Course,"
    96–98
Cross, William M., "Making Space for the
    Giants," 135–39
Crowe, Russell, 24
culture: and community, 246; definitions of,
    285n1; of higher education, 254; and student
    backgrounds, 201–2
curating, 225, 226, 282n25
curricula, 216–17
Curriki, 161
cyborg teacher, 170–71

decentralization, 10, 86, 87, 106, 108
decision-making process, 50n4, 115, 215
deep learning, 210–11
Denham, André R., "Instructor Communication and Feedback," 188–89
Department of Education, US, 68
Desire2Learn, 83, 249
dialogue, 189–91
DiBiase, D., 274n15
Dickens, Charles, 72
digital storytelling, 99, 199; Alexander on, 224–25
disabilities, 194–96, 201
discussion forums, 13, 89, 103–4, 118, 250
disruptive innovation, 255
distance learning, 7, 259–60n1
distributed-learning theory, 49, 87
Doering, Aaron, "Exploring Opportunities for Thoughtful Technology Transformation," 126–30
do-it-yourself (DIY) approach: in designing and choosing platform, 83, 85, 116; in designing websites, 203–4; in learning to teach online, 34, 37–38
Douglas, Michael, 24
Downes, Stephen, 78
drawing tools, 251
Drexler, Wendy, "Learning Instead of Teaching," 122–23
Dron, Jon, 231
Dublin City University (DCU), 18
Duguid, S., 50n3

Edgerton, Russell, 214
Edmodo, 176
EduBlogs, 85
educational access, 194–95; online learning and, 196–97, 201–2
EDUCAUSE, 95
EdX, 80, 83
Eesley, Chuck, "Venture Lab Online Education," 20–21
Ehrmann, Steve, 41
electronic gaming, 220–21
Ellis, H. J. C., 273n14
emotional connection, 244, 284n25
enrollment in online courses, 7, 78, 80–81, 104, 266n1
Entwistle, Noel, 211
Evans, B. J., 271n20

Evans, David, "An Open Introductory Computer Science Course," 102–5
evidence-based practices, 263n27
extreme learning, 61, 62–63

Facebook, 38, 40, 85, 129; as method to communicate with students, 174; and privacy issue, 198, 204, 206
faculty knowledge, 24–44, 262–64; about, 25–27; changes to, when teaching online, 27–32; DIY approaches to, 37–38; integration of, 30–32; levels of, 32–34; opportunities for developing, 32, 34, 263n18; popular depictions of, 24; and socialization, 34, 39–40; strategies for developing, 32–44; of technology, 29–30, 262n9; and TPACK framework, 30–31, 35–36, 263n19
faculty participation in online teaching, 8, 260n6
fair use, 134, 135, 145; copyright law on, 269n7; guidelines for, 133–34, 269–70n10; importance of, 138–39
Family Educational Rights and Privacy Act (FERPA), 197–99
Federal Virtual Worlds Challenge (FVWC), 221–22
feedback, 36, 102, 103, 123; and instructor communication, 188–89; promptness in, 41, 112, 213
Feenberg, Andrew, 14
Felder, Richard, 73
flaming, 248
Fleming, Neil, 73
Flickr, 224
Flipgrid, 129
Foley, Teresa, 201
for-profit universities, 140, 267–68n4
Forsythe, Giulia, "Adding Visual Practice to Your Online Course," 124–25
Freire, Paulo, 84
Friedman, Thomas, 255–56
Friesen, Norm, 28; "Establishing Persona Online," 172–73
fully autonomous approach, 105

Gabriel, Y., 261n19
Gamson, Zelda, 41
Garrison, D., 284n27
Garrison, Randy, 231
Gestalt psychology, 47, 48
GNU/Linux, 79

GoAnimate, 176
good practices, 41–42, 263n27
Goodyear, Peter, 168
Google+, 85, 176, 206
Google Docs, 217, 251
Google Hangout, 181, 247, 267n35
Google page ranking, 103
Grandin, Temple, 124
Grasha-Reichmann Student Learning Style Scales (GRLSS), 73, 268n15
Gravatar, 176–77
Groom, Jim, 99; "Blogging as a Form of Learning at the University of Mary Washington," 234–35
Guglielmo, T., 260n1

Harvard University, 80
Heidegger, Martin, 9
Herrington, Jan, 219, 223
Heydenrych, J. F., 259–60n1
highly specified approach, 105
Hill, Janette, 70
Hislop, G. W., 273n14
honesty, 235, 241, 283n20; Rabkin on, 236–41
honor codes, 238–39
Horizon Project, 60
Horizon report, 68
Houseman, John, 24
humor, 176, 181, 218
Hutchens, Neal H., "Who Owns Online Course Materials?," 142–44
hybrid courses, 81–82

identity, 166–67, 170
Ihde, Don, 9, 261n12
immediacy principle, 213–14
immersive worlds, 85, 267n29
Index of Learning Styles, 73
informal learning, 52, 59, 61; Bonk on, 62–63
informating, 15, 261n25
information-processing theory, 47, 48n8
information sharing, 41, 181, 198, 226, 234; strategies for, 247–48
innovation, 128, 220–21, 254; adoption and diffusion of, 8, 260n7; disruptive, 255
inquiry, communities of, 228, 231, 282nn2–3
Instagram, 175
instant messaging (IM), 88, 90, 153, 184, 250
instructional-design models, 109, 267n1
instructional time. *See* time, instructional
integration principle, 167, 283n24

intellectual property, 131–48, 269–71; about, 131–32, 269n1; changes to faculty experience with, 132–44; as issue in course planning, 110–11; ownership of, 139–41, 142–44; strategies for being mindful of, 144–48; student ownership of, 199–200, 204, 207; use of existing copyrighted materials, 132–34
interactivity, 89, 221, 284n29
Irvine, Valerie, 52; "Example of Three Multiaccess Courses," 53–59
iTunesU, 161, 175

Jacksonville State University, 99–100
Jigsaw, 253

Kansas State University, 99
Kearsley, G., 259n1
Keller, John, 109
Kennesaw State University, 99
Kern, S., 275n25
Khan Academy, 63
knowledge of teaching practices (PK), 31
knowledge of technological tools (TK), 31
Knowles, Malcolm, 217, 281n20
Koehler, Matthew J., 30–31, 263n19; "Learning by Design," 35–36
Kolb, David, 73
Koller, Daphne, 80
Kraken, 92

Lane, Lisa, 115–16, 117; "DIY Approaches to Faculty Development," 37–38; "Insidious Pedagogy," 13; "A Mature, Asynchronous Course," 88–91
Lang, James, 163
Lanier, M., 283n20
Lasky, S., 276n2
Latour, Bruno, 13
Lauzon, A. C., 259–60n1
Lave, Jean, 50n3, 228
Lazarus, B. D., 273–74n14
learning, views of, 45–75, 264–66; about, 45–48; activities and products of, 66–67; changes to faculty views of, 48–51; duration of, 64, 66; outcomes of, 67–68, 70, 72; as process of continuous change, 64, 66; route of, 61, 64; socio-technological constructivist views of, 49–50; strategies for taking stance toward, 73–74; timing and focus of, 51–52; types of, 52, 59, 61

learning analytics, 68; Campbell on, 71–72
learning communities, 50n4, 64, 228–29
learning environment, 67, 70, 127; creation of, 119–20; feedback in, 188–89; in hybrid courses, 81; social media and, 30, 83–84; students as participants in, 122, 216; and technology transformation, 127–28
learning management systems (LMSs), 13, 37, 83, 108, 235; and course planning, 116, 117–18, 119; and privacy, 198
learning pathways, 85–87
Learning Style Inventory (LSI), 73
learning-technology-by-design approach, 35–36
learni.st, 231–32
lectures, 8, 12, 89, 102, 103, 141, 157–58, 226, 270n15; pedagogy of, 115, 215, 223
Lee, Stan, 207
legal counsel, 207
Leh, A. C., 284n27, 284n29
Lessig, Larry, 147
Levine, Alan, "An Open Course (and Community) in Digital Storytelling," 98–101
Levine, Arthur, 150
licensing, 147–48
Lucas, Susan, "Being Present," 186–87

MacMurray, Fred, 24
Major, Ted, "Caution in Using Social Media," 205–6
Mappin, David, 53
Marra, Rose, "Planning: In and Out of the Box," 117–18
Marton, Ference, 210
Massachusetts Institute of Technology (MIT), 80
McCune, Velda, 211
McGuire, Joan, 201
McIsaac, M. S., 284n29
McLain, B., 274n14, 275n30
McLuhan, Marshall, 169, 261n23
McMillan, David, 241–42
McTighe, Jay, 109
Means, B., 264n12
Mediasite, 176
MediaWiki, 234
medium as message, 13, 168–69, 261n23
Mehrabian, Albert, 213–14
mentors, network, 79
Meyer, Katrina, "Research on Faculty Stories about Teaching Online," 43–44
microblogs, 38, 85, 250

Miller, Charles, "Exploring Opportunities for Thoughtful Technology Transformation," 126–30
mind mapping, 124, 251
MindMeister, 118
Mishra, Punya, 30–31, 263n19
mobile learning, 52, 264n1; Pachler on, 60–61
Montgomerie, Craig, 53
MOOCs (massive open online courses), 61, 62, 95, 99, 141, 180, 266n2; features of, 78; forms of, 80–81; plagiarism in, 236–38; Soltan on, 16–17
Moodle, 83, 88, 90, 116, 249
Moore, G. A. B., 259–60n1
Moore, M. G., 259n1
Moss, S., 277–78n2
motivation, 79–80, 102–3, 112, 122, 127; as factor in student engagement, 209, 211
MRUniversity.com, 157
multiaccess learning, 52, 53–59
Multiplayer Educational Role-Playing Games (MPERGs), 220–22
multiuser dungeons (MUDs), 267n29
multiuser virtual environments (MUVEs), 267n29

Nautilus Live, 63
netiquette, 188, 248
networks, 231. See also social networking
New Media Consortium (NMC), 60
Newton, Isaac, 135
Ng, Andrew, 80
Ning, 128, 129
norms: of community, 233, 235; need for creation of, 248–49
Norvig, Peter, 80
Nova Southeastern University, 266n1

Obas, Kenley, "Faculty Socialization," 39–40
OER Commons, 161
office hours, virtual, 159, 173, 277n16
Oliver, Ron, 219, 223
onsite teaching, 112, 141; blending of online and, 81–82; and community, 229, 230, 232, 233, 235, 242, 243, 244, 245; and copyright, 132, 134, 139; course planning in, 110, 111; durability of, 184–85; environment in, 66, 67, 85, 115, 119; lectures in, 115, 139; persona in, 164, 165, 166; student engagement, 212–13, 223; time spent in, 149, 151, 152, 153–54, 272–74nn13–14

open courses, 62, 78, 80–81, 85, 99, 106–7, 134; Couros on, 79–80
OpenCourseWare, 161
Open Education Resources (OER), 146–47, 271n20
OpenSimulator, 85
operant conditioning, 47, 48n5

Pachler, Norbert, "Mobile Learning," 60–61
Paciorek, Laura, "Matching Objectives and Assessments," 113–14
Paik, Nam Jun, 9
Palloff, Rena, 150
Palmer, P. J., 276n2
Paper Seminar, 253
Parini, Jay, 169, 277n12
participant pedagogy, 216–17
Pascarella, Ernest, 211
pathways, 108
Paulson, K., 267–68n4
Pavlov, Ivan, 48n4
pedagogical content knowledge (PCK), 26–27, 31
pedagogical knowledge (PK), 26; application of, 27–29
pedagogies, instructor- vs. student-led, 214–15
pedagogies of engagement, 214, 226
persona, teacher, 163–77, 276–77; about, 164; authenticity of, 164–65, 277n6; Blackmon on, 175–77; changes to faculty experience with, 164–69; Friesen on, 172–73; management of, 165, 167; and media, 168–69; scholarship on concept of, 163, 276n2; Stewart on, 170–71; strategies for, 169–77; and teacher roles, 167–68, 277nn8–9
personal learning network (PLN), 34, 38, 40–41
photo sharing, 175, 251
Photo Story, 176
pin boards, 252
Pinterest, 175, 231–32, 248
plagiarism, 144, 270–71n17; Rabkin on, 236–41
platform selection, 115–16
play concept, 64
Plupper, 90
podcasting, 183, 199, 224
poetry, 17
PowerPoint, 12, 168, 218, 261n19
practice, communities of, 228, 282n2

Pratt, Keith, 150
prescribed learning, 61, 64
presence concept, 187–88
Prinsloo, P., 259–60n1
prioritization, 156, 159
privacy, 248; social media and, 198, 204, 206; as student right, 197–99
problem-based learning (PBL), 44, 67, 128, 215
professor, origin of term, 25
professors, in film, 24, 262n1
punctuated lectures, 223
Puzziferro, Maria, 41–42

Rabkin, Eric, "Academic Honesty in an Online Course," 236–38
Raines, Deborah, 159
readiness assessment, 21–22
real simple syndication (RSS), 40
Reauthorized Rehabilitation Act of 1998, 194–95
Reeves, Thomas, 219, 223
research in online learning, 67–68, 264n12, 265n15; future, 69–70
Rheingold, Howard, 85, 216, 282n3; "Why Use Social Media to Teach Online?," 84
rhizomatic learning, 64, 66
Rogers, Everett, 8, 260n7
Ronaghi, Farnaz, 20

Säljö, Roger, 210
Samarawickrema, G., 275–76n33
Savin-Baden, Maggi, "Reflections on Identity in Virtual Worlds," 166–67
schema theory, 47, 48n9
Schwier, R. A., 282n9
Scott, Sally, 201
Seaman, Jeff, 82, 271–72n8
searches, 2, 259n1
Second Life, 85, 97, 176, 220
serious game, 220
sets, 231–32
"Seven Principles of Good Practice in Undergraduate Education" (Chickering and Gamson), 41
Shakespeare, William, A Midsummer Night's Dream, 167
Shelton, Kaye, 41–42
Showalter, Elaine, 169, 277n13
Shulman, Lee, 26, 31, 211
Siemens, George, 50n5, 78, 283n10
simulation, 219, 221–22

simultaneity, 153, 275n25
situated-learning theory, 49, 50n3
Sitzmann, T., 264n12
Skype, 181, 191
Sloan Foundation, 70, 72, 82, 271n8
social bookmarking, 40, 174, 250
social constructionism, 47, 48
socialization, faculty, 34, 39–40
social-learning theory, 47, 48n5, 70, 93
social media, 83, 85, 108; Biddix on, 92–95; creating online persona with, 173–77; and privacy issue, 198, 204, 205–6; Rheingold on, 84
social networking, 38, 85, 230, 252, 283n12
social presence, 247, 284nn26–29
social reading, 248
Socrates, 178
Soliya, 63
Soloman, Barbara, 73
Soltan, Margaret, "A Poetry MOOC," 16–17
Song, Liyan, 70
Squadron Officer College (SOC), 220–22
Stacey, E., 275–76n33
Staffo, Marilyn J., "Time Management for Online Instructors," 160–61
State University of New York–Cortland, 99–100
Stewart, Bonnie, 56; "Hybrids and Subversives," 170–71
Stommel, Jesse, "Participant Pedagogy," 216–17
student engagement, 208–26, 281–82; about, 208–11; changes to faculty experience with, 211–14; control of, 211–12; evidence of, 212–13; immediacy of, 213–14; pedagogies for, 214–15, 216–17, 218–19; strategies for designing, 214–26; student empowerment in, 215, 217
student learning. *See* learning, views of
student-readiness assessments, 112, 268n7
student rights, 193–207, 280–81; about, 193; changes related to, 194–200; educational access, 194–97, 201–2; ownership of intellectual property, 199–200, 204, 207; privacy, 197–99, 204, 206; strategies for ensuring, 200–207
study groups, 247
Study Process Questionnaire, 210–11
substitution, augmentation, modification, redefinition (SAMR), 123, 125
Suler, John, 167

Sullivan, Wanda, "Making Learning Meaningful to the Individual Learner," 218–19
Sun, Jeffrey, 150
syllabus, 204, 241, 268n12; development of, 114; as living document, 215, 216; online posting of, 82, 93, 188

Tabarrok, Alex, "New Medium, New Message," 157–58
Tait, Hilary, 211
Tan, Eloise, "Why Teach Online?," 18–19
task schedules, 93
Taylor, J. C., 260n1
teacher persona. *See* persona, teacher
teacher research, 42
teacher roles, 167–68, 277nn8–9
Teaching Literature (Showalter), 169, 277n13
teaching online: communication, 178–92, 277–80; community, 227–53, 282–85; course planning, 109–30, 267–69; course structure, 76–108, 266–67; faculty knowledge, 24–44, 262–64; as instructional change, 7–23, 259–62; instructional time, 149–62, 271–76; intellectual property, 131–48, 269–71; student engagement, 208–26, 281–82; student rights, 193–207, 280–81; teacher persona, 163–77, 276–77; views of learning, 45–75, 264–66
teaching-philosophy statements, 121, 268n16
team-based learning (TBL), 80, 215
technological content knowledge (TCK), 31
technological pedagogical content knowledge (TPACK), 30–31, 35–36, 128, 263n19
technology: changes to instruction by, 7, 9, 11–14, 28; and communication, 14–15, 179; as context, 9–10; and culture, 254, 285n3; as extension of selves, 10; faculty knowledge about, 29–30, 262n9; failure of, 185; as humanlike interface, 11; as interpretive lens, 10–11; and learning, 31, 46, 48; mediation of actions by, 12–13; mediation of interpretations by, 11–12; and temporality, 150; transformation of, 126–27; values implicit in, 254–55
Technology, Education, and Copyright Harmonization (TEACH) Act, 134, 145; institution's responsibilities under, 136–37; instructor's responsibilities under, 137–38; limits of, 138–39
Temple University, 99
Terenzini, Patrick, 211

text messaging, 250
Thomas, Douglas, 64
Thompson, M. M., 275n28
Thorndike, Edward, 48n5
Thurn, Sebastian, 80
time, instructional, 149–62, 271–76; about, 149–50; amount spent, 150–52, 271–74nn8–15; changes to faculty experience with, 150–56; efficiency and, 156; faculty focus on, 43–44; flexibility of, 153; fragmentation of, 153–54, 275nn28–30; freedom from, 155–56; prioritization of, 156, 159; separation by, 152–53; siphoning of, 155, 275–76n33; strategies for managing, 156–61
time/space relationship, 150, 271n3
timing, 82–83, 107
Tindol, Chad, "Advice for Navigating Ownership Issues," 145–46
Tomei, L., 272n13
Transformating Technology (Feenberg), 14
Tu, C. H., 284n27
Tubbs, S., 277–78n2
Tumblr, 40, 85, 206
Turnitin, 199
Twitter, 40, 56, 85, 99, 191, 224, 267n35; as method to communicate with students, 174; and privacy issue, 198, 204, 206

Udacity, 80, 83, 266n7
United States Distance Learning Association (USDLA), 40
universal design, 200, 201, 203–4
University of California at Berkeley, 80
University of Louisiana, 143
University of Mary Washington, 99–101, 234–35
University of Michigan, 236
University of Minnesota, 142–43
University of Phoenix, 267–68n4
University of Texas, 80
University of Victoria, 53
username, 169, 171

Van Manen, Max, 28
Venture Lab, 20–21, 83

verbal strategies, 173
video conferencing, 62–63, 247
Virilio, P., 275n28
virtual communities, 228–29, 230, 282nn3–7
virtual learning environments (VLEs), 83
Visser, J. A., 273n14
Visual, Auditory, Reading/Writing, Kinesthetic Learning Styles (VARK), 73
Voice over Internet Protocol (VoIP), 181, 251
VoiceThread, 118, 199, 224
Vredevoogd, J. D., 272n13

Web 2.0, 38, 116, 117, 118, 231
web-based learning environments (WBLEs), 70
WebBoard, 90
web conferencing, 39, 63, 181, 231, 249
webinars, 40, 63
website design, 203–4
Wells, H. G., 271n3
Wenger, Étienne, 50n3, 228, 282n2
West, Richard, 70
Western Governors University, 267–68n4
Wheeler, Steve, 226
Wiggins, Grant, 109
wikis, 38, 85, 217, 249, 251
Willinsky, J., 271n20
Wired Campus, 95
wisdom of practice, 41, 263n23
Wood, B. J., 272n13
WordPress, 85, 90, 199, 204, 234
work-for-hire, 139–41, 142–43, 270nn11–14
writing skills, 183–84

xMOOCs, 80–81, 83

Yahya, K., 263n19
York College, 99
Young, Jeffrey, 150
YouTube, 31, 63, 85, 199, 248

Zembylas, M., 276n2
zones for reflection, 153, 275n27
Zuboff, Shoshana, 14–15, 261n25